CALGARY PUBLIC LIBRARY

JUL 2018

Why We Need Religion

Why We Need Religion

Stephen T. Asma

OXFORD UNIVERSITY PRESS

Oxford University Press is a department of the University of Oxford. It furthers the University's objective of excellence in research, scholarship, and education by publishing worldwide. Oxford is a registered trade mark of Oxford University Press in the UK and certain other countries.

Published in the United States of America by Oxford University Press
198 Madison Avenue, New York, NY 10016, United States of America.

© Oxford University Press 2018

All rights reserved. No part of this publication may be reproduced, stored in a retrieval system, or transmitted, in any form or by any means, without the prior permission in writing of Oxford University Press, or as expressly permitted by law, by license, or under terms agreed with the appropriate reproduction rights organization. Inquiries concerning reproduction outside the scope of the above should be sent to the Rights Department, Oxford University Press, at the address above.

You must not circulate this work in any other form
and you must impose this same condition on any acquirer.

Library of Congress Cataloging-in-Publication Data
Names: Asma, Stephen T., author.
Title: Why we need religion / Stephen T. Asma.
Description: New York : Oxford University Press, 2018. | Includes index.
Identifiers: LCCN 2017042812 (print) | LCCN 2018016180 (ebook) |
ISBN 9780190469689 (updf) | ISBN 9780190469696 (epub) |
ISBN 9780190469672 (hardcover)
Subjects: LCSH: Emotions—Religious aspects. | Psychology, Religious.
Classification: LCC BL65.E46 (ebook) | LCC BL65.E46 A86 2018 (print) |
DDC 200.1/9--dc23
LC record available at https://lccn.loc.gov/2017042812

9 8 7 6 5 4 3 2 1

Printed by Edwards Brothers Malloy, United States of America

For Julien, my son

CONTENTS

ACKNOWLEDGMENTS

As always, I am deeply thankful to my parents, Edward and Carol, for their care and inspiration. When you grow up with close siblings, they seem more like parts of yourself than separate people. They are there at the beginning of life, and (gods willing) they make it all the way to the end with you. Brothers Dave and Dan are my lifelong co-travelers, and I feel very fortunate to have them. Thanks to my whole extended family for so much support: Keaton, Jackson, Maddy, Garrison, Nicole, Elaine, Waigong, and Waipo.

I have many friends to thank. Some have helped me directly with this project, while others have supported my work generally. Others have just bought me a whiskey when I really needed it: Rami Gabriel, Glennon Curran, the late great Tom Greif, Brigid Hains, Peter Catapano, Greg Brandenburgh, Alex Kafka, Riva Lehrer, Sam Weller, Robert Wright, Qiuxuan Lyu, Steve Corey, Erin McCarthy, Andrew Causey, Steve Mirsky, Teresa Prados-Torreira, Kate Hamerton, Rojhat Avsar, Tyrell Collins, Teri Campbell, Bob Vallier, Scott Wolfman, Elif Allenfort, Raymond Deeren, Michael Sims, Peter Altenberg, Michael Jackson, Ben Dauer, Ted Di Maria, Joanna Ebenstein, Peter Olson, Doug Johnson, Michael Paradiso-Michau, Abbas Raza, Jim Christopulos, Howard McCullum, Oscar Valdez, Joseph Carroll, Krista Rogers, Gerald Rizzer, Mathias Clasen, Lester Friedman, Kevin Berger, John Kaag, Kim Sterelny, Mark Johnson, Michael Caplan, William Irwin, Leigh Novak, Dario Maestripieri, Bob Zellman, Coltan Scrivner, Vlad Zaiets, Cheryl Johnson-Odim, all my old students in Beijing and Cambodia, and special thanks to the father of affective neuroscience and all-around mensch, Jaak Panksepp—RIP.

I wish to express my gratitude to my excellent editor at Oxford, Cynthia Read. Thanks also to Hannah Campeau and Joyce Helena Brusin for editorial help and manuscript preparation.

I feel intense gratitude to the incomparable Wen Jin, for giving me a beautiful son. And speaking of which, this book and my heart is dedicated to my son, Julien. When it's all done, I will meet you on the far shore. xoxo

Introduction

Opiate for the Masses?

It's a tough time to defend religion. The respectability of religion, among intellectuals, has ebbed away over the last decade, and the next generation of young people is the most unaffiliated demographic in memory. There are good reasons for this discontent, as a storm of bad behavior, bad press, and good criticism has marked the last decade.

On the negative side, abuse by priests and clerics, jihad campaigns against the infidels, and homegrown Christian hostility toward diversity and secular culture, have all converged into a tsunami of ignorance and violence. The convergence has led many intellectuals to echo E. O. Wilson's claim that "for the sake of human progress, the best thing we could possibly do would be to diminish, to the point of eliminating, religious faiths."[1]

It's hard to disagree with Wilson when we consider some recent cases. The 9/11 terrorists famously shouted "Allahu Akbar"—or "God is great" as they hijacked the planes. In January 2015, gunmen arrived at the *Charlie Hebdo* magazine offices, went to the third floor, and shot dead eight journalists, a guest, and a police officer who had been assigned to protect workers. The gunmen were heard saying "We avenged the Prophet Muhammad! We killed Charlie Hebdo," in French, and also shouting "Allahu Akbar."[2] And after the Islamic State (Daesh) attacked Paris on November 13, 2015, killing over 125 people, they released their "Statement about the Blessed Paris Invasion on the French Crusaders." In the statement, they quote the Qur'an repeatedly as a motivation and explanation of their violence, and also state, "In a blessed attack for which Allah facilitated the causes for success, a faithful group of the soldiers of the Caliphate, may Allah dignify it and make it victorious, launched out, targeting the capital of prostitution and obscenity, the carrier of the banner of the Cross in Europe, Paris."[3]

In May of 2014, the Catholic Church revealed that it defrocked 848 priests for rape or child molestation, and sanctioned another 2,572 clerics for lesser violations.[4] These dramatic figures represent only the ten years between 2004 and 2014. These kinds of negative cases lead many reflective people to question the sincerity of religious people (especially those in power), and the value of religion itself.

On the positive side of the antireligion trend, there has been a surge of important analyses coming from recent atheist and agnostic critics, and an arguable uptick in scientific literacy among the younger generation. For the first time in U.S. history, for example, the majority of young people believe that Darwinian evolution is a fact about the natural world.[5] I call these positive developments because they represent increases in critical thinking generally, although they've negatively impacted traditional religious belief.

These negative and positive developments, in turn, have generated a greater skepticism toward religion in the new millennium. It's a relative golden era for agnostics and atheists, and some of this is a welcome transformation.

On a personal note, it feels like the current zeitgeist has finally caught up with my own mindset of the 1990s. Most of my early publications were strenuously critical of religion, but it was a more credulous era then and the club of skeptics was tiny. I remember one of my mentors warning me in the early 1990s not to anger the gods and their servants too much before I secured tenure. It was good advice then, because I was scolded regularly in those days by Christians and New Age spiritualists for poking holes in Biblical literalism, mystical overreaches, and naïve supernaturalism. I wrote regularly for the *Skeptical Inquirer*, the *Humanist* magazine, *Skeptic* magazine, and my bestselling *Buddha for Beginners* (1996) exposed a wide audience to a demystified, nontheological Buddhism, long before it was standard. I even found myself listed as an entry in the reference work *Who's Who In Hell* (2000), and I'm still proud of my inclusion in that collection of august freethinkers and humanists. I'm relieved that the younger generation of skeptics has a smoother road now, and along with a generation of much better writers than myself, I take a sliver of credit for making skepticism more mainstream than ever.

So, now, it feels oddly familiar to be strangely out of step with my time, as I come around to write an appreciation of religion. But this will not be your typical, aging, return to religion, after a rebellious youth. I am not a religious apologist of that variety. Nor will this book use the old strategy of sweeping religious irrationality under the reassuring rug of "faith." The fideism or faithism tradition, from Kierkegaard to C.S. Lewis, has defended religion on the grounds that its truths are above and beyond the regular faculties of knowledge. I have no such allegiance to faith, as a special ability, or power, or window to the light.

So, what is my appreciation of religion based upon? Why do I think we need religion? Perhaps a story is a good way to begin.

After pompously lecturing a class of undergraduates about the incoherence of monotheism, I was approached by a shy student. He nervously stuttered through a heartbreaking story, one that slowly unraveled my own convictions and assumptions about religion.

Five years ago, he explained, his older teenage brother had been brutally stabbed to death. He was viciously attacked and mutilated by a perpetrator who was never caught. My student and his whole family were utterly shattered by their loss and the manner of their loss. He explained to me that his mother went insane for a while afterward, and would have been institutionalized if it were not for the fact that she expected to see her slain son again. She expected to be reunited with him in the afterlife, and—she stressed—his body would be made whole again. A powerful motivational force, hope, and a set of bolstering beliefs dragged her back from the brink of debilitating sorrow, and gave her the strength to keep raising her other two children—my student and his sister.

For the more extreme atheist, all this looks irrational and therefore unacceptable. Beliefs, we are told, must align themselves to evidence and not to mere yearning. Without rational standards, like those entrenched in science, we will all slouch toward chaos and end up in pre-Enlightenment darkness.

Strangely enough, I still agree with some of this, and will not spend much time trying to rescue religion as reasonable. It isn't terribly reasonable. But therein lies its secret power. Contrary to the radical atheists, the irrationality of religion does not render it unacceptable or valueless. Why not? Because the human brain is a kludge of three major operating systems; the ancient reptilian brain (motor functions, fight or flight types of instincts, etc.), the limbic or mammalian brain (emotions), and the most recent neocortex (rationality). Religion nourishes one of these operating systems, even while it irritates another.

In this book, I will argue that religion, like art, has direct access to our emotional lives in ways that science does not. Yes, science can give us emotional feelings of wonder and the majesty of nature (we can feel the sacred depths of nature), but there are many forms of human suffering that are beyond the reach of any scientific alleviation. Different emotional stresses require different kinds of rescue. Unlike previous secular paeans to religion that praise its ethical and civilizing function, I will be emphasizing its emotionally therapeutic power.

Of course, there is a well-documented dark side to spiritual emotions as well. Unlike scientific emotions of sublime interconnection (also still available in religion), the spiritual emotions tilt toward the melodramatic. Religion still trades readily in good-guy bad-guy narratives, and gives testosterone-fueled revenge fantasies every opportunity to vent aggression. But although much of this zealotry is undeniably dangerous, much of it is relatively harmless, and even the dreaded tribalism has some benign aspects. Moreover, I will argue (based on recent social science and psychology data) that the positive dimensions outweigh the negative. I will argue that traditional religion recruits and channels the mammalian emotions of *fear* and *rage* adaptively in premodern small group collectives, but in state-level global societies fresh challenges and obstacles arise. The lamentable story of religious zealotry is used by the enemies of religion to damn the whole enterprise, but this critique oversimplifies both the emotional palette (much of which is prosocial) and the religious modes of emotional management.

The New Atheists, like Richard Dawkins and Sam Harris, are evaluating religion at the neocortical level—their criteria for assessing it is the hypothetico-deductive method.[6] I agree with them that religion fails miserably at the bar of rational validity, but we're at the wrong bar. The older brain, built by natural selection for solving survival challenges, was not built for rationality. Emotions like fear, love, rage, even hope or anticipation, were selected for because they helped early mammals flourish. Fear is a great prod to escape predators, for example, and aggression is useful in the defense of resources and offspring. Care or feelings of love (oxytocin and opioid based) strengthen bonds between mammal parents and offspring, and so on. In many cases, emotions offer quicker ways to solve problems than deliberative cognition. Moreover, our own human emotions are retained from our animal past and represent deep homologies with other mammals.

Of course, the tripartite brain is not a strict distribution of functions, and many systems interpenetrate one another, but affective neuroscience has located a subcortical headquarters of mammal emotion. This, I will argue, is where religion thrives. For us humans the interesting puzzle is how the old animal operating system interacts with the new operating system of cognition. How do our feelings and our thoughts blend together to compose our mental lives and our behaviors? Our cognitive ability to formulate representations of the external world, and manipulate them, is immersed in a sea of emotions. When I think about a heinous serial killer, for example, my blood runs cold. When I call up images of my loved ones in my mind's eye, I am flooded with warm emotions. Neuroscientist Antonio Damasio has shown that emotions saturate even the seemingly pure information-processing aspects of rational deliberation.[7] So, something complicated is happening when my student's mother remembers and projects her deceased son, and further embeds him in a metaphysical narrative that helps her soldier on.

I will argue that religion helps people, rightly or wrongly, manage their emotional lives. No amount of scientific explanation or sociopolitical theorizing is going to console the mother of the stabbed boy. But the irrational hope that she would see her murdered son again sustained her, according to my student. If this emotionally grounded belief gave her the energy and vitality to continue caring for her other children, then we can envision a selective pressure for such emotional beliefs at the individual and kin levels of natural selection.

Those of us in the secular world who critique such emotional responses and strategies with the refrain, "But is it true?" are missing the point. Most religious beliefs are not true. But here's the crux. The emotional brain doesn't care. It doesn't operate on the grounds of true and false. An emotion is not a representation or a judgment, so it cannot be evaluated like a theory. Emotions are not true or false. Even a terrible fear inside a dream is still a terrible fear. This means that the criteria for measuring a healthy theory are not the criteria for measuring a healthy emotion. Unlike a healthy theory, which must correspond to empirical facts, a "healthy emotion" might be one that contributes to neurochemical homeostasis or other affective states that promote biological flourishing.

The definition of an emotion is almost as contentious as the definition of religion. For our purposes we will acknowledge that emotions involve complex combinations of (a) physiological sensations, (b) cognitive appraisals of situations, (c) cultural labels, and (d) expressions or behaviors of those feelings and appraisals (Simon and Nath 2004, following Peggy Thoits 1989). I will sometimes refer to the physiological aspect of emotions as "affects" to distinguish them from the more cognitive emotions of modern humans.

The intellectual life answers to the all-important criterion: Is this or that claim *accurate*? Do our views of the world carve nature at its joints? But the emotional life has a different master. It answers to the more ancient criterion: Does this or that feeling help the organism *thrive*? Often an accurate belief also produces thriving (how else could intelligence be selected for in *Homo sapiens*?). But frequently there is no such happy correlation. Mixing up these criteria is a common category mistake that fuels a lot of the theist/atheist debate.

Some skeptics suggest that my appreciation of emotional well-being (independent of questions of veracity and truth) is tantamount to "drinking the Kool-Aid" or "taking the blue pill" (from the *Matrix* scenario). But the real tension is not between delusion and truth—that's an easy one. And that easy debate dominates the conversation, preventing a more nuanced discussion. The real tension is between the needs of one part of the brain (limbic) and the needs of another (the neocortical). Evolution shaped them both, and the older one does not get out of the way when the newbie comes on the scene.

William James understood this tension, long before we had a neurological way of framing it. And I will draw heavily on James's still powerful "middle way" between the excesses of both secularism and theism. James recognized that faith is not *knowledge* in the strict sense, but since it is deeply meaningful it is important to see how and why it might be justified. He also understood, long before Damasio, that secular reason is more feeling-laden than we usually admit—there is a sentiment of rationality. The recent debates about religion, like polarizing political rhetoric, have lacked James's refined understanding of the real stakes involved. John Dewey's pragmatic *A Common Faith* also tried to preserve aspects of religious experience, while jettisoning the troubling metaphysics. "The religious," Dewey explained, "is any activity pursued in behalf of an ideal end against obstacles and in spite of threats of personal loss because of its general and enduring value."[8] In this more capacious definition, he laid down a template for both today's moderate skeptics and interfaith optimists.[9]

I will build a case for religious tolerance and appreciation, without neutering metaphysical traditions entirely. I will argue that there are *indicative* metaphysical commitments of religion (e.g., "Jesus is God," "Shiva is destroyer," "the soul exists"). But these are not the primary elements of religion. Our indicative beliefs are derived instead from our *imperative* emotional social experiences. Adaptive emotions, folk psychology, and cultural transmission are enough to generate most religious life. The metaphysical beliefs become part of a feedback loop, but they are not the prime movers or motivators of religious life. Dewey's insight, that almost anything can be "religious" if we understand its unique blend of enthusiasm and existential scope, can be updated and revitalized with recent insights from social psychology, neuroscience, and cross-cultural philosophy.

I never had much use for magical thinking . . . until, eventually, I did. In the years since my student told me of his slain brother and unbreakable mother, my own troubles amplified in disturbing albeit illuminating ways. My personal suffering in the last decade, together with my experience living in Cambodia, strengthened my respect for religion, while leaving my agnosticism fully intact. There's no need to go into confessional mode here, except to express an emotional solidarity with believers who find meaning in the intellectually awkward domain of religion. The relationship between suffering and religion is old and obvious, but we now have new tools (philosophical and scientific) to assess the relationship better. Moreover, this book will couch the issue of suffering in the wider web of religious necessity, namely human vulnerability. The need for religion is frequently proportional to the stakes involved—the householder/parent, for example, has a level of high-stakes vulnerability largely unknown to the bohemian ascetic, or the teenager, or even the twenty-something citizen. And sure enough, their religious interests follow quite different paths. My book will offer an explanation of and modest justification for these religious impulses. It will be a respectful, rather than reductionist, psychologizing of religion. As Roger Scruton has pointed out, "consolation from imaginary things is not an imaginary consolation."

Importantly, this book is not just a defense of religion on the grounds that it comforts. It certainly has this function, and it is a crucial aspect of why we need religion. But many thinkers, from Lucretius and David Hume to Pascal Boyer, have noticed that religions inculcate some uncomfortable, harrowing psychological states.[10] Sometimes religion creates more distress for believers than consolation. Jonathan Edwards (1703–1758) famously set the bar for American religious horror, when he said, "The God that holds you over the pit of hell, much as one holds a spider, or some loathsome insect over the fire, abhors you, and is dreadfully provoked: his wrath towards you burns like fire; he looks upon you as worthy of nothing else, but to be cast into the fire; he is of purer eyes than to bear to have you in his sight; you are ten thousand times more abominable in his eyes, than the most hateful venomous serpent is in ours."[11] I will endeavor to show that even these negative feelings are part of the larger therapeutic mission of religion to manage the emotional life.

How one *feels* is as vital to one's survival as how one *thinks*. This argument, premised on the view that emotions are largely adaptive, will be made throughout the chapters. Running through the text then will be two sets of data and argument. One will be the evidence and argument for adaptive lust, care, panic, fear, equanimity, rage, and so on. How exactly are these adaptive (from the Pleistocene to the present)? Secondly, how exactly do religions manage and modulate these affective powers? How do some of the religious universals (e.g., ritual, sacrifice, forgiveness, soteriology) regulate the emotions into successful survival resources?

Before we begin, we need to define some important terms, and also introduce the idea of the *religious imagination*. Not only are there many different global religions, such as Christianity, Islam, and Buddhism, but there are also many definitions of religion. Some definitions are too narrow or provincial, and exclude religions from unfamiliar regions (e.g., monotheists frequently ignore animism). On the other hand, some definitions are so capacious as to include every kind of human endeavor, and do not successfully limit the domain (e.g., Dewey's definition may be too broad in this sense).

The etymology of the word "religion" is unclear. Some scholars claim it is derived from the Latin *religio*, a modification of *ligare*, "to bind." This makes sense, given that religion unites or binds people together into a cultural unit, and religion binds the believer with behavioral constraints. The ancient Roman philosopher Lucretius uses the term in this way, as does St. Augustine. But Cicero offers a slightly different etymology when he suggests that religion comes from *relegere*, "to read through" or "to go through again." And this suggests a crucial liturgical or ritual element of religion.[12]

If we think of religion as a "family resemblance" of ideas, behaviors, feelings, and so on, then we find a general likeness in many features (like a family nose or forehead, for example) but not an exhaustive required set of properties. Most religions, for example, bind a social group together and provide a sense of identity. Most religions commit to a belief in supernatural beings. Most religions have ritual or sacred objects and conduct ceremonies around those objects. Most religions promote an ethical or moral code. Religions engender rare feeling states, such as awe, reverence, guilt, and so on. Religions have a story about the origin of the cosmos or the origin of a people. They involve modes of communication to other divine realms, such as prayer, divination, or meditation. And although theologians might stress the scriptural notions of the gods, and anthropologists might stress the ritual ceremonies, religion is all of these things.

If a cultural system exemplifies many of the above features, then it is most likely a religion, even though some systems share few features and no systems are complete exemplifications. In addition to a list of defining features, religion also can be analyzed using two different approaches; namely, *essential* or *functional* methods. Crudely put, the essentialist approach to religion is concerned with *what* a particular religion is about, while the functionalist approach tracks what a religion *does*. If I'm analyzing the Christian idea of "original sin," for example, then I can investigate the scriptural story of Adam's rebellion in Eden, and examine St. Augustine's and Martin Luther's interpretation of original sin as an ongoing expression of human desire (concupiscence), and so on. These would be essentialist approaches to religion, because they examine the nature of the ideas and beliefs directly—taking them as explicit statements about the self, the world, and God. Essentialist approaches are deeply concerned with the content of religion, and track the variations of religious systems as constitutive (e.g., polytheism vs. monotheism or Catholicism vs. Protestantism).

By contrast, functionalist approaches to religion tend to look beyond the specific doctrines and unique rituals, to focus on the social uses or purposes of religious behavior. One might take a functionalist approach to original sin, for example, by arguing that the doctrine helps believers take a cautious or pejorative attitude toward their own desires and appetites, which in turn reduces selfish behavior. Or one might take a functionalist approach to religious sacrifice on the grounds that such activity signals group membership and solidarity. Notice, however, that it's not just anthropologists who are functionalists about religion. Even the growing interfaith movement, like what one finds in the Interfaith Youth Core, looks beyond the specific essentials of denominational religion to find underlying purposes in all religions. For example, it is common for interfaith proponents to identify "love your neighbor" as an underlying function beneath specific Christian, Jewish, and Muslim doctrines. One needs some functionalism in order to find some of the common or shared goals and values in diverse religions. But most functionalists, like psychologists and social scientists, are examining beliefs and practices as extrinsically valuable or useful.

I will be making many functionalist arguments about religion, because I will be arguing that it is part of a broader adaptive strategy for human beings. But the division between essential and functional should not be overstated. In reality, there is no function or use of religion without the essential or substantive ideas and behaviors. We can abstract the deeper functions from the specific rituals or scriptures, but this is an analytical move that comes from a metalevel of detachment and does not represent the lived experience of the believer. We will discuss both the essential beliefs and behaviors of specific religions, as well as their functions and uses.

Human beings are meaning-seeking animals. And from this perspective we see the marriage of form and content, or religious function and substance. The *religious imagination* is a broad field that contains the various methods of religious analysis within it, and then some. Religion is about making and finding meaning, in the sense that it's about issues of ultimate concern, existential exploration, or what philosopher Bernard Williams called our "ground projects."[13] The religious imagination is a way of understanding the world and ourselves, that draws upon our visual and narrative capacities (underwritten by perceptual and cognitive faculties). The religious imagination sees the world as it is, but also a second universe, infusing the facts.

Philosopher Charles Taylor broadened the definition of religion to the larger project—the system of meaning. He suggested that religion is not really about supernatural beings and big sacrifices, but about frameworks that give us values. These values give us norms, and ways of behaving that define us as a social group, and thereby increase cohesion. Such value frameworks are inescapable for humans, and even our Western secular framework is just another one (Western secular liberalism is a religion that doesn't know it's a religion, according to this view).[14] The main reason for thinking of contemporary liberalism (**W**estern, **E**ducated, **I**ndustrialized, **R**ich, **D**emocracy) as "religious" is because it has certain fundamental values (e.g., individual rights) that are not demonstrable, or derivable, or provable. Our values are not obviously derived from scientific investigation, Taylor points out, and therefore they are similar to the faith-based first principles of traditional religions (e.g., God made nature).

Although I'm sympathetic to Taylor's emphasis on meaningful value systems, I think he has broadened the notion of religion too much. The frameworks that give meaningful values for Christians, Muslims, and Buddhists, for example, are intimately metaphysical (and often tend toward the supernatural). The values and the meanings flow from the metaphysics. The belief in a God, or a soul, or karma, or an afterlife, makes up the foundational content that anchors the values.

I take it as obvious that we can have values, and very good values, without religion. It's time to acknowledge that although this was once a pressing point of contention, it is thankfully now a no-brainer. Human reason and sentiment, properly cultivated, are sufficient to provide us the golden rule, and many other ethical norms. I will not waste time rehashing this tired debate. We will be focusing on the relationship between religion and values, because that is one of the key elements of the book, but it's a given that nonreligious people can be, and are, deeply ethical.

The relation between secular and sacred values is not a purely academic issue, because we need a social world that appreciates the multicultural diversity of different religions in the United States or Europe, but also limits and constrains those beliefs/practices when they occasionally contradict the values of Western liberalism (e.g., polygamy, honor killings, or no education for females). Competing value systems and their metaphysical assumptions are difficult to reconcile, even in a pluralistic culture.

For now, we only want to acknowledge the importance of imagination as a force of religious life. We're wrong to think that the imagination is only a fantasy fabricator. I will argue throughout this book that the imagination has epistemic power—that is to say, power to construct knowledge and also change behavior. Yes, there is an aspect of imagination that spins unreality, but there is another aspect that *investigates*. And another aspect that synthesizes or composes from disparate parts. And yet another aspect of imagination motivates behavior, conduct, and even conversion. The religious imagination is a mediating faculty between facts and values on the one hand, and cognition and affect on the other. The nature of this imagination has been misunderstood by both proponents and detractors of religion.

Mark Twain tells of the fascinating case of Reverend Thomas Beecher (brother of Henry Ward Beecher), who came from Connecticut to Elmira, New York, (Twain's summer hometown) to take charge of a Congregational church. Beecher served as pastor there for many decades, and became Twain's friend.

"He had a fine mind," Twain reports in his *Autobiography*. When he came to Elmira to take over the parish, Beecher was a "strenuous and decided unbeliever." But, he reported to Twain, his upbringing required him eventually to come to believe in Christian doctrine, or he would never be happy or free from terrors. So, the atheist Beecher had accepted the parish confidently, knowing that he had made up his mind to compel himself to become a believer. Twain says that he was astonished by this strange confession, and found it stranger still that Beecher managed to pull it off. Beecher claimed that within twelve months of coming to Elmira, he had "perfectly succeeded in his extraordinary enterprise, and that thence forth he was as complete and as thorough a believer as any Christian that ever lived. He was one of the best men I've ever known. Also he was one of the best citizens I've ever known."[15]

It's hard to interpret this credulous compulsion, this self-imposed conversion. If we take Twain and Beecher at face value, then the conversion represents a kind of tour de force of the will-to-believe. But belief on demand seems, forgive the irony, hard to believe. This is an important issue for us, because we will be considering the possibility of religious belief or commitment, without satisfaction of truth requirements, and even in the face of truth failure.

There is full-on belief, without doubt. And there is complete disbelief. But there are also many fine-grained intermediate positions that need more exploration. The religious imagination has a powerful role in the construction of an unseen, meaningful world—one that structures life, even as it fails to deliver on its literal promissory notes.

Philosopher Jean Kazez writes, "I am a religious fictionalist. I don't just banish all religious sentences to the flames. I make believe some of them are true, and I think that's all to the good."[16] At her family's religious feast, the Seder, she pretends there is a deity to be praised for various things. "I like pretending the Passover story is true," she explains, "because of the continuity it creates—it ties me to the other people at the table, past years that I've celebrated Passover (in many different ways, with different people). I like feeling tied to Jews over the centuries and across the world. I also like the themes of liberation and freedom that can be tied to the basic story."

Many people take a fictionalist approach to God. They accept the existence of God, but they do not really believe God exists. As philosopher William Irwin puts it, "They accept that God is love and that (the concept of) God has shaped human history and guides human lives, but when pinned down they admit that they do not really believe in the actual existence of such a God. Their considered judgment is that the existence of God is not literally true but is mythologically true."[17]

Many nonbelievers dismiss this kind of fictionalism as bad thinking, but many of these same nonbelievers accept the moral power of imagination. In his song *Imagine*, John Lennon famously entreated us to imagine "no countries," "no religion," "no possessions," and a subsequent "brotherhood of man." And Martin Luther King, Jr. invited us to project a "dream" into future reality, and make it so.

Imagination helps us find empathy for other people, by putting us in their shoes. It helps us envision an alternative reality where greater social justice exists. Dreaming our ideals helps us organize our daily lives and institutions to bring about those ideals. But, of course, the imagination is not intrinsically positive and affirmative. Nightmares are also dreams, after all. In contrast to the egalitarian dreams of liberalism, imagination-based xenophobia drives cultures to imagine the worst, and fear tears apart communities and fosters "us versus them" dynamics. So, the religious imagination is a double-edged sword, and we must try to ascertain which direction it is cutting throughout the specific cases of this book.

Finally, we need just a word or two about opiates. The modern condemnation of religion has followed the Marxian rebuke that religion is an opiate administered indirectly by State power in order to secure a docile populace—one that accommodates poverty and political powerlessness, in hopes of posthumous supernatural rewards. "Religion is the sigh of the oppressed creature," Marx claimed, "the heart of a heartless world, and the soul of soulless conditions. It is the opium of the people."[18]

Marx, Mao, and even Malcolm X leveled this critique against traditional religion, and the critique lives on as a disdainful last insult to be hurled at the believer. I hurled it myself many times, thinking that it was a decisive weapon. In recent years, however, I've changed my mind about this criticism.

First, the opiate critique was born during the rise of industrial urban culture, and it trades on a particular image of "the masses"—an image that doesn't really hold up. Yes, the State can use religion to anesthetize the disenfranchised, but we need to rethink the role of religion for the "elemental social unit"—the family. Nineteenth-century theories, such as Friedrich Engels's, suggested that the nuclear family was a product of industrialization, but more recent anthropology reverses this order and suggests that industrialization was so successful in Europe because nuclear families facilitated it. Anthropologists Timothy Earl and Allen W. Johnson studied hundreds of human societies, in their *Evolution of Human Societies*, and discovered that the nuclear family is the default form of human organization, because it allows for maximally flexible management of resources, limited demands on those resources, and trustworthy social ties.[19] Religion, then, may be analgesic, but it is managed more by the family, not a faceless bourgeois State or even a centralized Vatican or other power hub. When the family unit is making selective use of the images, stories, and rituals of the local religious culture, then insidious Big-Brother interpretations are politically expedient but inaccurate.

Secondly, religion is energizing as often as it is anesthetizing. As often as it numbs or sedates, religion also riles-up and invigorates the believer. Indeed, one might argue that this animating quality of religion makes it more dangerous than any tranquilizing property.

Finally, what's so bad about some opiates, anyway? If my view of religion is primarily therapeutic, then I can hardly despair when some of that therapy takes the form of palliative pain management. If atheists think it's enough to dismiss the believer on the grounds that he should never buffer the pains of life, then I'll assume the atheist has no recourse to any pain management in his own life. In which case, I envy his remarkably good fortune. For the rest of us, there is aspirin, alcohol, religion, hobbies, work, love, friendship, and other analgesic therapies. After all, opioids—like endorphins—are innate chemical ingredients in the human brain and body, and they evolved, in part, to occasionally relieve the organism from misery. Freud, in his *Civilization and Its Discontents,* quotes the well-known phrase, "He who has cares, has brandy too."

We need a more clear-eyed appreciation of the role of cultural analgesics. It is not enough to dismiss religion on the grounds of some puritanical moral judgment about the weakness of the devotee. The irony is too rich. In this book, I will endeavor a charitable interpretation of the believer and religion, one that couches such convictions in the universal emotional life that connects us all.

CHAPTER 1
Adventures at the Creation Museum

FOR THE BIBLE TELLS ME SO

Driving from my home in Chicago to the Creation Museum in Kentucky (six hours away) is, itself, a kind of espionage foray in the American culture wars. The culture-shock goes both ways and I'm sure that natives of the rural heartlands also feel like they're entering "enemy territory" when they roll up to the urban jungle.

Just as the skyscrapers recede in the rearview mirror and the now verdant landscape begins to flatten out, the radio acquires considerably more twang—and more sincerity, too. Whether it's melodramatic arena-rock ballads or modern country, the music loses all the tongue-in-cheek irony of urban college rock and the cynical posturing of hip-hop. The music becomes heartfelt, strident, almost embarrassingly earnest.

Suddenly, around Hebron, Indiana, there are eight or nine Christian stations pumping a combination of power ballads (with lyrics such as, "you are my one redeemer"), personal inspirational confessions, and inflammatory conservative talk-shows. By the time I get to Petersburg, Kentucky, I feel as though I'm in a foreign country, excited by the different customs and the distinctive aesthetic.

Inside the $30 million Creation Museum I am immediately confronted by a bizarre animatronic scene—a small girl plays next to a raptor dinosaur (unaware that her species arose 64 million years *after* the extinction of dinosaurs). But this is only the first in a long line of polemical "challenge exhibits" designed to undercut the idea that the earth is billions of years old. This evangelical museum is an offshoot of Answers in Genesis

(AiG), which is run by Ken Ham, president and CEO. Ham, who holds a BS in applied science from the University of Queensland, is author of titles such as *The Lie: Evolution*, and *Walking Through Shadows: Finding Hope in a World of Pain*. In addition to books, AiG produces a creationist magazine, and a variety of Christian DVDs, CDs, and so on. He and his board of directors, each of whom he describes as "a godly man who walks with the Lord in wisdom and maturity," have been "upholding the authority of the Bible" since 1994.

In 2014, Ken Ham famously challenged science educator Bill Nye (the Science Guy) to a debate about creationism versus evolution. The event, held at the Creation Museum, sold out instantly and garnered several million video stream viewers. Ironically, donations to Ham's organization spiked after the debate and may have enabled Ham to open his Noah's Ark theme park in Williamstown, Kentucky. The ark and the Creation Museum are counter-punches from the deep American culture war.

Ham and his organization believe that the time is ripe for rebuttal museums and theme parks. The promotional material on the AiG website states, "Almost all natural history museums proclaim an evolutionary, humanistic worldview. For example, they will typically place dinosaurs on an evolutionary timeline millions of years before man. AiG's museum will proclaim the authority and accuracy of the Bible from Genesis to Revelation, and will show that there is a Creator, and that this Creator is Jesus Christ (Colossians 1:15–20), who is our Savior."

After the foyer animatronics of humans and dinosaurs, I am quickly shuttled into a high-tech movie theater to watch *Men in White*, a "humorous" and awkwardly preachy spoof of the Hollywood film, *Men in Black*. Here the hip sunglass-wearing protagonists are actually archangels Michael and Gabriel ("Mike" and "Gabe"), and they give us (and an animatronic purpose-driven searcher named Wendy) a quick tour of the "problems" with modern science. Science is represented entirely by a congregation of dogmatic egg-headed teachers, who espouse (shriek actually) such "dubious" doctrines as geology, evolution, fossil-dating methodology, and basic cosmology. They are all vanquished by the lovable wise-cracking Mike and Gabe, while we the audience are thumped and rocked by motorized theater chairs and even sprayed with water during the jocular Flood sequence.

From here it's just one unsettling display of edutainment after another, culminating in a relatively gory film about Jesus's bloody sacrifice for "you and me." Along the way, we get to walk inside a scaled section of Noah's ark; we learn that pornography, suicide, and abortion are on the rise due to evolution's nihilism; and the Grand Canyon was formed in a few weeks. One spends two to three hours touring the "Seven Cs, in God's Eternal Plan"; Creation, Corruption, Catastrophe, Confusion, Christ, Cross, and

Consummation. And there is no way to break off the tour at any point prior to consummation, as I learned the hard way. About two hours in, I start to get claustrophobic (the spaces seem to get tighter and darker as one walks the eschatological narrative). I decide to step away (just when genocide, racism, and crime were being blamed on Adam's imprudent taste for forbidden fruit), in order to find an exit to the cafeteria ("Noah's Café") so that I might nourish my weakening spirit. To my horror, I discover that one cannot actually exit anywhere along the pathway. The herding is so absolute that when you attempt to backtrack, you find that the doors you've been entering have no handles of any kind on the opposite side. Unlike any other museum, you must (like someone who has entered a haunted house) complete the entire circuit in order to stop the experience.

It's not quite accurate to call this evangelical center a "museum" at all. It contains almost no "information," unless one counts speculations on how Noah kept dinosaurs on the ark as information. It offers no new observations about nature, unless inferring its Designer can be called observational. Unlike most other nature museums, it has no "research" component whatsoever. When I asked Mark Looy, vice president for "Answers in Genesis" ministry relations, where the research labs and archive collections were located, he stuttered and confessed that he didn't understand the question. "This is a museum," he finally said, chuckling.

What the Creation Museum *does* have, however, are copious ways of needling accepted and established theories of science with juvenile conspiracies and misguided quests for certainty. Some of their hostility toward geology and evolution is understandable on the cultural (as opposed to evidentiary) grounds that some science educators are dogmatic (i.e., bad educators). But Americans, even American evangelicals, believe that the power of "choice" is supreme, and so a growing number of Christians feel comfortable choosing a different origin story than the materialist one. The Creation Museum emboldens them to do so because it invokes a naive "show me" empiricism (e.g., "hey, I don't *see* evolution happening"). The exhibits repeatedly ask visitors, for example, to consider that: dinosaur bones don't come out of the ground with their dates printed on them, so why should we believe the crazy scientists with their theoretical dating methods? It's an "empiricism" that gives them just enough skepticism to doubt the secular culture they're immersed in, but not enough to doubt their own Biblical culture.

> How many sheep, I carefully asked "would a dinosaur need to eat per day while living on the Ark?"

I had done my homework in order to interview Ken Ham, the director of the Creation Museum. I had the good fortune to interview him during the first month of the museum's opening. But in order to be up-to-date with "ark science," my "homework" had to go back to the 1660s. Here, particularly in John Wilkins's *An Essay Towards a Real Character and a Philosophical Language* (1668), I learned that "atheistical scoffers" had been rolling their eyes, of late, at the notion that so many animals could fit on so small a boat (300 cubits = 450 feet long, 75 feet wide, and 45 feet high; Genesis 6:15). Bishop Wilkins, who acted as the first secretary of the Royal Society, set about demonstrating once and for all that the ark could indeed hold the menagerie. Creating elaborate charts based on scriptural descriptions of Noah's craft and cargo, Wilkins established that the middle floor of the three-floor ark was just under 15 feet tall and held foodstuffs for all the passengers, including 1,600 sheep for carnivore consumption. So naturally, when I learned that Ham's new exhibit diorama would show visitors how the dinosaurs lived on the ark (something Wilkins couldn't have predicted), it seemed reasonable to ask how many sheep they'd be digging into.

It is exceedingly hard to ask this question with a straight face. Even now when I think about it, I start smiling. When I asked this surreal query of Ham, I was sure I had edged over some boundary of tact and would now be perceived as mocking him. But he didn't miss a beat, and replied, Well, that's an interesting question.

"We don't know for sure," he said, "but from a biblical perspective we know that all animals were originally herbivores." (Carnivore activity only happens as a result of the Fall—no animals experience death before Adam's sin.) "So it is possible that carnivores ate plants and grains while they lived on the ark. Even today we know that grizzly bears eat grass and vegetation primarily, so it's not true that an animal with sharp teeth and claws must eat meat or must be a carnivore. At the very least, the carnivores could survive on vegetation for a significant time span."

I was relieved to find Ham unfazed by my line of inquiry. The fact is that I was drawn into the ark issue more fully than I had ever expected. Something slowly happens to your criteria of "reasonableness" the more you become immersed into this creationist worldview. Ham and I were having a perfectly reasonable conversation, had we been living in the 1600s. Ham's speculation on the possibility of ark-bound vegetarianism seemed, at least for a moment, ingenious because it simultaneously cut down on the physical space needed for food (grains and vegetables can be compressed to take up less space than sheep) and eliminated another 1,600 mouths to feed. Bishop Wilkins would be proud.

The museum has an elaborate walk-through exhibit of Noah's ark. As you enter the giant exhibit you encounter twelve animatronic figures building the vessel. You can then meander around two floors of animal pairs, walking both inside and outside the ark. There is also a display of the design plan of the ark to lend scale—demonstrating to visitors that this massive diorama represents only 1% of the total ark space. The walls are covered with mural paintings that show how Noah's family took care of the animals, including engineering speculations about food and waste management. And crucial to the logic of the entire ark display is the exhibit showing how two of every "kind" of animal was brought on board, not two of every "species."

If Noah had to get every species on board, then Ham and the other Creationists would be in deep trouble. The Amazon rain forest alone, according to some researchers, may contain as many as 20 million species of arthropods, which are themselves only a piece of the rain forest biosphere. The popular college textbook *Biology* (Campbell, Reece, and Mitchell, 2012) sums up the numbers by saying that, "To date, scientists have described and formally named about 1.8 million species of organisms. Some biologists think that about 10 million more species currently exist; others estimate the number to be as high as 100 million" (p. 1245). Even if we take the most conservative numbers of species and then add the staggering numbers of now extinct species (such as the dinosaurs), we have an insane number of animals to fit on a boat that's less than two football fields long.

But the Creation Museum argues that Noah never had to take two of every species, but only two of every "kind," and that cuts the numbers enough to reasonably pack the boat. What is a "kind"? Creationists are invoking the next level up on the ladder of taxonomy, the genus. To the skeptic who thinks there were too many species of dinosaur, for example, to fit on the ark, Ken Ham responds by saying that "there were not very many different kinds of dinosaurs. There are certainly hundreds of dinosaur names, but many of these were given to just a bit of bone or skeletons of the same dinosaur found in other countries. It is also reasonable to assume that different sizes, varieties, and sexes of the same dinosaur have ended up with different names. For example, look at the many different varieties and sizes of dogs, but they are all the same kind—the dog kind! In reality, there may have been fewer than 50 kinds of dinosaurs." In contrast to the Creation Museum, scientists estimate that there may have been over 2,000 genera of dinosaurs.

I asked Ham if just a handful of dinosaurs wouldn't be too big (even in smaller genera numbers) to accommodate on the ark.

"We want people to understand," he responded, "that, of all the fossil skeletons found around the earth, the average size of dinosaurs is only the size of a sheep. We also want to point out that dinosaurs probably don't have a growth spurt until after five years, so they could be quite small when young. Therefore, it's not ridiculous to think that two of every kind were on the ark."

It's worth noting that while Ham and others are trying to make the animal kingdom smaller so it will fit into the boat, earlier exegetes entertained the idea of making the ark much bigger in order to accomplish the same goal. Augustine argued for example that the biblical "cubit" was really more like 9 feet long, rather than the 1.5 feet that we usually accept. But John Wilkins put the brakes on that when he applied this new cubit to other biblical passages, pointing out that if Augustine and others were correct, it would also make Goliath's head nine feet tall, simply too big for David to carry.

The Museum teaches that plants would have survived the flood as floating mats of vegetation, and insects and invertebrates would have lived on them, instead of inside the ark. And so on. My purpose here isn't to refute each and every such claim, but to highlight that the main agenda behind all this pseudoscience is to make the world a much smaller place. The Creation Museum is not just trying to shrink the animal kingdom, it is also scaling back the universe.

The world I live in is ancient and vast. The Big Bang occurred around 14 billion years ago; the earth is approximately 4.5 billion years old; life itself (single-cell organisms) emerged a few hundred million years later; dinosaurs went extinct 65 million years ago; and modern humans developed from ancestral hominids around 100,000 years ago. The Creation Museum, however, is speaking to the Americans who live in a much smaller world. That world was created by God 6,000 years ago; a great deluge covered the earth 4,400 years ago; species have gone extinct within the last several thousand years, but no new species have evolved; and the savior came 2,000 years ago and will come again soon to wrap up the whole enchilada.

To maintain this smaller-scale picture of nature (i.e., a human-centered, young cosmos), the Creation Museum offers an exhibit illustrating the rapid formation of the Grand Canyon. Near the museum bookstore, a hallway wall is covered with a replica of Grand Canyon strata, complete with dinosaur fossils lodged in situ. But the exhibit explains to visitors that the Grand Canyon was formed quickly during the great flood, rather than over the course of millions of years as current geology contends. (Scientists believe the Colorado River probably began carving the canyon around 20 million years ago.)

When I asked Ham if there was any particular museum exhibit that might prove conversionary for the skeptic, he underscored the importance of the young-earth doctrine.

"I think one of the big issues in this whole topic is obviously the age of the earth—the question of millions of years versus thousands of years. That issue is even more key than the business of Darwinian evolution. And I believe that there is very compelling evidence in our displays, and in the DVD's that we produce, to show that the earth is not millions of years old."

The socially conservative political stance of the museum is prevalent in almost every exhibit, but the *coup de grâce* is the "Culture in Crisis" exhibit. Here the museum gives us a "natural history" of the breakdown of the American family. Visitors are invited to look through three windows of a contemporary American home. Videos loop to show two young boys looking at porn on the computer and experimenting with drugs. Another window shows a young girl crying, surrounded by abortion pamphlets. And finally, the parents are shown arguing. A recreated church facade stands at the other end of the room, but the foundation of the church has been damaged by a large wrecking-ball labeled "millions of years." The signage explains that the cause of all this misery is our move away from Genesis and toward the scientific ideas of geology and evolution. Ideas about an old earth make people feel small and insignificant, so naturally they do drugs and have abortions.

To play on Max Weber's famous terminology, the Creation Museum exhibits the world as an "enchanted garden." It may be defiled temporarily by the sins of man, but the world is a magical place wherein God cares about human beings and codes nature with secrets and signs of his power and purpose. The evolutionist, on the other hand, lives in a much larger, older, and more mechanical version of nature. The late Stephen Jay Gould once described his metaphysical worldview as "the 'cold bath' theory that nature can be truly 'cruel' and 'indifferent' . . . because nature was not constructed as our eventual abode, didn't know we were coming (we are, after all, interlopers of the latest geological microsecond), and doesn't give a damn about us (speaking metaphorically)." And Gould writes, "I regard such a position as liberating, not depressing."

The Creation Museum, on the other hand, finds this "cold bath" view very depressing, and it is the reason, the organizers say, why the American family is disintegrating. Ham's "Answers in Genesis" website laments that "the devastating effect that evolutionary humanism has had on society, and even the church, makes it clear that everyone—including Christians—needs to return to the clear teachings of Scripture and Genesis and acknowledge Christ as our Creator and Savior. In fact, Genesis has the answer to many of the problems facing the compromising church and questioning world today."

One of the developers of an evolution exhibit at Chicago's Field Museum, Eric D. Gyllenhaal, told me that curators will often do front-end surveys and exit surveys of visitors to see what they knew before going through the exhibit and what they knew and felt afterward. Curators do this to see whether their "message" is getting through. Unprompted, patrons exiting the Field's evolution exhibit reported a strong sense of their own "fragility" as a species, and many visitors reported feeling very "small" in comparison with the vast scales of geological time.

In that vein, I asked Mark Looy, vice president for Answers in Genesis ministry relations, what the intended "message" was for the whole museum.

"The message is that the Bible is true. We're not trying to hide that from anyone—the museum will be an evangelistic center."

Many mainstream moderate Christians read the Bible figuratively rather than literally and they see God as the maker of natural laws, from the Big Bang to natural selection. They are comfortable with modern science and for them God is not a micromanager of nature, nor an intruder on the free-will affairs of the human species. But the Creation Museum characterizes those moderates as part of the problem.

I asked Looy if moderate Christians, or any "theistic evolutionists," would enjoy the museum.

"Well, we welcome them to the museum," he said, "to observe two things; one, the evidence that supports Genesis and shows them that they don't need to compromise with the evolutionists. And two, we'll also challenge them with the question, 'Why would an all-powerful, all-knowing God use something so cruel and wasteful as Darwinian evolution?'"

The museum does not shy away from the traditional "problem of evil" by saying that suffering does not exist, or by saying that it only looks like suffering to us but it's really good from a God's-eye perspective. Instead, it offers a disturbing progression of exhibits that move the visitor from the "Cave of Sorrows," where Eve eats from the Tree of Knowledge, to "The First Shedding of Blood," where images and text explain how animals began to suffer and die after God's wrath at the fallen Adam and Eve. So, the museum accepts the reality of natural selection's brutality (all organisms tend to make more offspring than can survive to procreative age), but it places the blame for this unpleasantness on man's shoulders, not the Deity's.

Scientists observe the "carnage" of natural selection and see it as the engine of adaptation and speciation. Creationists observe the same carnage and explain it as divine punishment, with no evolutionary significance. The gap reminds us that data usually underdetermine the theories that are proffered to explain them. In other words, we can usually give more than one coherent explanation for the same data. The people at the Creation Museum were eager to point that out to me, whenever they could.

"The big issue in the museum that we deal with," Ham said, "is helping people to see the difference between using the scientific method in the present—what's called operational science—and one's origin beliefs."

"An evolutionist," said Looy, "looks at a dinosaur bone and says it must be 65 million years old. We look at the same bone and say the creature was probably covered by a global flood about 4,400 years ago. Same evidence, same bone, just a different interpretation."

Never mind, I guess, that the different interpretation flouts the facts of all the sciences combined. Creationists believe that since an observable dinosaur bone must be explained by an unobservable story, we are all legitimately entitled to choose the story we like best. Choosing a Biblical story of origins brings with it comforting cultural baggage—kindred spirits who live in a cozy, young, enchanted world, comprised of obvious good guys and bad guys. Choosing an evolutionary story of the bone brings its own cultural baggage, but also the immeasurable advantage of consistency with established discoveries, observations, and stories from the scientific brain trust. Not all stories are made equal.[1]

HABITS OF MIND

How does a modern person come to dismiss science and history in favor of an Iron Age book, like the Bible? Answering, as some secularists do, that the person is stupid or crazy tells us nothing and closes down a real investigation. We need to delve into how the mind works—some psychology and epistemology—in order to understand a seemingly pathological view of nature.

It is typical of Blue-State urbanites and college-educated liberals to feel quite superior to the superstitions of Red-State Bible thumpers. My own students in Chicago chuckle with ironic dismissal about the Creation Museum. But now it gets interesting. My students believe in ghosts.

It's not just a few students, or an odd cohort, that believe in ghosts. It's a vast majority. Over the last decade, I have informally polled my students and discovered that around 80 percent of them believe in ghosts. I suspect that most other American college students also believe in ghosts, but their college professors have had no pressing reason to ask them. The topic doesn't come up in geology, or economics, or math classes. I have occasion to ask them because I teach critical thinking and philosophy, and I ask them a whole battery of bizarre questions.

If you are surprised to find such a high number of ghost believers, you might be alarmed to discover that almost half my students also believe in astrology, and around one-third believe a variety of conspiracies, including alien cover-ups, the intentional murder of Princess Di, the man-made origin of AIDS, and the U.S. government's secret role in hatching the 9/11 events. Interestingly, almost none of them believe that global warming is a hoax. This last volte-face of sober conviction might seem like a rare triumph of logic and evidence, but it seems to stem more from their being urban liberals than from scientific literacy.

Much has been made recently of the nonreligious nature of the Millennials, given that they self-identify as "unaffiliated" when polls ask them about religion. They are indeed disaffected about organized institutional religion, but we would be mistaken if we read this as an Enlightenment style triumph of scientific literacy. They are as devoted to mysticism, supernaturalism, pseudoscience, and conspiracy as Generation X and Baby Boomers, perhaps more so. Their postmodern childhoods have made the lines of belief and doubt unpredictable and idiosyncratic, but not more rational. They are not better thinkers, in the sense of evaluating evidence.

Several of my students laughed and mocked the ludicrous beliefs of creationists, but presented their ghost and alien beliefs with implacable gravitas. And the same ones who think the idea of heaven and hell is ridiculous, see karma and reincarnation as manifestly obvious. This haphazard mix of credulity and skepticism is not a result of critical thinking or systematic investigation, or anything educators promote as legitimate justification for belief. It's just an accidental grab bag of opinions, accumulated by parental influence, the sway of peers, cable television, and the Internet. Of course, most adults, including professors, are victims of the same mental hodgepodgery.

No doubt, some naive pedagogues are harrumphing about "evidence and logic"—that's all you need to sort good thinking from bad! This is the sort of person who hasn't studied much history of science. When you look at the development of good thinking (like a good scientific theory), it only looks more logical and evidenced after decades of hindsight. Additionally, consider how informed and educated many of the conspiracy theorists are. They're not suffering from backwoods myopia. The 9/11 deniers know more about engineering than most people, and there are now over 2,000 architects and engineers (AE9/11Truth) who have signed a petition for an independent investigation of the towers collapse. I point this out, not because I think they're right, but because the "obviousness" of evidence is never very obvious. One can always interpret data in multiple ways. And for every expert witness in a legal case, the opposition can always find a counter expert. Also, life is short, and no one can crosscheck and fact-check everything coming at us, even if the crosschecking is reliable. This is a fundamental challenge for all critical thinking, because there does not appear to be any algorithm for churning out believable facts from a contentious tide of "evidence."

The traditional criteria used to distinguish good thinking from bad include things like Karl Popper's criterion of "falsifiability" and William of Occam's "Occam's razor." The simple-minded rationalist suggests that competing explanatory claims (such as creationism and evolution) are easily resolved—creationism is usually dismissed on the grounds that its claims cannot be falsified (evidence cannot prove or disprove its natural theology beliefs). Popper's criterion of "falsifiability" seems, at first blush, like a good one—it nicely rules out the spooky claims of pseudoscientists and snake oil salesmen. It's probably enough to rule out creationism and ghosts. Or is it?

Philosopher Larry Laudan thinks we've failed to give credible criteria for demarcating science from pseudoscience. Even falsifiability, the benchmark for positivist science, rules *out* many of the legitimate theoretical claims of cutting-edge physics (e.g., string theory) and rules *in* many wacky claims, such as astrology—if the proponents are clever about which observations corroborate their predictions. Moreover, historians of science since Thomas Kuhn have pointed out that legitimate science rarely abandons a theory the moment falsifying observations come in—preferring instead (sometimes for decades) to chalk up counterevidence to experimental error. Philosopher Paul Feyerabend even gave up altogether on a so-called scientific method, arguing that science is not a special technique for producing truth but a flawed species of regular human reasoning (loaded with error, bias, and rhetorical persuasion). And finally, increased rationality in one domain doesn't always decrease credulity in other domains. We like to think that a rigorous application of logic will eliminate kooky ideas. But let's not forget Arthur Conan Doyle, who was well versed with induction and deduction, and yet also believed that a pharaoh's curse may have caused the death of Lord Carnarvon, the patron of the Tutankhamun expedition.[2]

None of this is designed to suggest the reasonableness of creationism per se. Compare creationism for a moment with another controversial contender for scientific status, namely Traditional Chinese Medicine (TCM). The possibility that TCM may turn out to be true hinges on the possibility that current Western medicine fails to explain *x* (say, "frozen shoulder" or some other ailment) but TCM succeeds in explaining and fixing *x*. Let's say I get frozen shoulder, and Western doctors can't figure out the causal matrix and can't seem to treat it, but the acupuncturist has a *qi* theory and a treatment that fixes my shoulder. That might happen. This is not the situation with creationism and evolution.

Evolution has been providing superior explanations (testable) for most natural history data for a century and a half (e.g., the fossil record, anatomical homology, genetics, immunology), while creationism has not shown a track record or even a promise of explaining an "x" that evolution cannot explain. On these grounds, TCM—while contentious—looks like a much better contender for believability than creationism or ghosts. On the other hand, for Ken Ham and like minds, God is the most fruitful and capacious explanatory strategy because He explains not only the fossil record and genetics, but also geology, historical change, and even moral truth. God's will potentially explains everything. What creationism lacks in empirical falsifiability, it makes up for in its ability to unify disparate domains of explanation under one umbrella of ultimate causation. Is that a virtue or a vice? Here the problem with creationist explanation is that it seems unlikely to help us make predictions about nature. God's will doesn't help us predict the weather. But, then again, evolution is also better at explaining the *history* of life than at making useful *predictions* about the future.

One way radical religious beliefs might be explained (e.g., the cosmos is 6,000 years old) is via a poverty of information. Maybe the religious fundamentalist is not getting the quantity or quality of information needed, and is making the best belief commitment she can, given the available info. The remedy for this, presumably, is to give the fundamentalist better information. And this makes sense when the believer is socially, geographically, or culturally isolated. But two problems arise immediately. First, there are many cases in which the relevant information is introduced and patiently explained (e.g., Bill Nye detailing the science of evolution to Ken Ham in a debate), and the person remains unmoved and does not revise his beliefs. And secondly, many believers in ghosts, or gods, or conspiracies, have extensive access to copious information (via the Internet, urban resources, media, etc.) and yet hold firm to radical beliefs. Remember that some of the 9/11 conspiracy proponents are engineers and architects. And my Chicago students, for example, live in an information-rich environment, yet still readily believe in ghosts and conspiracies.

The issue, as I see it, is not the quantity of information but how the person uses or weighs the information. This is not a simple story of how a person deduces (well or badly) from premises or starting points. This explains some issues, like when Ken Ham reasons (quite sensibly) about how to fit dinosaurs on the ark. But starting points or first premises—for all of us, not just Ken Ham—are already bound up in a messy amalgam of mutually reinforcing assumptions, values, articles of faith, emotions, and so on.

The general failures of finding an unambiguous set of criteria for distinguishing sense from nonsense have led some philosophers to shift from the pursuit of criteria to the pursuit of psychology. If there are no clear rules to settle the good thinking question, then are there good habits of mind? Are creationists sloppy thinkers in general? What about ghost believers? Are secular humanists tidy or orderly thinkers? Or are they unimaginative?

Intellectual vices include things like being overly rigid in one's thinking, gullibility, prejudice, carelessness, and so on. Just as there are moral virtues (such as courage or temperance), there are intellectual virtues, including things like mental flexibility, moderate skepticism, carefulness, attention focus, and so on.

When a person doggedly commits to conspiracies, ghosts, or young earth creationism, despite overwhelming evidence to the contrary, they may be revealing a poor intellectual character. But this is not some inborn character; rather, it flows from habitual practice, or lack of practice. On this account, the creationist belief in "ark science" is not about a specific data point, or information gap, or deduction error, but about a flabby intellectual character. The way we handle knowledge is the result of habit. Additionally, our beliefs never stand alone, but have a holistic integration with many other beliefs and feelings.

Someone believes *x* presumably because they have reasons for believing it. If I ask Ken Ham why he believes that dinosaurs were on the ark, he gives me reasons why—a combination of logic and evidence that, at least in his own mind, justifies the belief. But stand-alone reasons are a myth, and our inner world is not so simple. Trying to reason a believer out of their belief is not very successful, as any specific reason must come up against a whole network of intertwining beliefs, where some of them are quite deep and existential in nature. A creationist, for example, believes *x* in part because his mother, whom he loves, believes in *x*. This is not irrelevant. Your critique of *x* is also, in his mind, a critique of his mother. We could divorce the logic of creationism or evolution from the psychology of its proponents, but that won't help us understand each other. And it won't help us understand how knowledge really works.

Imagine the mind as a collection of complex "pictures" or paintings, rather than as a computer. A picture is a composition of various forms and patterns. Sometimes the forms are related to one another in a concordant way, sometimes not. Sometimes small parts of the overall composition seem to coordinate well, while other parts hang together in a haphazard way. The individual human mind and life are like this. The gestalt composition of our ideas, emotions, beliefs, background assumptions, and experiences cannot be completely sifted into two realms of facts and values.

At bottom, Ken Ham and I have two very different pictures that govern our lives. In my picture, I can't get the random mutation pattern to coordinate with an all-good God pattern. The combination clashes too much for me, but Ham can pull it off. This difference has to do, in large part, with what other forms or patterns (i.e., ideas, experiences, or emotions) these two beliefs are attached to or mixed with. Isolating one feature of Ham's picture, or my picture, and showing all the ways it doesn't make sense, can be legitimate and fair in some cases, but it also fails to recognize how that feature is connected to other important ways of living and being in the world. The belief in a nonrandom nature is connected in an important way, for Ham, to a feeling or attitude of gratefulness or a general appreciation of life itself. Whereas, my feelings of appreciation and existential gratitude are connected to completely different parts of my picture. One's organizing picture structures the way one thinks, imagines, and behaves. And while that picture might include a very large section that is given over to a pattern called logic, we should not be so naive as to think that the picture itself is constructed on the foundation of logic.

When the believer in randomness and the believer in design go head to head, they bring with them their respective pictures. If ontological beliefs existed in an isolated way within people's minds, then straightforward refutations would work; people would hold up their belief to specific tests, see that a specific belief doesn't accord, and happily discard it. But because the belief is tied to so many other things, some of which may be very precious commitments, people will hold fast to the belief and reinterpret the tests instead. This happens as much in the sciences as it does in the religions.

One of the positive outcomes of this metaphor, of human organizing pictures, is that people who disagree with you cannot be easily dismissed as either stupid or deceptive. Some deep disagreements between people may have more to do with the picture contexts, than the isolated terms under discussion. Does this mean that there is no shared vantage point from which to critique each other's beliefs or even pictures? Are Ken Ham and I simply two ships passing in the night; two incommensurable pictures? No.

Two things are clear about the pictures that organize our respective lives: they are revisable, and they have many features in common with other people's pictures. Although our core picture of life is built up by gradual accretion and is slow to change, it is not immovable. New experiences, persuasion, and logic are always tinkering with our picture. Secondly, our common humanity gives us very similar raw materials for our pictures (needs, wants, hopes, etc.), and this allows each of us to gain some entry into another person's mode of life. My picture and Ken Ham's picture are deeply rooted things, but they are not unchangeable, and they are not totally incommensurable.

So, the question of "Who's right?" comes down to the issue of what's at stake. If Ham and I are having a lively debate over coffee somewhere, and he's advocating for design and creationism and I'm championing randomness and Darwin, then there's probably not much at stake. If we both walk away from our exchange with unchanged pictures, then it's no big deal. But if Ham is lobbying the local school board to censor the parts of biology textbooks that discuss random mutation, then I'm going to work very hard to block his move and get him to revise his picture. Much more is at stake in this second scenario.

On this picture theory of the mind, we can see that habituation is a crucial aspect. We do sometimes come to reject an old belief and adopt a new one. That's the good news. But the bad news, for the rationalist, is that such change is usually the result of new habituation (fresh habit patterns), not enlightening flashes of insight or computational crunching. The good news is in the realm of pragmatism—you can, with great effort, get an antisocial or antinomian group of believers to change their views by retraining them (habituation via carrots and sticks), but not by some simple exposure to "the truth." This suggests an unsettling dominance of rhetoric over truth. If you want to convert creationists to evolutionists, then you should make it "cool" or "profitable" to be an evolutionist, rather than comparing their competing theories. Of course, this cuts both ways, and also explains why evolutionists—like my Chicago students—believe in evolution, despite not really studying it much or knowing it explicitly. What they believe, I suspect, is that Bill Nye is cool, and Ken Ham and the other Bible thumpers are decidedly not cool. Moreover, ghosts and reincarnation are cool for them, when skepticism about such fun stuff is really killjoy. I'm not sure we can give them credit for accidentally agreeing with evolution theory.

I conclude from all this that creationists are not stupid or crazy, nor do they have flabby intellectual characters. Instead, our mental lives contain complex pictures that connect some beliefs with powerful emotions, and idiosyncratic personal (and cultural) histories. This picture theory explains why some people are deeply attached to some beliefs that have no evidence or even significant counterevidence. And it explains how our mental lives can be very compartmentalized. I can have very tight reasoning in one domain and very sloppy reasoning in another, depending on the mixed-in or interconnecting biases. Perhaps habitual cultivation of intellectual virtues has to happen piecemeal, in different domains, but it's not clear that all domains are influenced by some generic intellectual character.

REHEARSING TO BELIEVE

The critic of religion is always horrified by the idea that I can will myself to believe something, and I can accept an idea because it makes me feel good, or comforts me, or otherwise improves my psyche. It looks like cowardice to the brave secularist whose courage, he tells himself, steels him to sustain doubt until all the facts are in. The disdainful skeptic (not all skeptics are of this variety) sees himself entirely motivated by the unbiased search for truth, but there is a hidden affective or emotional component to this ascetic approach.

As William James pointed out, the skeptic has an emotional center, despite himself. According to James, "he who says, 'Better go without belief forever than believe a lie!' merely shows his own preponderant private horror of becoming a dupe. He may be critical of many of his desires and fears, but this fear he slavishly obeys."[3] He fears, more than anything, the possibility of being fooled, and he gambles that he would rather be inconsolable and suffer the pains of doubt, than become a boob. This withholding of belief is insurance against the final discovery that there is no God after all, or soul, or afterlife. The skeptic is afraid of humiliation, whereas the believer is ready to risk such humiliation. I hasten to add that such humiliation or vindication is a mental invention, given that the skeptic is proved right and vindicated only by being scattered into nothingness after his death—an event he cannot enjoy or lord over his duped colleagues.

Now the defense I am mounting of the believer is not just an appreciation of positive thinking, or a personality type. Instead, I want to suggest an important insight about the nature of knowledge. The ideal function of knowledge, for the secularist, is to ascertain the best possible description of nature. Among contenders like creationism or evolution, for example, the secularist thinks about knowledge as the accurate description of how nature works, and in this case, it is Darwin's natural selection. Of course this is correct, and I myself have spilt significant ink promoting the Darwinian description of nature. Its description of the world is right. But notice something important. For most human beings, the purpose of knowledge is not to describe the world, but to help them navigate it. From Joe Six-Pack to the scientist (when he's not explicitly "sciencing"), what most of us need are beliefs that help us *act* in the world, not *describe* it.

The secularist will protest that he has the correct model of the world and this helps him make accurate predications about nature, so it is useful and helpful in navigating the world. But is this really the case? In my classroom, I use Darwinian natural selection on a regular basis to describe the way birds' wings evolved, or the way human skin color developed as an adaptation to environment, but I can't remember the last time I used natural selection to help me navigate a difficult social encounter, or hiking expedition, or real-time animal interaction, or any practical life challenge. I've used it many times to understand nature writ large, and I've used it to browbeat people at cocktail parties, and so on, but I don't need it much in the world of daily struggle. I submit that this fact is as true for Richard Dawkins as it is for me.

This isolates the key point about knowledge. It appears to have two different aspects, an indicative function and the imperative function. The mind itself has two mental pathways—dorsal and ventral, cold and hot, indicative and imperative. To appreciate the interwoven pathways of mind, consider briefly an experience like fear of a predator—part cognitive and part emotional. The emotion/cognition complex in predator fear is a two-faced experience, partly *imperative* (e.g., I should run away) and partly *indicative* (e.g., that creature is a snake). According to some philosophers, this two-faced representation is strongly coupled together in lower animals—mice, for example, simultaneously recognize cats as a kind of thing (in a category) *and* as dangerous (fear affect).[4] A gazelle sees a cheetah as a specific kind of thing (i.e., not a crocodile, not a giraffe, etc.) but also as a fast approaching threat (imperative). Humans, on the other hand, can decouple these two pathways (indicative and imperative) and fear can be reattached to alternative kinds of creatures or perceptions.[5] Sometimes the indicative face of "crocodile," for example, can be so mentally decoupled from fear and active response, that we can simply study it in a cool unemotional way. This is the foundation of science.

Psychologists refer to these cognitive pathways, imperative and indicative, as "hot" and "cold" cognition, respectfully. Let's adopt this helpful language to capture the distinction I'm drawing. Knowledge that describes the world, and endeavors to describe it with increasing accuracy (science), is processed as cold cognition. It is slow, careful, reflective, deliberative, logical, and based in language and abstraction. Hot cognition, on the other hand, is fast, emotional, embodied, and more habitual than reflective.

The distinction I'm drawing between kinds of knowledge and belief is one we already recognize in other domains. Compare, for example, the way a good violin player uses musical knowledge. Her goal is not to describe the world. As she performs a piece of music, her beliefs and her habits of thought are enlisted for the imperative action of performing. Her beliefs and her habits of mind (and muscle memory) are adaptive, in the sense that they fit with the musicians around her and with the musical environment. But there is no meaningful sense in which her descriptive picture of the world is failing or succeeding against competing beliefs.

Now, let's be clear. Some people are indeed *acting on* (and *navigating with*) the correct *descriptions* of nature. They are applying the indicative knowledge to the imperative struggle. When a NASA physicist needs to calculate a launch trajectory, she uses the best description we have of nature, and when an immunologist works on a disease she uses adaptation models from evolution. That is not disputed. But you and I, and even these scientists, leave the office and reenter the fast spinning world of real-time problem solving and do not have the luxury of describing nature. Beliefs in that fast-spinning world are for something else, namely, survival.

I have no interest in defending the Creation Museum here. The problem with the Creation Museum, and creationism generally, is that creationists have made the error from the other side. They are trying to justify their imperative beliefs on the grounds of an alternative indicative description of the world (an Iron Age description). Why do some believers bother to do this? Many mainstream Christians, for example, are comfortable with imperative beliefs (e.g., moral norms, values) needing no validation in the indicative description of nature. Most moderate religious people accept some version of Galileo's famous division of labor: "The intention of the Holy Ghost is to teach us how one goes to heaven, not how heaven goes."[6] Ironically, the creationist, and fundamentalist generally, has accepted the dominance of the indicative model of knowledge (which describes facts). Fundamentalists unknowingly embrace the logic that norms and values (imperative beliefs) must be built upon a description of the world (indicative beliefs). In that doomed project, creationists and atheists share the mistaken assumption that an accurate description of the world will unroll the rules of moral and social behavior.

I want to propose that it's the other way around. The imperative hot cognition approach to life is very ancient, predating the rise of language, logic, and even the expanded neocortex. It's how animals get around in the world. It's the limbic life of gut feelings, and rapid responses, helping us detect quickly who is a friend, an enemy, a sexual partner, and subtler social relations, such as who is a good hunter, who is reliable, who owes me, and how I should treat this approaching person right now.

In this imperative world, memories, instincts, and emotional systems guide me, not logic or science. Eventually, of course, we evolved language and developed symbol-based ways of navigating the world. But generally speaking, the symbols that rule this imperative world of action are *stories* and *images*, not the later descriptive language of science. Stories and images don't just describe the world, they inspire action in the world. They push our emotions in specific directions. They motivate us, rather than just label, organize, and model the world. From this perspective, a factual description of the world comes after the hot cognition interaction with the social world. Or at least they are parallel tracks of knowledge.

William James (1879) goes even further and argues that even our scientific concepts and descriptions only make sense in the context of our very human purposes and needs. Even a *concept* only has essential or defining properties in light of the goals or purposes we are pursuing. "What now is a *conception*? It is a *teleological instrument*. It is a partial aspect of a thing which *for our purpose* we regard as its essential aspect, as the representative of the entire thing." "But," he continues, "the essence, the ground of conception, varies with the end we have in view. A substance like oil has as many different essences as it has uses to different individuals. One man conceives it as a combustible, another as a lubricator, another as a food; the chemist thinks of it as a hydro-carbon; the furniture maker as a darkener of wood . . ." (p. 319).[7] And following this logic, history also admits of alternative conceptions. For the believer, whose purpose is relating to God, history is a record of the Deity's plan, while for the skeptic, history is a sequence of events, with causal connections but not destiny.

The religious person is living more in the imperative world than in the indicative one. We are all living in both worlds, but we tend to spend more time in one rather than the other. For the fundamentalist the world is a drama first and a material system second. Their world already is populated with good guys and bad guys, fates, destinies, sacred missions, and other literary and mythic aspects. For the secularist, the indicative mode is more dominant, and the material system of impersonal laws is primary. Norms, values, and the imperative life generally should follow the contours of the objective description.

The irony I mentioned above is clearer. Moderate religious people are happy to treat their imperative knowledge as a fundamental reality—needing no further foundation but faith, or social experience, or emotional validation. The average Christian, for example, doesn't need the Moses story of Ten Commandments to be true in order to believe strongly in the value of telling the truth. But fundamentalists have incorrectly accepted the modern secular framework (despite their best intentions) by insisting on the objective "truth" of their Iron-Age description of the world. They betray their anxiety about their imperative beliefs by trying to tether them to the indicative world. It's a bad strategy twice over. First, the Iron-Age description of the world can't hold water in our era of upgraded description. And secondly, imperative beliefs about ethics and values don't even need scientific or indicative validation.[8] Their validation comes from the complex world of social emotions, but more on that later.

In many aspects of life we want to avoid make-believe scenarios because they smack of intellectual cowardice, but in some aspects we actively cultivate the primordial imagination. There's no reason why this has to be consistent—only the secular mind craves law-like consistency anyway.

An important feature of grown-up pretending is that it can bring about the real thing. In some cases, imagining and pretending may be the only way to realize an actual change in the world. Stanford anthropologist Tanya Luhrmann has separately studied the rich counterfactual lives of evangelical Christians and schizophrenics. The usual barrier between the counterfactual and factual world, which most of us maintain with ease, is not as robust or distinct in some people. When the counterfactual second universe bleeds too far into the factual world, we recognize pathologies like schizophrenia. But otherwise healthy minds also will voluntarily cultivate a breakdown of the barrier, in service of religious insight.

God has no face, no obvious form, no clear and unambiguous voice. When you pray, Professor Luhrmann points out, "you cannot look him in the eye, and judge that he hears you back."[9] This is a perennial problem for the believer, according to Luhrmann, but there is an imaginative remedy. For one thing, believers engage in a process of imagining that their dominant ideas, mental events, and feelings are coming from God directly, rather than just their own associational mind. This requires the believer to pick out dominant thoughts from the stream of mental events during reflection and prayer, and it also requires the believer to assign God as the agent responsible for those mental events. Both these requirements get easier with practice and cultivation. Luhrmann discovered that many evangelical women practice this process by doing imaginary "dates" and other "couples" activities, all the while in a virtual "conversation" with Jesus—their imaginary companion. Moreover, following a point made by Christian apologist C.S. Lewis, in his book *Mere Christianity*, Lurhmann finds that many evangelicals "pretend" or imagine themselves to be Christ (or Christ-like) as they interact with people throughout the day.

I'm not sure that we can *choose* to believe things in a straightforward manner, nor am I sure this is an advisable path toward intellectual virtue. But this example of habituation (e.g., talking to Jesus) reveals how an initially counterfactual belief can be slowly normalized and added to one's cognitive/emotional picture of the world. Even some of our more respectable and seemingly justified beliefs may be the result of brute habituation, rather than investigation, logic, and method (e.g., my Chicago students who are habituated to evolution). But one thing is clear—pretending you are Christ (or Buddha, or Martin Luther King, Jr.) can transform the world of action and policy.

If I pretend that I am a dog, I do not eventually become a dog. If I pretend that the world is only 6,000 years old, nothing changes in the structure of the universe. But if I pretend that I am good for long enough, I actually become good. Also, if I pretend that we are friends in the early days of our acquaintance, then slowly we become friends—not solely by an act of imagination, but by the activities that such pretending galvanizes. In the dramatic imperative world (which is primary in the religious person and secondary in the secular), imaginative habituation is transformative. It helps people survive tragedies, motivate action, and dance through complex social experiences.

Lastly, we need to briefly acknowledge a specific emotional nexus that nourishes and is nourished by being a marginal community. Creationists, conspiracy theorists, ghost believers, and more serious groups like jihadi fundamentalists share an emotional life. The pleasures of being a rebel, which were once the provenance of atheists, have now become the bread-and-butter of religious subcultures. Conspiracy and creationism give believers a great emotional sense of being elite cognoscenti, in a world of misguided sheep (and/or infidels). Moreover, it feels uniquely good to be right, in the face of tempting alternatives, and it activates the emotions of pride and resolution to wake up every day and resist. Feelings of outrage, aggression, vanity, as well as positive effects of gratitude, generosity, vitality, and so on, crystallize around the eccentric size of the group. We'll have more to say on these and other emotions in the coming chapters.

CHAPTER 2

Sorrow, Death, and Emotional Management

No one ever told me that grief felt so like fear.

— C.S. Lewis, *A Grief Observed*

To weep is to make less the depth of grief.

— William Shakespeare, *King Henry VI, Part 3*

Losing a family member or a lover is one of the greatest injuries that life can throw at you. Of course, dying is not great either, but at least you're not left behind to writhe in grief. Existential dread of one's own death is a well-known impetus for religious belief, and the preponderance of elderly people at church, temple, and shrine betrays the universal anxiety. Fear is a language in which religion is fluent, and we will examine it carefully later. But religion is also remarkably helpful in consoling sorrow.

When I was in primary school, I was a Catholic altar boy. My brothers and I were dutifully driven, in rain or snow, to Immaculate Conception church, where we would serve mass. The duties of altar boys are largely ornamental, and we performed ritual tasks, such as standing at the lectern during gospel readings, ringing bells at key moments in the liturgy, holding a metal dish under the parishioner chin in case of fumbled communion hosts. In addition to weekday morning masses, and of course Sunday services, we also served a huge number of funerals. This brought me into close proximity with death at an early age, and gave my brothers and me a weird mix of reverence and offhanded indifference. Most altar boys were more concerned with the possibility of a postfuneral tip—a few dollars—from a relative of the deceased, than with the journey of the dearly departed.

Still, I learned one thing of great importance—a thing one cannot learn by only occasional funeral attendance. I learned the shtick or the sell of funerals. Like a roadie who goes on tour with a band and sees every cliché repeated nightly to an unsuspecting audience, the altar boy sees the clichés of the priest and Catholicism reiterated ad nauseam. Of course, there is wisdom in some of these clichés. They are tried-and-true rituals and messages of consolation for grieving families.

At each homily, the priest would insert the name of the deceased into a road-tested, generic, eulogy. And the broken hearts of the audience would interpret even the most artless tribute into a beautiful homage. But the priest's overall message was unwavering: "Your beloved (fill in name here) is not really dead, but lives on in the next world." The shtick of the funeral, and of Western religion generally, is that death is an illusion.

Wanting my dead loved one to be alive in a place where I can see her again is not about my gullibility. My rational mind, after all, may feel quite awkward about such a belief. But I am reminded, in the very moment of such wishful thinking, how much I loved that person. The burn of that hopeful and ludicrous desire, even amidst the contempt of my own reason, is evidence that our bond was essential and fundamental. I loved that person so much that I am willing to deny death, on the outside chance that we can reunite. The triumph of magical thinking during the grieving period is nothing to be ashamed about, and it has nothing to do with weakness.

Critics of religion are quick to interpret the denial of death as "fear" and then it's a quick step to calling it cowardice. Christopher Hitchens (2007), for example, says that religion will not die out until we "get over our fear of death" (p. 12), and Sam Harris (2004) says, "without death, the influence of faith-based religion would be unthinkable" (p. 39).[1]

But sorrow is not the same as fear, nor is it motivated by fear. The two emotions sometimes become mixed, and our cultural activities surrounding death can reinforce the mixture. C.S. Lewis famously said, "No one ever told me that grief felt so like fear."[2] But grief and fear are two distinct emotional systems. And it is grief or sorrow that concerns us in this chapter.

THE BIOLOGY OF GRIEF

Sorrow and grief are part of our emotional inheritance, as mammals. Darwin, in his book *The Expression of Emotions in Man and Animals* (1872), describes the unique facial changes that humans undergo just before weeping.[3] The eyebrows invariably arch up into a peak, furrowing the brow, and the corners of the mouth turn down dramatically. These expressions are so universal that Darwin calls their underlying causes "grief muscles." Of course, uncontrollable tears often follow.

Most mammals produce tears as a way to clean their eyes, and keep them moist. But do animals cry? Do they produce tears in response to emotional sadness? "The Indian elephant," Darwin reports, "is known sometimes to weep." Darwin quotes Sir E. Tennent's description of a bound elephant: "When overpowered and made fast, his grief was most affecting; his violence sank to utter prostration, and he lay on the ground, uttering choking cries, with tears trickling down his cheeks." And Darwin adds that, "In the Zoological Gardens the keeper of the Indian elephants positively asserts that he has several times seen tears rolling down the face of the old female, when distressed by the removal of the young one" (p. 59).

In 2013, at the Shendiaoshan wild animal reserve in Rongcheng, China, a baby elephant was rejected by its mother just after being born. The mother actually tried to kill the baby. Once rescued from the cage, the baby reportedly cried tears for five hours, leading many to wonder about the emotional similarity with human sorrow.[4] Of course, it is always dangerous to anthropomorphize animals, when data is so anecdotal. But as Marc Bekoff reminds us, "the plural of anecdote is data," so enough of these stories can stack up to something.

An expert in animal cognition, Marc Bekoff, cofounder with Jane Goodall of Ethologists for the Ethical Treatment of Animals, suggests that elephant tears are emotionally significant and might express real grief or sorrow. Bekoff says, "we are not 100% certain, solid scientific research supports the view that elephants and other nonhuman animals weep as part of an emotional response. Rather than dismissing this possibility as merely storytelling, we need to study it in more detail."[5] Examining the case of the crying elephant in Rongcheng, Bekoff points out that mammals are hardwired to pursue "contact comfort"—the calming comfort of a caregiver's touch. When denied this comfort, the animal shows all the signs of stress and even sorrow. Henry Harlow's famous experiments with rhesus monkeys, in the early 1960s, tragically showed us how babies without comforting touch go insane, even if their other needs are fully met.

Human babies also need contact comfort, and develop attachment disorders when they fail to get caregiver touch. Discomfort and sadness in the face of social isolation (i.e., isolation from touch, warmth, smell, visual and auditory stimuli, etc.), is extremely traumatic for mammals because we are social creatures. Unlike some reptiles and insects, we mammals evolved in a highly dependent relation with other members of our species.

Mammals evolved social glue that first bonds mothers and infants, and later helps establish family and friendship affiliations. Bonding is an essential skill for any animal born into a hostile environment. Prey animals, especially herd animals, are born with remarkable physical adeptness. They can walk and even run within minutes of birth. This mobility is important in a predator-filled world, but it puts these animals at great risk of potential separation from their mothers. So, it's not surprising that herd animals have very tight windows of opportunity for identifying their mothers and latching on to them. Other animals, such as rats, humans, and predators, have extended periods of bonding—the window for latching onto Mom closes very slowly. Failure to lock onto Mom means death for the offspring, and possible termination of gene line for the parents. So the natural selection pressures for attachment are intense.

Babies don't rationally decide who their Mom is and then pledge devotion to her. The process is not rational in that way. Nor is the bonding process a simple case of behavioral conditioning—a view that dominated psychology for decades. Behaviorists assumed that we form social bonds because we are conditioned by the pleasant rewards of food, water, shelter, and so on. According to this view, I love my parents because of reinforced associations with pleasurable (hedonic) rewards. Some of this conditioning is genuine, but emotional neuroscience has recently discovered a bonding circuit in the brain. Specific internal chemical changes spike during the window of opportunity in the brains and bodies of parents and offspring, cementing them together in ways that are not comparable to other relationships.

Specific neuropeptides—oxytocin, prolactin, and opiates like endorphins—all rise sharply in the last days of a mother's pregnancy. Oxytocin and opioids regulate several aspects of maternal biology (facilitating labor and breastfeeding), but also play a crucial role in nurturing behavior—what Dr. Jaak Panksepp calls the CARE system. Simply introducing these neuropeptides in high doses into a nonpregnant female mammal will actually produce mothering behaviors. Nonpregnant female rats, given blood transfusions from females who had just given birth, immediately began engaging in new maternal behaviors (e.g., building nests, gathering another mother's dispersed pups together, or hovering over them to provide warmth).[6]

Many mammals imprint through the "Jacobson's organ" (vomeronasal organ) at the roof of the mouth. Chemicals from offspring are taken up by the mother's Jacobson's organ (through smell or oral contact), usually during the cleaning of the newborn baby, and signals are conducted upstream to target brain sites in the amygdala and hypothalamus. Humans have a vestigial Jacobson's organ, observable in embryogenesis but largely inactive in adulthood. Different species have diverse ways of harvesting the chemical information that bonds them together, but for mammals the resulting brain chemistry of oxytocin is strikingly similar.

Sheep have a very short window for the mother to bond with offspring, only an hour or two. If a lamb is removed from its mother for two hours, the mother will not be bonded and will subsequently reject the lamb. Remarkably, after the bonding window has closed, scientists can *reopen* it again for a couple of hours by injecting oxytocin into the mother's brain. Once oxytocin is flooding the system again, the mother can lock onto her offspring and engage in maternal behaviors.[7] The mother elephant that rejected her baby and caused the crying fit in China probably had a failure in her oxytocin-based CARE system.

Oxytocin is more than a lever or switch for turning on motherhood. It also plays an important role in the brain (it's made in the hypothalamus, stored in the posterior pituitary, and then released into circulation). Discovery of oxytocin receptors in the brain signify that the brain is also a target organ for oxytocin. Oxytocin has been shown to reduce many forms of aggression. It is, among other things, a general anxiety reducer. Oxytocin calms down aggression and dramatically reduces irritability—important mood alterations for new parents. Male moods are equally transformed by oxytocin, which floods the male brain after sex.[8] Some recent research alternatively suggest that oxytocin is more like an emotional amplifier, rather than a reliable anxiety reducer, but the role in bonding is well established.

Humans are like other mammals in their development of separation distress. Of course, babies cry out for their caregivers from an early age, but we don't exhibit the more profound forms of separation distress until our motor skills have matured enough to give us walk-around independence, and therefore the ability to get lost. Our early childhood emotional experience contours the kind of attachment style we take into later life. Starting in the late 1950s, John Bowlby began articulating attachment theory, developing it further with a trilogy of books in 1969, 1972, and 1980.[9] Bowlby argued that infants are born with a psychobiological need to turn to their caregiver when experiencing fear or stress. We are born primed for intimacy, and that bond is forged with touch, eye contact, vocal soothing, and general attentiveness of the caregiver to the needs and emotional states of the child. Infants continue to explore their environment when they sense that their caregiver is nearby and vigilant. When the mother or father provides this safe haven, then adaptive attachment occurs, otherwise known as *secure base* attachment. This secure bonding, however, is often disrupted, or fails to develop (insecure attachment), because of neglect or abuse. Insecure attachment often leads to less successful social navigation in later life. Oxytocin underlies these experiences of social attachment.

Dr. Seth Pollak and other psychologists at the University of Wisconsin, Madison, discovered that oxytocin is absolutely vital in *human* bonding.[10] Researchers wanted to know why some kids fail to bond with their parents. Many kids suffer from "attachment disorders," failing to seek comfort in others, even their own families. Using a control group of nonadopted kids, the researchers collected baseline oxytocin (and vasopressin) levels in eighteen 4-year-old kids who were adopted from Russian and Romanian orphanages. The children from the orphanages had a history of neglect.

Dr. Pollak devised a test in which oxytocin levels were checked before and after comfort/play time with parents. The children were held on the laps of their mothers and played a computer game together, engaging in intimate play, like whispering, tickling, petting, and so on. Immediately after this, the pleasurable oxytocin levels spiked in the nonadopted children, but remained the same in the adopted children. It appears that the anxiety reducing, calming effects of oxytocin have been *primed* in us by our earliest nurturing experiences. If a child is neglected, in an overpopulated orphanage, or in a cold family situation, they fail to form the normal attachment chemistry. Early experience with a loving caregiver "wires" the brain to associate a specific person or people with pleasurable, happy states. This association, which is both chemical and psychological, is the template for positive social bonding in later life.

In the same way that we can be hungry and even starved for food nutrition, the brain can be starved for emotional nutrition—and close family and friends provide that sustenance by simply being present. Like other mammals, we go into panic mode when we are lost and when we lose someone.

Human grief and sorrow are more complex and subtle forms of mammalian separation distress. Our grief has elaborate cognitive dimensions, because humans can ruminate on dashed hopes and also replay memories at will, but deep down, the emotional brain is undergoing a major reduction in opioids, oxytocin, and prolactin. "Brain opioids were the first neurochemistries discovered to powerfully reduce separation distress. As predicted by the opiate theory of social attachment, drugs such as morphine that powerfully reduce crying in animals are also powerful alleviators of grief and loneliness in humans."[11] Dr. Panksepp suggests that human drug addictions may emerge in part because our brains evolved to seek and take pleasure in social bonds (via internal opioids), but when a person fails to forge those bonds (for many diverse reasons) they turn to substituting those satisfactions via pharmacological means.

All this takes the sting out of the common Marxist critique of religion—that it is nothing but an "opiate of the masses." If affective neuroscience is correct, then the lion's share of our social life also is underpinned by internal opiates. Our brains evolved an endogenous opioid system that blocks pain and produces euphoria, and this feedback loop became the motivational system underlying our social interactions. Maybe religion is the opiate of the masses, but then so is friendship and love. No one is condemning friendship because of its pain-killing, pleasure-producing aspects. And it's easy to see that religion and friendship are healthier external triggers of the internal system, than say morphine, heroine, Vicodin, and OxyContin (unless of course you're injured, in which case the pharmacy trumps social euphoria). It's true that the "opiate objection" to religion is more about political oppression and we shall come to that shortly, but it's important to forestall the merely puritanical distaste for analgesia.

HOW DOES RELIGION RELIEVE SORROW?

Separation distress is part of our mammalian operating system. It drives us to be with other human beings, and to seek the contact comfort of intimacy. It evolved long before rational cooperation (conscious cost-benefit assessment), as the emotional glue that held families and tribes together against a hostile world. Unfortunately, as the Buddha was fond of pointing out, being attached to others opens us up to great suffering, because of course they will die. In the words of folksinger Slaid Cleaves, "Everything you love will be taken away."

Sorrow is elemental for us, and, as such, needs emotional management. The task of cultural technologies like religion is not to repress sorrow, deny it, or repudiate it. The task is to process it in a manner that leaves the grieving person relatively vital, functioning, and even potentially happy, albeit transformed by the nontrivial loss of the loved one. Sadness of loss must be accepted, but then it must eventually be blended into the wholeness of life. This is complex and necessary therapeutic work, and it is adaptive for the individual and the species.

I want to suggest five ways in which religion successfully manages sorrow. First, let's consider the placebo effect. The placebo has been a long-time methodological tool in medical research. A fake or false treatment, or an inactive substance (such as saline solution or a sugar pill), or even an authoritarian suggestion, can improve a patient's condition just because the patient believes or expects it to be helpful or effective. The placebo often has been used as the methodological contrast (together with no treatment) to demonstrate the objective effectiveness of some active ingredient. More recently, however, psychologists have noticed how surprisingly powerful the placebo effect can be.[12]

A study in 2007 demonstrated the impact of mindset on health, by testing hotel room cleaners.[13] Eighty-four female workers from seven different hotels were medically assessed and then half of them were told that their regular cleaning work was extremely healthy, and satisfied the Surgeon General's recommendations for an active lifestyle. The other half of the group was not given this informational pep-talk. Both groups did the same quantity and quality of work, but after four weeks the pep-talk group showed a decrease in weight, waist-to-hip ratio, blood pressure, body fat, and body mass index. The investigators concluded, "these results support the hypothesis that exercise affects health in part or in whole via the placebo effect." This conclusion seems a bit overstated, but it's clear that mental attitude and belief have measurable physical effects.

In 2014, a study showed how cognition also can be heavily influenced by placebo suggestion.[14] One-hundred and sixty-four students were hooked up to fancy brain-wave reading machines as they went to sleep. They were told that the machine measured the quality of their sleep, but it really did nothing. When they woke they were informed (randomly) that their REM sleep had been excellent (28% of their total sleep) or poor (only 16%). Following this bogus information, the students were administered a battery of cognitive tests, and those who believed they had excellent sleep (via placebo suggestion) did markedly better on the exams.

Religious responses to grief may be similar to these placebo cases, where mindset helps to improve overall health and emotional wellbeing. The Catholic funeral liturgy, for example, is formulaic and most clerics read aloud some version of this passage: "In the face of death, the Church confidently proclaims that God has created each person for eternal life and that Jesus, the Son of God, by his death and resurrection, has broken the chains of sin and death that bound humanity. Christians celebrate the funeral rites to offer worship, praise, and thanksgiving to God for the gift of a life which has now been returned to God, the author of life and the hope of the just."[15]

My brothers and I heard something like this a hundred times, as we lit candles and rang bells according to our altar boy duties. And the line that drops like a placebo seed into the hearts of the grieving, only to grow and flower later is: "At the rite of final commendation and farewell, the community acknowledges the reality of separation and commends the deceased to God. In this way it recognizes the spiritual bond that still exists between the living and the dead and proclaims its belief that all the faithful will be raised up and reunited in the new heavens and a new earth, where death will be no more." There it is. Bold, blockbuster even, and deeply consoling, however improbable. The placebo may unfold and grow slowly, as the fresh pain subsides, but the placebo of "death will be no more" makes the inspirational power 28% REM sleep pale by comparison.

Placebos are around 60% as effective in reducing pain as most active medications (e.g., codeine or aspirin).[16] Cultural mechanisms of suggestion, like religion (e.g., liturgy, clerical commands, blessings, group and personal rituals, and shaman healing), have historically delivered the palliative therapies. Historically, pills have not been needed for placebo suggestion, although many religious rituals do involve ingesting some pseudomagical substance (e.g., communion, ghee, halva, matzo, ayahuasca, or peyote). The effectiveness of placebo cultural mechanisms should give pause to any facile rejection of ritual as outmoded and useless. Remarkably, several studies have found that faithful believers live longer and healthier than skeptics.[17]

A second way that religion successfully manages sorrow, can be seen in the social traditions of most funerary and grieving customs. In the same way that social touch, collective feeding, and grooming restore mammals to health after separation distress, so, too, human grieving customs involve these same soothing prosocial mechanisms. We comfort-touch and embrace a person who has lost a loved one. Our bodies give ancient comfort directly to the grieving body. We also share food with them. We provision the bereaved with food and drink, and we break bread with them, too (e.g., the Jewish tradition of shiva). We also groom the griever with language, by sharing stories about the loved one, and giving encouraging words to help them reframe their pain in larger optimistic narratives. Even music, in the form of consoling melodies and collective singing, helps to express shared sorrow and also transforms it from an unbearable and lonely experience to a bearable communal one.

The Order of Christian Funerals summarizes the kind of social grooming we see in most religions. "Members of the community should console the mourners with words of faith and support and with acts of kindness, for example, assisting them with some of the routine tasks of daily living." These seemingly mundane activities bring the positive affect/emotional ingredients we discussed earlier (i.e., oxytocin, endogenous opioids) and push negative affect out of the suffering mind. It's also possible that religious ways of framing social interaction increase serotonin, dopamine, and norepinephrine, though we don't have much data on this yet. Brain science aside, however, we can appreciate that positive social involvement from the community after a death can act as an antidepressant, boosting adaptive emotional changes in the bereaved.

Obviously, hugging someone after they've lost a loved one is not some exclusive behavior of religious persons. Indeed, my claim is that positive social touch goes back to our mammal ancestry, and predates religion by a long shot. But religion is a cultural codification of these evolved grief-consoling strategies. Religion formally organizes many of these prosocial behaviors—consoling stories, handshakes, hugs, food, music, collective shared emotional expressions, and so on. There are secular ways to harness and organize some of the therapeutic prosocial emotions after a sorrowful loss—for example, see The Moyer Foundation's "Camp Erin" for grieving children[18]—but these are few and far between.

A third way that religion helps to manage sorrow is something I'll call "existential shaping" or more precisely "existential debt." It is common for Westerners, and Americans in particular, to think of themselves as individuals first and as members of a community second. There are cultural and historic reasons for this emphasis, but our ideology of the lone protagonist—fulfilling his individual destiny—is more fiction than fact.[19] Even the most independent among us are usually tied in a web of social relations that make us who we are. Losing someone (or even losing at one of life's many other trials) reminds us of our dependence on others and our frailty and vulnerability. Sometimes it is important to remember our vulnerability, because it reconnects us to the people we need, and teaches us some humility toward the larger challenges of life. Long after your parents have died, for example, religion helps you memorialize them and acknowledge your existential debt to them.

Grief, failure, and sorrow, without religion will probably still remind you of your vulnerability, but religion can help to structure our cognition and emotion—turning us toward the web of relations rather than away from it. Religion has ceremonial ways of reminding us of our existential debts, and this does two important things. It takes us out of the depression and self-pity mode, and it also reminds us that the web of existential debt is still vital among the living. The rather obvious debt for the believer is, of course, her gratitude to a divine being that brought about her existence. But that is only the most obvious form of indebtedness and the humanist critique of such deference drowns out religion's subtler forms of social commemoration.

Religious management of death helps us remember and celebrate, but not perseverate or despair. As the famous psychiatrist Elisabeth Kubler-Ross, puts it, "the reality is that you will grieve forever. You will not 'get over' the loss of a loved one; you will learn to live with it. You will heal and you will rebuild yourself around the loss you have suffered. You will be whole again but you will never be the same. Nor should you be the same nor would you want to."[20]

Formalizing memory of the dead person, through funerary rites, or tomb-sweeping holidays in Asia (Qingming), or Day of the Dead in Mexico, or annual honorary masses in Catholicism, is important because it keeps reminding us, even through the sorrow, of the meaningful influence of these deceased loved ones. This is meaningful sorrow. It is not a self-deception about the unreality of death, but an artful way of learning to live with it.

Who I am is tied up inexorably with my people—my family, friends, and tribe. Losing them is losing some part of me. Religion helps me see such loss as both tragic and beautiful. It's not beautiful because the person is still alive in the beatific beyond (although some believers speak this way). The grief becomes beautiful in the sincere acknowledgment of the value of the loved one, and religious rituals help people set aside time and mental space for that acknowledgment. When you are experiencing the gratitude of your existential debt to departed family and friends, then you are momentarily reuniting with them. As Philip K. Dick puts it, "grief reunites you with what you've lost. It's a merging; you go with the loved thing or person that's going away. You follow it as far as you can go."[21]

As grief slowly gives way to acceptance, we still share deep connections with the dead—connections called "spiritual" by believers and even agnostics, who find no better vocabulary to emphasize their depth. There are duties and privileges in honoring the dead. The poet Galway Kinnell offers a powerful articulation of the ongoing relationship that we living have with the dead. The heart of the relationship is not supernatural or metaphysical, but based upon memory. Religion, like poetry, employs supernatural language because literal language fails to capture the emotional profundity.

> If I die before you . . .
> I will cross over into you
> and ask you to carry
> not only your own memories
> but mine too until you
> too lie down and erase us
> both together into oblivion.[22]

A fourth way that religion helps relieve sorrow is more controversial. In short, there are levels of tragedy that cannot be healed, or rehabilitated, or assuaged, by anything secular or scientific. There is no scientific or secular sop to a parent who has lost her child. Only a magical "solution" will work. Religion excels in this domain.

The Islamic funeral prayer, for example, states, "O God, admit him to Paradise and protect him from the torment of the grave and the torment of Hell-fire; make his grave spacious and fill it with light." This sort of thing abounds in many religions, and gives hope to the hopeless. We learn in the *Bhagavad Gita*, for example, that the soul cannot be pierced with sword, or burnt, or otherwise harmed, or destroyed. If a parent can think of the essence of her child as this immaterial soul, then she can imagine that some essential part of her child escaped the brutal physical death she sees in the morgue.

The relevance of magical consolation can be seen clearly when we move from the obviously religious cases to the pseudoreligious scientific attempts to overcome death. The history of science reveals more irrational hope than one might expect. The point of this example is to foil the atheist accusation that religion causes magical hope and to underscore that such universal hope inspires science, too. Setting aside the many cranium-freezing, transhumanist longevity projects, consider a moving story of physicist Ron Mallett.[23]

For most of his life, physicist Ron Mallett has been motivated by a deep desire to see his dead father again. In the 1950s, Ron's dad died suddenly of a heart attack when Ron was ten years old. Ron says it is impossible to describe the overwhelming sense of loss and anguish that he felt, and still feels. "He was the center of my universe."

After his father's death, Ron slowly forged his big plan. The plan started from reading a comic book based on H.G. Wells's *The Time Machine*. If Ron could really make this machine, he could go back to be with his father again. He would go back in time and warn his father to take care of his health, so he could live on. He knew that he had to keep this plan a secret, because others would think he was crazy.

Ron started small, with childish machines built in the basement, but slowly he began reading more sophisticated science books, including Einstein's discussion of the Lorentz Transformation, and then he kept delving into ordinary calculus, tensor calculus, group theory, differential equations, multivariable calculus, vector analysis, matrix analysis, physics, quantum mechanics, electrodynamics, general relativity, and so on. He eventually became a professor of physics at the University of Connecticut. At the core of his interest was the obsession with time travel, but he could not reveal this passion to the public or his professional colleagues, and he grew increasingly depressed. After many years, he took up the challenge again, and actually built a small machine that uses light to bend gravity and potentially alter time. The experiment drops a neutron into the machine and looks for tiny changes. When he presented his work to an elite group of physicists, a contemporary of Einstein's—a hero of Ron's—told him, "I don't know if you'll get to see your father again, but he would have been proud of you."

We can dismiss Ron's work and passion as neurotic or obsessive, but one thing the absurd project did for Ron was help him feel close to his father. He frequently fantasized about going back in time to see his father, and bringing a photo album to show him his future family. He rehearsed their conversations. Imagined the sound of his voice. And he rehearsed how he would scold him to stop smoking and take better care of his health. Finally, he would tell him what he had not told him in childhood—that he loved him.

This is a moving story of sorrow, devotion, and determination. But the scientific aspects and the higher math do not hide the fact that Ron is engaged in magical consolation. Time travel to see our dead loved ones is as realistic and rational as soul communion in the afterlife. Scientists who have suffered great loss are as unrealistic as the rest of us. Don't let the PhDs after their names fool you.

Lastly, religion is helpful in managing sorrow and grief because it provides unique appraisals. As we mentioned in the Introduction, emotions are partly physiological change or arousal and partly cognitive evaluations or appraisals of events. The classic experiment, demonstrating the importance of appraisal in emotion, was done by Stanley Schachter and Jerome Singer in 1962. They injected test subjects with adrenalin (telling them it was an eyesight medication). Next they separated the subjects into groups and put them in different rooms. The adrenalin raised their physiological arousal to a high degree (respiration, blood pressure, heart rate), but each room was given a different confederate actor; one was angry and hostile, while the other was humorous and fun. The test subjects did not feel a specific emotion based on arousal alone, but instead read their immediate environment for clues about what they were feeling. The fun room led them to label their aroused state as joyful, while the other group labeled their heightened arousal as negative emotion. The appraisal helps to make the emotion specific.

An emotion like grief has many ingredients. The physiological arousal of grief is accompanied by cognitive evaluations: I will never see my friend again; I could have done something to prevent this; she was the love of my life; he still owed me money, and so on. But emotional appraisals are also proactive, according to psychologists Phoebe Ellsworth and Klaus Scherer.[24] Appraisal is going "beyond the immediate situation and assessing the probability of possible outcomes by taking into account the ability to change the situation and its consequences" (p. 580). This is called "secondary appraisal" and it goes beyond the primary appraisal "this is very sad" to assess our ability to deal with the situation: "this is too much for me"; "this will break me"; "I don't know how to deal with this"; or positively, "I will survive this" or "I am ready for this."

According to emotions research, part of our ability to cope is our sense of power or agency. There are many sources of power when we are dealing with pain. For example, physical strength can give people the sense that they can cope with a threat or a particular kind of pain, or that money is a source of power when we feel stressed about certain trials and tribulations. Having knowledge is another important source of power, as is feeling attractive. These sources of power can greatly improve our coping abilities when disaster strikes.

In addition, the way we understand agency or responsibility can shape the specific emotion we're experiencing. "The attribution of agency has been shown to be particularly important in distinguishing among the negative emotions of anger (other agency), guilt (self agency), and sorrow (circumstance agency)" (p. 580). In many cases of grief (death from cancer, car accident, etc.) the agency is diffused to a wide realm of accidental circumstances (e.g., the laws of nature, and chance). But it is also common in the early stages of grief to assign other agency (thus feeling angry) and self agency (guilt).

The point is that more power generally means better coping ability. And having God on your side must be a huge sense of power. Being religious can be an important part of the grieving person's proactive appraisal. Believing that your benevolent God is aware of your current misfortunes, and perhaps even an inscrutable architect of those misfortunes, gives the believer a sense that the appearance of capricious calamity is only that—appearance. Belief that some deeper design or plan is at work makes the uncontrollable world seem controlled and may buttress a nearly defeated griever. The old saw, "God won't give you any more than you can handle" (vaguely derived from 1 Corinthians 10:13), is a source of power for many religious bereaved. Power, even if it's only perceived or imagined power, is instrumental in successful coping.

Psychologist Kenneth Pargament and others have amassed a fair amount of empirical data that confirm the role of religion in coping with life's hardships.[25] Generally speaking, religious believers engage in one of three styles or types of coping; the deferring style (where all hardships are referred to God for resolution), the self-directing style (where individuals employ their God-given powers to resolve issues), and finally the collaborative style (where God is treated as a teammate in the resolution of difficult issues). According to Pargament's colleagues, R.E. Phillips et al., the collaborative style correlated well with improved self-esteem, and reduced depression.[26] In other words, believing that God or a divine power is along with you in your travails, lending a hand so to speak (e.g., God is my copilot) improves your ability to meet challenges.

It's common for critics of religion to acknowledge its occasional therapeutic aspect, but quickly remind us that religion is a form of "reality denial" or "reality avoidance." No doubt this is true in some cases, but Dr. Pargament found substantial data that religion's main power lies in its "ability to appraise negative events from a different vantage point. Crises become an opportunity for closeness with God . . . Even the most desperate situations can be appraised in a more benevolent light from the religious perspective."[27]

According to this view, religion does not increase coping by denying reality, but by reframing it in a manner that inspires resolve, or courage, or whatever is needed. In this regard it functions like the friend who helps you see your troubles in a more positive light. No doubt, our friends have been performing this vital function since the dawn of language, and we even see it clearly in the earliest work of literature, *The Epic of Gilgamesh* (c. 2100 BCE). On the eve of facing a dreadful monster, Gilgamesh has a series of frightening dreams that dispirit him and render him weak, but his best friend Enkidu reinterprets each dream in a positive manner, such that Gilgamesh is emboldened for the battle. His fear dissipates, and he is nourished by the benevolent spin that his friend offers. Like the friend, religion helps one reframe obstacles as opportunities.

Of course I'm not naive, religion can also help you see your troubles in a more negative light (e.g., "God hates you because you're attracted to the same sex," etc.). But these more stressful reappraisals are common to extremist traditions (a loud minority) rather than mainstream stakeholders who are just trying to make it through the daily travails of life. There is an undeniable masochistic streak in religion, but it is only a streak.

ALL THINGS ARE IMPERMANENT?

Most religions proffer some version of immortality. I've been suggesting that this is particularly consoling in the face of sorrow and grief, when we lose people we love. Of course, many people have pointed out that belief in immortality also acts to neutralize fear of our own death (or at least reduce it), and such belief has the added function of keeping believers honest or ethically upright (through fear of hell-fire and desire for posthumous bliss).

The great outlier religion is Buddhism, which denies the existence of immortality, the soul, and other consoling metaphysical notions. I've lived in Buddhist countries extensively, however, and the story is more complicated than many Westerners imagine.

Once, when I was living and teaching in Phnom Penh, Cambodia, I returned home to find that the eighty-year-old man who lived across the street from my guesthouse had died that afternoon. I didn't know the man personally, but I had seen him many times sitting on his front steps. I found the street filled with mourners. Relatives set up a makeshift kitchen on the sidewalk, and they were cooking furiously for the arriving family and friends. A man was chanting Pali Buddhist scriptures into a microphone, and a cheap public-address speaker was croaking it into the street. The chants were about the impermanence of all things.[28]

I sat with the taxi moto drivers, who were taking a respectful break from their routine card game, and watched as the family organized round plastic tables and chairs for a funeral meal. They carefully placed blue tablecloths and hung a black and white mourner's banner across the open entry of the house. Inside the home (the first floors of most Khmer houses are wide open, like garages), they hung a large colorful painting of the Buddha on his lotus flower, and they built a makeshift shrine there. At the shrine, family members were dropping pieces of paper into a flaming pot, as a symbolic offering of money to the gods. The body of the dead man was sprinkled with flower petals.

The motorcycle traffic from nearby Sihanouk Boulevard drowned out the old man's chanting. People consoled one another. Two wild dogs got into a fight in the street, until a woman threw an empty coconut shell with contusional accuracy. A bold prostitute from the park approached and solicited the moto drivers. After awhile the old man's throat gave out, and the mourners started to play some beautiful Khmer folk music over the loud speaker—very simple repetitions (like a drunken Philip Glass) on a marimba dulcimer.

The mourners closed off the street and lit a bonfire in the dirt road. I noticed, from my vantage point, that the perfectly full moon could be seen just over the dead man's house. I thought about my own son who was growing rapidly inside his mother back in Chicago. I thought about the babies who were being conceived at that very moment and I wondered about reincarnation. Even though official Buddhism rejects the idea, many Khmer people cling to the pre-Buddhist belief that the old man's soul will wander for a week before it transmigrates.

The Buddha offers us Four Noble Truths. First, he says "All life is suffering, or all life is unsatisfactory (dukkha)." This seems pessimistic at first, but he's simply pointing out that to have a biological body is to be subject to pain, illness, and eventually death. And to have family and friends means that we are open to inevitable loss, disappointment, and also betrayal. But more importantly, even when we feel joy and happiness, these, too, are transient experiences that will fade away because all things are impermanent. Secondly, the Buddha says "Suffering is caused by craving or attachment." When we have a pleasurable experience we try to repeat it over and over or try to hang on to it and turn it into a permanent thing. Sensual experiences are not themselves the causes of suffering—they are inherently neutral phenomena. It is the psychological state of craving that rises up in the wake of sensations that causes us to have unrealistic expectations of those feelings—sending us chasing after fleeting experiences that cannot be possessed. The Third Noble Truth states that the cure for suffering is nonattachment or the cessation of craving. In the *Samyutta Nikaya* text, the Buddha says that the wise person "regards the delightful and pleasurable things of this world as impermanent, unsatisfactory and without *atman* (permanent essence), as a disease and sorrow—it is he who overcomes the craving" (12:66). Lastly, the Fourth Noble Truth is an eightfold path that helps the follower to steer a Middle Way of ethical moderation. Following the simple eightfold path allows the follower to overcome egoistic craving.

Perhaps the most important craving that must be overcome, according to Buddha, is the craving for immortality. The Buddha claimed that giving up transcendental tendencies would help us better see the people all around us who need our help. We would become more compassionate, he argued, because we would not be distracted by cravings for the "other world."

In the *Potthapada sutta* (*Digha Nikaya*), Buddha retells a debate he had with some "philosophers and Brahmins" who believed that "the soul is perfectly happy and healthy after death." The Buddha says, "I asked them whether, so far as they knew it or perceived it, the human world was perfectly happy, and they answered 'No.' Then I asked them: 'Moreover, can you maintain that you yourselves for a whole night, or for a whole day, or even for half a night or day, have ever been perfectly happy?' And they answered: 'No.' Then I said to them: 'Further, do you know a way or a method, by which you can realize a state that is altogether happy?' And still to that question they answered: 'No.' And then I said: 'Sirs, have you ever heard the voices of heavenly beings who had realized rebirth in a perfectly happy world, saying: 'there is a right path, a true path, which is in human capacity to follow, a path to the world of unfailing bliss, for we ourselves by following it have come to this world of bliss?' They still answered: 'No.'"

The Buddha concludes from this Socratic questioning, that, although their mouths are moving and words are coming out, these philosophers and

Brahmins are really speaking nonsense. He says that people who dedicate themselves to an incoherent doctrine of eternal paradise are like carpenters who build staircases for mansions they've never seen, and for which they have no dimensions or measurements. In other words, they labor, but their misunderstanding renders the work absurd.

This epistemic argument here is compelling, but the real point is the metaphysical one. Why can't you be perfectly happy? Why can't you even be happy for more than a few hours? The answer is because happiness is inherently impermanent (*anicca*). Like all other feelings, happiness comes and goes, and like all other things in the world, it cannot last. Treating a moment as if it were a thing to be possessed is a kind of regular human tendency and a regular human mistake.

In the same way that paradise crumbles upon further inspection, so, too, the Buddha thinks that the soul (*atman*) is nowhere to be found, except in the literary inventions of Hinduism and the confused heads of its followers. Buddhism, contrary to all dualistic theories, asserts that we are not made up of two metaphysically different parts, permanent spirit and impermanent body. Buddhism breaks with most religions, East and West, by recognizing that man is a finite tangle of qualities, all of which eventually exhaust themselves, and no part, conscious or otherwise, carries on independently.

All humans, according to Buddha, are composed of the five aggregates (*khandas*); body (*rupa*), feeling (*vedana*), perception (*sanna*), volition (*sankhara*), and consciousness (*vinnana*). The Buddha is skeptical of the immortal essential soul that goes on after death. Show me this permanent entity, the Buddha would demand. Is the body permanent? Are feelings permanent? What about perceptions, or volitions, or even consciousness? Buddha examines all the elements of the human being, finds that they are all manifestly ephemeral, and finds no additional permanent entity or soul amidst the tangle of human faculties. There is no ghost in the machine.

Buddhism has a more obscure doctrine of rebirth. The soul does not go on after death, because there is no soul in Buddhism. So what is getting reborn? This was a common mystery even during the Buddha's lifetime and in the subsequent centuries of Buddhist philosophy. Instead of thinking of a permanent substance or ghost continuing on, the Buddha says we should understand that the five aggregates (the khandas) continue on. Body, sensation, perception, volition, and consciousness are like flowing streams of energy. They coalesce for a time and make up persons, but they also keep flowing when those persons cease. It is like our contemporary scientific idea of the conservation of matter—matter/energy gets rearranged but it does not disappear during these transformations. The Buddha's commitment to a kind of natural causality means that *later* events are heavily (some might say deterministically) influenced by the paths of *earlier* ones. In this way, Buddha believes that karma can hold across lifetimes. Perhaps the most famous analogy to make sense of this flowing rebirth model is the flame simile. When challenged on the coherence of his doctrine, the Buddha and subsequent philosophers have described a candle or a lamp. Imagine that we light the candle and it burns for a time. Now we use the candle to light a second candle and blow out the first. After a time we do the same with a third, fourth, and fifth candle. It does not make sense, the Buddha suggests, to ask whether it is the *same* flame at candle five as it was at candle one. It is not even the *same* flame as it burns on the first candle, because it is a dependent convergence of combustion processes. So, too, rebirth of living beings is not a movement of a self-same soul, but a causal process that links earlier and later (temporary) unities.

This is relatively sophisticated philosophy. It reorients us from thinking about substances to thinking about processes or functions instead. But anyone can see that it is also deeply unsatisfying to our emotional desires for immortality. Yes, energy will go on and on, but *I* won't be there to experience it. Despite the warm and fuzzy way that such rebirth is discussed in New Age literature, there is, in fact, nothing very consoling about the idea that I and my loved ones will die, disintegrate, and get rearranged into other stuff. Of course, for Buddhism, that's the point. The Buddha is not interested in stroking our egos, comforting us, or feeding our emotional cravings.

Given all this, we can wonder what consolation, if any, Buddhism offers the grieving family. Is Buddhism a cold-bath religion that asks its practitioners to suck it up and face the nonexistence of our loved ones with hard-hearted resolve? And does Buddhism confound my overall argument that people need religious metaphysics for emotional consolation?

No, I don't think Buddhism is a damaging counterexample to my overall theory. Closer examination reveals that it comfortably fits the thesis. Contrary to many recent Western popularizations, Buddhism in practice is a good deal more magical than Buddhism on paper. Most traditional Buddhist cultures practice a form of devotional religion largely disconnected from the original, agnostic philosophical ideas. Lay Buddhists in Asia rarely meditate or philosophize, instead making offerings at the temple for prosperity and favor. Meanwhile, many Western converts cleave to the meditation practices and the bookish inspirations of decontextualized scriptural aphorisms. All this makes for a humorous lost-in-translation, and vaguely dissonant, fellowship of Eastern and Western Buddhists. And we must add to this *funkstille* the fact that most Western Buddhists focus on the moral teachings of the dharma, or they focus instead on the private cultivation of virtuoso consciousness—neither of which figure much in the daily Buddhism of Asians.

Buddhism is a highly complex and naturalistic philosophical system, but it is also a beautiful cultural mess with supernatural assumptions and self-contradictory convictions—just like Christianity or Islam. Moreover, there is no such thing as Buddhism, but rather *Buddhisms*. The various forms of Buddhism that exist in radically diverse geographic, economic, and ethnic regions all have a kind of family resemblance, but some of the distant cousins have almost no commonly recognizable features.[29] For example, Buddhist cultures like Theravada in Thailand, Qing Dynasty Buddhism in China, Zen in Japan, and Vajrayana in Tibet contain diverse metaphysical assumptions.

A recent genre of Buddhism books has proven to be very popular lately. These can be called the "secular distillation" books: Stephen Batchelor's *Confessions of a Buddhist Atheist*, Steve Hagen's *Buddhism Plain and Simple*, Sam Harris's *Waking Up: A Guide to Spirituality Without Religion*.[30] These books have been helpful in articulating the logic of Buddha's arguments and the relation of dharma to scientific naturalism and philosophy generally. They come at a cost, however, in the sense that they abstract Buddhism out of its cultural milieu and treat its devotional and folk aspects as embarrassing and nonessential.

These supposedly "embarrassing" aspects of Buddhism, however, are the meat and potatoes of cultural Buddhism, practiced by hundreds of millions of adherents. *Boran* Buddhism, for example, is a magical form of Theravada, but it is emblematic of many magical threads in Buddhism, from Cambodia to Tibet to Japan. Boran Buddhism is an amalgamation of pre-Buddhist animism—which recognizes spirit-beings in the local trees, rivers, mountains, even buildings—and pre-Buddhist Hindu Brahminism, which reintroduces the permanent soul idea (atman), along with myriad supernatural deities.

The psychological attraction of magical Buddhism (like *boran*) is not hard to see. Let's say a loved one in your family becomes terminally ill. According to strict Buddhist philosophy, you and the doctor do your best to heal them and try to make them comfortable, but in the end you must come to the realization that you're ultimately powerless against a reality in which all things are impermanent (and that's a tough pill to swallow and takes years of dharma discipline). In the more esoteric *boran* traditions, however, there are many more "weapons" in your "arsenal"; you can pour water over a lingam-Shiva statue (thereby charging the water with holy power) and then sprinkle your sick family member with it; you can pray and make offerings to the animistic spirits, *neak ta,* to chase away evil forces and grant your relative peace; you can ask Vishnu, Ganesh, and Brahman to heal your loved one; you can have a monk come and chant over your relative in order to undo the damage; you can negotiate with a fortune teller; you can have holy mendicants bless totems and amulets and lay the energized objects on the body, and so on and so forth. I'm not saying all this in a condescending way—I suspect this magic, mystery, and authority helps ease people's grief and sense of helplessness. Of course, on balance, a good medical doctor is in the patient's best interest—but it's not the victim that's interesting in the above scenario, it's the relatively helpless family. And when your loved one eventually dies of this illness, magical Buddhism supplies all the immortality consolations we've already detailed in Western religion.

The world is a tough place (First Noble Truth of *dukkha*), if only in the sense that you can't control most of what happens to you. The most prevalent response to this is to find ways to negotiate with these forces (prayers, offerings, sacrifices, rituals, etc.). The road less traveled, however, is to give up trying to control the Fates and, instead, just learn to control your mind and your desires (which requires years of meditational training). Most people, however, do not have the luxury of restructuring their minds over many years of strict training. Most of us with families, and jobs, and mortgages, have to take the road more traveled.

When I was living in Southeast Asia, I interviewed two young *Bhikkhus* (monks), Venerables Amnann and Sovanratana, about the current tensions between Buddhism's philosophical principles and its superstitious culture. On the rooftop of my building, we drank iced tea and talked shop. Both of these monks had just finished an eight-year intensive program in Buddhist philosophy in Sri Lanka—they're Khmer, but they had to go to Sri Lanka to study philosophy because after Pol Pot, little higher-level Buddhist education remained in Cambodia. These monks, unlike the cultural Buddhists I met every day in Asia, are very well versed in the philosophical concepts and scriptures. Since our meeting, Ven Sovanratana has become an important leader at Preah Sihanouk Raja Buddhist University.

In the course of our lengthy discussion we delved into the main topics of Buddhist philosophy: *anatta* (the theory that we have no permanent soul, or lasting personal essence); *anicca* (the theory that all things, including ultimate reality, are impermanent); and *paticca samuppada* (the theory of dependent arising—all beings are dependent on other beings in an ecological "web" of relations).

When asked whether the average Khmer Buddhist has familiarity with these philosophical concepts, the Ven. Sovanratana laughed. The young monk said he could not teach the no-soul doctrine (anatta) to the average Buddhist, because it was too disturbing to them. He explained that if he actually taught real Buddhism to the people, then he would go hungry! Remember, every monk depends upon the daily donations of food made by the local devotees, who give as merit-making behavior (karma points). If laypeople are not happy with the monk, they don't donate food to him.

"Honestly," he explained, "lay people would have no part of it. Real Buddhism is too rational, not magical enough, for most practicing Buddhists." If the Buddha came back today, one wonders if the lay people would ask him to go away, so they could return to their miracle, mystery, and authority.[31]

One response to all this hypocrisy is derision, and atheists as well as Western secular Buddhists are quick to heap the disdain. But not me. I love the flawed, vulnerable, and desperate humanity of the cultural Buddhists. I am one of them.

The vast majority of Buddhists do not live up to the no-soul doctrine (anatta, or *anatman*), and instead focus on the Four Noble Truths. Often, they just revert to Hindu-like beliefs that the soul is immortal and will go on. But their failure to live up to anatta is not because they are hypocrites or too weak. It's because they're human.

As we know intuitively, and the science of bonding and separation distress confirms, to be human is to be attached. Consider, for example, that Gandhi condoned a Buddha-like detachment from family and friends, because such attachment reduced universal compassion for *all* beings. When George Orwell read Gandhi's autobiography in 1948, he was deeply troubled by the Indian saint's "anti-humanism." Orwell remained impressed by Gandhi's political achievements, but he was stunned by Gandhi's views on friendship and family. Saintly detachment seemed repugnant to Orwell, who reminded us that "love means nothing if it does not mean loving some people more than others."[32]

Many of us side definitively with Orwell here, and cannot follow the Indian saint to his lofty conclusion. Many of us agree with Orwell's claim that "the essence of being human is that one does not seek perfection, that one is sometimes willing to commit sins for the sake of loyalty . . . and that one is prepared in the end to be defeated and broken up by life, which is the inevitable price of fastening one's love upon other human individuals."

My point is that the soul concept, for all its faults, has the consoling implication that I will be able to stay fastened (in some essential way) to my deceased child, lover, friend, sister, parent. Scoff all you wish, but most people cannot adopt the no-soul (anatta) part of the dharma because they learn it long after it's too late. Even Buddhists in Tibet and Cambodia learn their Buddhism *after* they're hopelessly attached and bonded to their families. It's an uphill battle after that, and not because we're afraid and want to live forever, but because we love some people so much that we can't bear to let them go.

There are two interesting exceptions to my generalization here. For whatever reason—be it insecure attachment in early life, or mild Asperger syndrome—some of us are naturally detached people. This is not a value judgment, but an observation. Some people are less bonded, less involved, less entangled, and more emotionally aloof, than others. Buddhist detachment comes easier to them. I consider them lucky, because they must be spared substantial misery by this accidental advantage of disposition. They can acquire and sustain the no-soul doctrine more easily. And their agnosticism about the soul seems to bleed quite naturally into other metaphysical and religious domains.

The second small group that manages to actually live the anatta doctrine is select monks. The monks make up a tiny fraction of Buddhists, which is a confusing fact for Westerners, who mostly see stereotypes of Buddhism in the form of robed monks. This relatively tiny group spends many hours a day meditating, for years on end. It is a hard life, and not luxurious by any material means, but it is luxurious in the sense that they can practice detachment and dharma generally for most of their day. They're on the same path as the rest of us, but monks, with all their training, fly toward the target (*nibbana*) like straight, well-crafted arrows, whereas the rest of us are crooked timber. Meditating all day is an indulgence that no lay Buddhist can afford. Subsequently, the monks are able to reprogram their brains and their emotions to really adopt the anatta doctrine (and other difficult features of the dharma).[33] The rest of us are stuck in the fly-paper of life.

Interestingly, recent empirical research suggests that Buddhist monks who reject the soul and the self are not less fearful of death, but possibly more fearful of death. Experimental philosopher Shaun Nichols interviewed the no-selfers (Buddhist monks) and the selfers (everyone else), and found that concentrating on your own impermanence all day long (as monks do) can actually increase your fear of death (instead of liberate you from such anxiety).[34] This research is new and inconclusive, but it gives us pause. My argument has been that most human beings cannot reprogram themselves to stop believing in the soul/self. But even if you could attain this extreme form of mental reprogramming, it might not give you the freedom and equanimity you had expected.[35]

CAN THE STATE MANAGE SORROW?

If we eliminated religious funerals would people be better or worse off, in terms of grief management? Given that many critics of religion think religious funerals infantilize us with death-denying dogmas, it might be interesting to consider the elimination of them. Religion is not the only way to assuage the sorrow of loss. Successful grieving is possible without religion. But religion is a readymade part of deep culture. Religion is usually old enough to have a long trial-and-error period, in which the emotional management (the adaptive aspects) has been relatively debugged, so to speak. Its therapeutic work is relatively efficient in high-stakes situations (i.e., debilitating pain). Like a native language, religion is already around you and available to express and communicate some new experience, or in this case, tragedy.

If the death of loved ones could be memorialized without explicit religion (e.g., a purely secular funeral), that ceremony would need to adopt the highly ritualized, devotional qualities that traditional religion usually stages. It will need this because, according to my argument, ritual contains the body movements (e.g., genuflecting, dancing, power poses), the objects (e.g., flowers, images), and the activities (e.g., singing, eating) that coax *positive* affect or emotion out of its hiding place in order to mix with and even overtake *negative* affect. Some of this will be accomplished vis-à-vis catharsis of negative affect (e.g., collective weeping) and some of it vis-à-vis affect replacement (positive for negative). And some of it will be accomplished by pep talk (possibly placebo) about overcoming death itself in the next life.

Consider the well-known New Orleans jazz funeral, which demonstrates the emotional management of well-crafted ritual. The jazz funeral is a mélange of Yoruba African spiritual practices, Haitian Voudoo, Mardi Gras Indian culture, and Protestant Christianity. It starts with a slow sad procession and dirge music, but after the body is entombed, the mourners shift emotional gears. The music becomes up-tempo and joyful, and the parade of mourners dances and celebrates. The ritual itself is an expression of the irrational feeling that love conquers death; but because it is a hybrid of religious traditions, it cannot be considered a secular form of grieving. It simply distills the best of the spiritual traditions in New Orleans history.

Twentieth-century China, however, did abolish religious funerals and pursued a more secular approach to grief. In traditional Chinese culture, it was important to bury the dead. Confucianism claimed that immediate and careful disposal of a relation was a sign of virtue and respect for one's family. A grandiose funeral was a symbol of *xiao*—a virtue that we translate as filial devotion.

A Chinese funeral song, known to most Chinese people even today, expresses the deep longing and the social healing of the traditional rite. Written by artist and Buddhist monk Hong Yi (1880–1942), its lyrics include: "Friends have scattered to the reaches of heaven and the ends of the sea, with only very few left. Let's enjoy this pot of murky wine to indulge ourselves in the remaining joy we have. Dreaming in the chilling night, I wave goodbye."

During the Mao era, however, funerals were discouraged, and cremation was insisted upon. Like other aspects of traditional culture (i.e., Buddhism, Confucianism, etc.) funerals were redefined as Old World, antimodern, and superstitious. Graves and cemeteries were considered wasteful, and the land deemed better used for farming. Likewise, coffins were a waste of wood, and funerals in general drew people away from work and also burdened everyone with extra costs, depleting resources.

But like the other attempts to break nuclear family ties, the communists failed to reshape the deep emotional springs of human life. Religious grieving traditionally enshrines the filial love of families. Religion at this level is not for the State or for the oppression of the underclass. It is for the proximate bonds of family members who have shed blood, tears, and sweat together over the course of family history. It is precisely because of this celebration and strengthening of filial bonds that the communists prohibited funerals. The Maoist logic—also practiced by the Khmer Rouge in the 1970s—sought to dismantle the nuclear family bonds (which are biologically natural but also hallowed in Confucianism) and refasten those bonds onto The Party.

Ostensibly, The Party forbade traditional funerals as a way of preventing financial waste of resources (as well as traditional superstition), but the veneer is transparent when we realize that visitors to traditional Chinese funerals are supposed to donate money, thereby demonstrating respect and defraying costs for the bereaved family. The traditional system—evolved over thousands of years—puts financial resources at the level of families, rather than the State. The Party was bound to re-engineer such traditions. Even as recently as 2016, The Party issued guidelines to party members that recommended greater frugality and less ceremony at funerals.[36]

This brings us to an important point about most religion. Its primary therapeutic function is observable at the microlevel of neighborhoods, not the macrolevel of nations. The Left, even today, sees religion as a State tool, but this fails to grasp its true power. For example, Terry Eagleton, in *Culture and the Death of God* (2014), argues that the reason all previous substitutions for religion have failed is because the primary function of religion is to justify and uphold political authority. Religion is sadly inevitable in modern nation states, according to Eagleton's Marxist approach, because power elites need to dispense their opium to the masses. But postmodernism, Eagleton suggests, has finally come to the rescue and offered up the real possibility of atheism. How does it do this? By dethroning all culture (including religion) from a place of elite privilege, thereby decentralizing all meaning. Postmodernism democratizes culture and dethrones its socially coercive theologies. "If postmodern culture is depthless, anti-tragic, non-linear, anti-numinous, non-foundational and anti-universalist, suspicious of absolutes and averse to interiority, one might claim that it is genuinely post-religious, as modernism most certainly is not."[37]

The major problem with this argument is that it's hard to see *who* Eagleton is talking about. His very own analysis acknowledges that the bloodless literati option could never compete with the full-blooded body of meaning provided by working class religion. But then he seems to mistake the ostensible research into working class culture (so beloved by cultural studies scholars) for actual working class consciousness. Working class consciousness, I submit, has as much postmodern awareness as Justin Bieber has maturity. Postmodern irony will never replace a religious funeral, for example, unless our emotional lives become as empty as postmodern art.

As anthropologists Allen W. Johnson and Timothy Earle point out, the meaning of religion is quite different in communities under 300 people (called local groups) compared with large groups in the thousands (regional polities). "If sanctity at the local group level is mainly about highlighting and reinforcing the ties that bind families into groups, at the level of the regional polity sanctity is mainly about encouraging the compliance of commoners with elite policies and privilege."[38]

Eagleton is exclusively concerned with this large-scale political function and, like Mao and Marx before, he is both impressed by its power and depressed by its anesthetizing effects. But Eagleton, while professing a more sympathetic view, fails just like the new atheists to appreciate the proximate prosocial benefits and existential advantages of local group religion. Yes, big time Statist religion is an opiate, but people are not really religious in that way. It's small-time religion (local community) that provides all the motivation for membership. And no matter how big the State gets, the local family-based pockets (affective communities) still do their living and dying in service of each other and God, rather than abstractions like the "industrial capitalist system." Moreover, I suspect these smaller affective communities have not heard word-one about postmodern liberation, nor would they make sense of it if they did. For them, a religious funeral is a way to say goodbye to their brother, or mother, not a waste of State resources, a postmodern irony, or a distraction from political oppression.

The most interesting part of Eagleton's analysis of religion hovers near this issue and acknowledges that none of the modern surrogates for religion (e.g., culture, rationality, nationalism) hold a candle to the *imaginative* magnetism of religion. Our imagination is fed directly and powerfully by the motivating stories, ceremonies, and images of religion. But Eagleton lacks the main ingredients (insights from biology and anthropology) for understanding the sort of inevitability that goes beyond modern politics.[39] We'll have more to say later about the role of imagination in therapeutic religion.

In closing, I want to suggest that rationality does not help the grieving child, or parent. It cannot do the heavy lifting that is required in the face of devastating loss. Cognitive reframing—in the form of scientific facts or Buddhist teachings about inevitable mortality—only goes so far to ameliorate the emotional state. What is needed is positive affect, and pain reduction.

Most contemporary critics of religion are Enlightenment-styled rationalists, who see religion as a dark cloud, obscuring the light of reason. Supernaturalism is the great delusion that distracts our otherwise optimal, rational calculations of life. It is a sunny picture of human nature, one that is optimistic and universally reconcilable with all agents/cultures, if only religion could get out of the way. I've tried to show, in the case of sorrow, why religion will always speak to the deeper and more desperate recesses of the human psyche. From Freud to affective neuroscience we have a picture of the human mind that is irrational and vulnerable, no matter how trained and mature the rational mind becomes.

The Christian celebration of Easter is itself an international, annual enactment of emotional management. Yes, the story of Jesus's resurrection has all the supernatural qualities that give hope to the hopeless, but the elaborate global celebrations of Holy Week also embody the techniques of affect catharsis and replacement. Whole communities gather to acknowledge death, mourn, and then celebrate rebirth. There is a grieving cycle of abandonment, sadness, acceptance, hope, assurance, and then joy. Holy Week is a global funeral rite, and Easter is a party—where people give each other transfusions of positive affect (via song, dance, eating, drinking, etc.). As 1 Corinthians 15:54 proclaims: "Now, when what is decaying is clothed with what cannot decay, and what is dying is clothed with what cannot die, then the written word will be fulfilled: Death has been swallowed up by victory!"

Easter is uniquely Christian of course, but it echoes ancient pagan ceremonies and celebrations of spring. Before Christian ceremonies of sorrow and hope, there was Sumerian Ishtar, Egyptian Horus, Persian Mithra, and even older animistic traditions of fertility.

Sorrow is well documented in the mammal clade, and we find primate mothers grieving their dead babies, and elephants mourning their fallen friends. Distress vocalization and panic during social separation are correlated with glutamate and corticotropin-releasing hormone increase, but restoration of social contact floods the mammal brain with pacifying opioids and oxytocin. Internal opiates reduce mammal grief. As we've seen, humans have this same basic operating system. Religion responds to our emotional tragedies with the ameliorating rituals of social grooming, but it also responds to the greater demands of sophisticated angst that only neocortical reflection can produce. Will I see my child again? Is my departed father proud of me? Will I finally be able to tell him that I love him?

CHAPTER 3

Forgiveness and the Restart Button

Forgive us our sins, as we forgive those who sin against us.

—Lord's Prayer (Matthew 6:12)

What is true of individuals is true of nations. One cannot forgive too much. The weak can never forgive. Forgiveness is the attribute of the strong.

—Mahatma Gandhi (*Young India,* April 1931)

I know forgiveness is a man's duty; but to my thinking, that can only mean that you're to give up all thoughts of taking revenge; it can never mean that you're to have your old feelings back again, for that's not possible.

—George Elliot, *Adam Bede*

In the ninth level of hell, Virgil leads Dante on a tour of the frozen lake (Canto xxxiii). In this gruesome section of the *Inferno*, we meet sinners, particularly traitors, who are trapped in the frozen water. Parts of their bodies are exposed and moveable, but mostly they are submerged in the cold, concrete-like ice. Dante notices a pair of unfortunate men, because one is gnawing on the skull of the other. Wiping his mouth off on the hair of his victim, Count Ugolino takes a break from his grisly repast to introduce himself. He is chewing on the head of Archbishop Ruggieri, a man who betrayed him in mortal life. Ruggieri and Ugolino were colleagues, but in a trick move, Ruggieri had Ugolino and his sons arrested and put in prison where they all starved to death. Ugolino had to watch his children writhe in pain and beg for mercy until they perished one by one. Unable to forgive or forget this terrible injustice, Ugolino is frozen in the same hole with his archenemy—forever tied to him through an unquenchable hunger for vengeance.

Dante shows us, in this graphic example, how the victim can be further victimized by his own psychology. We are invited to consider the two modes of suffering—first, the injury done to us or our family, and second, the continued suffering we endure by our own subsequent psychological response of hate, revenge, and endless rumination. For most of us it would be hard to respond other than Ugolino. If you were forced to watch your children die, it could be the very end of your psychological well-being. Philosopher Martha Nussbaum (2001) argues that some tragedies might befall you that are so horrible, you actually lose your humanity afterward (as in the case of Greek tragedy character Hecuba, whose friend betrays her, leading to the murder of her son).[1] These kinds of tragedies remind us of the fragility of human flourishing and the vulnerability of human happiness.

For many of us, forgiving an enemy of Ruggieri's stature is nigh impossible. I, too, might have to gnaw his head for all eternity if he wronged me so. Turning the other cheek is an essential feature of Christianity, however, and may represent a zenith of clemency and mercy. Of course, many other religions have a similar spiritual commitment to mercy. Judaism has its day of atonement (Yom Kippur), Buddhism teaches us to unburden ourselves of the slavery of retaliation and vengeance, and Sikh scriptures advise "Where there is forgiveness, there God resides."

This chapter will consider the adaptive power of forgiveness, understood at the level of personal psychology and the level of social evolution. Forgiveness is a complex adaptation that helps restore social cooperation in groups, and also alleviates negative affect and destructive perseveration—restoring existential value, meaning, and vitality. Catharsis is an important religious emotion that encapsulates diverse phenomena such as ritual purification and cleansing, but also includes psychological acts of mercy (both receiving and dispensing forgiveness). Reintegration of individuals who have transgressed social norms is a crucial feature of a successful community, but reintegration of the wronged party (now overwhelmed by negative affect) is also at stake. Forgiveness rescues many such potential disasters.

Forgiveness is simultaneously a behavior, a state of being, a philosophy, and an emotional feeling (i.e., catharsis, relief, freedom). According to the American Psychological Association's United Nations document *Forgiveness* (2006), it is a "process (or the result of a process) that involves a change in emotion and attitude regarding an offender . . . the process results in decreased motivation to retaliate or maintain estrangement from an offender despite their actions, and requires letting go of negative emotions toward the offender."[2]

Forgiveness may entail reconciliation or the restoration of a former relationship, but it need not. Whereas reconciliation requires both parties to come together (and may occur grudgingly and without absolution), forgiveness can be a one-sided process or change, with no acknowledgment or even awareness on the part of the offending party. In fact, it is somewhat common for deceased offenders to be forgiven by the injured party.

Religious forgiveness is one of the many cultural mechanisms that help us manage or regulate our emotional lives. I made this same argument about religious views/rituals surrounding death and grief, but now is a good time to get more explicit about emotional regulation. Before we examine forgiveness more carefully, we need to clarify emotional management. What is it, and how does it work?

EMOTIONAL REGULATION

It is common for us to adjust, regulate, redirect, and even fine-tune our emotional states. When I am very angry, I count to ten before I speak. When I am afraid, I give myself a quiet pep talk, reminding myself that it's not as bad as it seems. When my friend is overwhelmed with anxiety, as the plane takes off from the runway, I hold her hand.

We are so competent at emotional regulation, that we often do not notice our own techniques. Some of our methods were explicitly taught to us, like when parents teach us to focus on positive memories when we are stressed out. And some of our methods emerge naturally through our personal development, like discovering the value of deep breaths when we are feeling overwhelmed. In the same way that we learn to stimulate ourselves, or up-regulate emotion, we also experiment with behaviors and thought patterns that calm and down-regulate affect.

Psychologist James Gross studies emotional regulation and suggests that there are five basic kinds of management.[3] One way we keep negative emotions at bay is by controlling our situation or context. If I know that I become very anxious in a large crowd of people, then I avoid the sold-out Rolling Stones concert. If I have a strong fear of grizzly bears, then I do not accept my friend's invitation to camp in the remote areas of Glacier National Park. And positively speaking, if I feel down and lonely, I may force myself to attend a party, in hopes of enjoying some social pleasures.

Secondly, I may modify the situation I'm in, so as to regulate my emotions. Perhaps I cannot avoid the huge crowd that I'm forced to endure. In this case, I migrate to the back of the room or seek a less trafficked hallway. But much more commonly, I find myself in an unpleasant conversation—one that I cannot simply walk away from—and I up-regulate my positive affect by tactfully changing the topic. We've all shifted an unhappy conversation by bringing up a new subject or by steering the other person away from painful themes.

A third way to regulate our emotions is to deploy our attention. Sometimes we are filled with negative affect—for example, sadness, or anger, or anxiety—and we find a way to distract ourselves. We refocus our attention on something positive or even neutral, such that the negative feelings abate. Perhaps I'm on a horrible date, with a person who is boring me to tears, or whose political views are enraging me. I might notice that the meal is particularly tasty or the wine is excellent, and keeping my attention focused on the meal successfully down-regulates the negative affect. Likewise, we are sometimes in a terrible state of stress or worry, but we immerse our attention in a novel or a film. In this way the negative emotion dissipates as our consciousness becomes filled with someone else's real or fictional story.

The fourth method of emotional regulation is to change our cognition. By rethinking an experience, we can sometimes engender positive feelings where negative ones previously dominated. This can be trivial—like when my friend, who hated spicy food, began to think of curry as a "roller-coaster for the mouth," and subsequently converted to Indian food. Or it can be serious—like when I begin to think about my high school bully as a person who is also suffering and confused, and thereby transform dread and fear to pity and possibly compassion.

A fifth way that we often adjust our emotional experience is by modulating our responses or expressions. For example, counting to ten before responding to an insult (cooling the response), or laughing when you feel like crying. These methods regulate the emotion by altering the expressive behavioral pattern. You might be bursting with joy that you've won the award, but then you realize your nearby friend has lost, and you downplay your enthusiastic expression. The modification actually reduces some of the intensity of your joy, but you're glad you regulated your emotion.

This last example reveals something important about emotional management. It is not always in service of the ego. Regulating our emotions is often a socially directed good. Emotional modulation has a great deal to do with how we protect, serve, and provision our children. Indeed, it's hard to imagine the existence and evolution of altruism without powerful emotional regulation. Some scholars have pointed out that our evolutionary transition to nuclear families and our cultural leap in information transfer (e.g., teaching skills to kids) was only possible when parents became emotionally patient.[4] Impulse control is a form of emotional regulation. Fathers who could scale back their aggression—which comes in high volumes because of intermale competition—could better teach their children, cooperate with their mates, and provision their tribes. Cooperation requires emotional regulation. "Keeping your cool" and "getting a hold of yourself" are necessary ingredients for increasingly complex social projects.

When we consider all these adjustments of emotion—usually done quickly, in real-time—we begin to appreciate how emotions are evaluations or pseudojudgments. An emotion such as anger is a strong feeling that seems to burn in the body, but it is also a judgment that someone has wronged us. From Stoic philosophers such as Epictetus and Seneca to contemporary psychologists such as Jaak Panksepp (2012) and Joseph LeDoux (2015), we have recognized that anger or fear is not just the instinctual physiological response to stimuli (e.g., fight or freeze), but also the cognitive judgment that "I have been injured" or "I am disrespected," and so on.[5] Aristotle defines anger as "an impulse, accompanied by pain, to a conspicuous revenge for a conspicuous slight directed without justification towards what concerns oneself or towards what concerns one's friends." And he adds, "It must be felt because the other has done or intended to do something to him or one of his friends" (Rhetoric Bk. II, Ch. 2). The uniquely human form of anger, on this view, requires the angry person to judge a willful malevolent intention on the part of the offender. Human emotion is so intimately tied with higher cognition that Seneca thought it was impossible for animals to feel anger or other emotions (De Ira I.3).[6]

Contemporary versions of this cognitive approach abound. Philosopher Martha Nussbaum (2001) describes the deeply emotional episode of her mother's death.[7] Her feelings of grief were not just physiological plummets of positive affect, but also beliefs and judgments that this most important character of her life was now gone. An existential value judgment—that the whole world was now less—gave true scope and meaning to her grief.

The idea that emotions are judgments is important, but many philosophers (like Nussbaum) overemphasize the cognitive aspect of emotions—mistaking the uniquely human emotions (which are heavily intellectualized) with all emotion. Instead, emotion should be seen in layers, all of which reside in the human psyche. Yes, the top layer of grief is enmeshed in cognition (about the loved one's personality, history, and meaning), but below that is the older mammalian operating system—the limbic system.

As we've already seen, social emotions such as grief and care/bonding are deep, physiologically based feelings that evolved as adaptations for social creatures such as primates, cetaceans, elephants, and dogs. When our whole body is crying out to reconnect with our deceased loved one, it is this lower layer of emotion infusing the more intellectual layer.

The layer cake of emotion has three levels. At the very bottom are the instinctual drives, such as fight or flight, and seeking. This layer is housed primarily in our subcortical brain, and neuroscientists call it primary emotion.[8] We share these primordial affective systems with all other vertebrates. This layer heavily influences the layer above it, secondary emotion, which is more developed in mammals. Secondary emotion resembles the kind of animal grief we described in the elephant story from the previous chapter. This layer includes social emotions, such as grief, play, and care. It is distinguished from the primary level because it is sculpted by learning and conditioning. It is the layer of soft-wiring (part native instinct and part learned association), as compared with the hard-wiring of primary level emotion. Emotions in primary and secondary layers are sometimes unconscious, and even when we are regulating them, we do not have clear introspective conscious access to the process.[9]

Last comes the top layer, or tertiary emotion. This is the layer that Nussbaum and other philosophers tend to focus on exclusively. Here the emotions are still connected to the limbic system, but they are intertwined in the cognitive powers of the neocortex. Ruminations and thoughts, underwritten by language, symbolic ability, executive control, and future planning, are energized by lower-level emotion. And these ruminations and thoughts also serve as top-down regulators and directors of emotion. At this third level, we arrive at uniquely human emotions, like the elaborate feelings of introspective savants such as Marcel Proust and Fyodor Dostoyevsky.

SHAME AND GUILT

Shame and guilt are the important psychological and existential corollaries to forgiveness. Though we will see that forgiveness does not require the wrongdoer to acknowledge his culpability, the social reality of forgiveness often ties the injured and the injuring party together. If I fail to see my action as wrong and in need of forgiveness, I can still be forgiven and then the benefits (psychological and social) fall primarily on the side of the forgiver. Nonetheless, a brief discussion of shame and guilt is helpful for understanding the motivations and processes of forgiveness.

To be in a state of shame or guilt is to be in search of forgiveness, or release. Is shame or guilt a natural emotional instinct? In the last chapter, we considered whether nonhuman animals feel grief, and now we can ask the same about shame and forgiveness.

In his Notebook N (c. 1838), Darwin pondered the feeling and expression of shame. He asked himself, "What difference is there between Squib [Darwin's dog] after having eaten meat on the table and a criminal, who has stolen? Neither of them feel fear [in this case], but have shame." Much later, in the *Descent of Man* (1871) he expands on his comparative, and possibly anthropomorphic, views. "Most of the more complex emotions are common to the higher animals and ourselves. Everyone has seen how jealous a dog is of his master's affection, if lavished on any other creature . . . animals not only love, but have desire to be loved. Animals manifestly feel emulation. They love approbation or praise; and a dog carrying a basket for his master exhibits in a high degree self-complacency or pride. There can, I think, be no doubt that a dog feels shame, as distinct from fear, and something very like modesty when begging too often for food" (p. 17).

Many of us have seen our pet dog looking very guilty after some furniture has been mysteriously chewed up, or some other infraction committed. Several recent studies, however, have established that dogs are not feeling real shame or guilt when they give us those regretful eyes.[10] In two related studies, researchers had dog owners leave a room, while their dog remained behind. The dog was sometimes invited to break a rule (e.g., eat a forbidden treat) and sometimes not. If the dog was indeed guilty, then she should have signaled that fact on her face when the owner returned. But owners were never able to tell whether their dog had violated the rule, and dogs never initiated shame-face spontaneously if they had. Instead, the shame-face emerged rapidly if and when the owner began disapproving tones and body gestures. In other words, owners trigger shame-face by being angry. Dogs immediately go into contrition faces and gestures (submission signals) as a way of soothing the social situation, rather than acknowledging guilt. They don't know why you're mad, they just want to fix it. In fact, when several dogs are tested together, the one that offers up the shame-face is rarely the offending dog, but rather the one who is most timid and responsive to human hostility. The people-pleaser dog acts ashamed, whether she chewed up the furniture or not.

Although some dog owners, eager to humanize their pets, find these data disappointing, they are, in fact, remarkable. The experiment shows that the dog is adjusting her face in order to re-establish social harmony. This suggests that even when they don't know what they've done, and they don't know why you're mad, and they don't feel remorse, they do nonetheless want to be "forgiven." They want you to "love" them again—allow them re-entry into your mutually positive emotional world. In a way, this is even more endearing than discovering doggie guilt. We see that the animal is devoted to the positive emotional state of its human family. Of course, this devotion is not a conscious choice, but an unfolding of the affective CARE system that we articulated in the previous chapter.

Dogs don't seem to have a guilty conscience, in the sense of an internalized superego. They may possess the first stage of superego formation—like a toddler who realizes that dad is mad, and then makes submissive face gestures to soothe the anger. But it's remarkable that dogs have the emotional expression (shame-face) without the inner feeling. Presumably this is because they only need the face (for social navigation with humans). But the face only works on us because we ascribe the feeling that goes along with the face (we anthropomorphize the inner feeling). But we're being played. They evolved a face that works on us, because we read the signal a certain way (i.e., "oh, he feels shame, so I'll stop punishing"). The expression is decoupled from the feeling, but selected for because the expression is beneficial in the human environment (where it is misread; it's not contrition, but it is emotion-based social surrender).

The origin of shame-face, however, is an important puzzle. How did the expression first arise? In humans, the feeling is first, and then the expression.[11] So if the human expression is favored by natural selection, it is indirectly carrying along (in the same selective pressure) the feeling of guilt/shame. If dog expressions are tied to feelings in a similar manner as ours, then the dog is feeling something, because that feeling is the natural cause of the favored expression. Alternatively, dog ancestors might have tried every kind of face in response to hostility and just settled on the one that stopped all the social strife. Then this would be "remembered." When many social animals fight one another, they afterward try to smooth things over with additional grooming and conciliatory behaviors. And this might be the most primitive pursuit of forgiveness.

The dog's emotional/behavioral response reflects the limbic impulse to bond and avoid separation anxiety. We add a layer in our human version that assigns a cause to the social separation (the sin), a responsible party (the offender), and a cognitive repetition of those features ad nauseam. Our tertiary layer of emotion contains these more cognitive ingredients. But the feelings of shame and guilt are at bottom the limbic feelings of privation and social alienation. These feelings might be explicit in the overt ostracism of the community, or they might be implicit in the virtual ostracism of the penitent's mind.

Religion is a cultural organization of this tertiary layer of emotion (which also includes the lower layers). Religion, for example, expands the reach of superego scrutiny. It expands the realm of things for which we are sorry and need forgiveness. Now it's not just murder, but lying, too. And then it's not just lying but thinking bad thoughts, and so on. Then we have religious ways to supplicate and roll over with submission: asking for forgiveness, lighting candle offerings, saying penance, giving money, time, resources. All these might mask the deep function of guilt and penance, and no doubt it takes on a life of its own and can become neurotically maladaptive. But essentially the goal is to knit the group back together. Forgiveness becomes increasingly necessary in the evolution of human social groups.

Philosophers and psychologists disagree about the difference between shame and guilt. For example, June Price Tangney and Ronda L. Dearing, authors of *Shame and Guilt*, suggest that shame is a more damaging emotion because it focuses on the failure of the person himself.[12] Shame ascribes very negative emotional evaluation to the character or the "self" that is doing the offending action. When I feel shame, I feel that *I* am bad. Guilt, in their view, focuses not on the person so much as the sin or offending behavior. In their view, shame is older and more primitive, and it demonizes the person, whereas guilt is a feeling that judges the actor's behavior, rather than the actor. The authors amass evidence from clinical and developmental psychology in order to conclude, "the pattern is pretty clear-cut: guilt is good; shame is bad" (p. 136).

I suspect that Tangney and Dearing are correct in claiming that shame is older than guilt. A major reason for agreeing is that shame seems much more dominant in the ancient ethics of the Greeks and Romans, as well as in the Warring States period of Chinese ethics (e.g., Confucius). The way I would characterize this is that shame is public and requires the disapproval of other people, so it thrives in "face-cultures" such as Rome and China. The Judeo-Christian tradition, by contrast, stressed a deeply private sense of contrition—between you and God directly. Even if no one knew of your sin and your penitent heart, God still knew. Guilt has no escape. Guilt is an inner state of pain, whether or not the community passes judgment. For this reason, some have argued—including Nietzsche and Freud—that guilt is a much more damaging emotion, because it tilts toward perseveration, and neurosis, very easily.

Friedrich Nietzsche was the first to notice that religious emotions, like guilt and indignation, are still with us, even if we're not very religious. He claimed that we live in a post-Christian world—the Church no longer dominates political/economic life—but we, as a culture, are still dominated by Judeo-Christian values. And these values are not obvious—they are not the Ten Commandments or any particular doctrine, but a general moral outlook.

We can see our veiled value system better if we contrast it with the one that preceded Christianity. The pagans valued honor and pride, but the Christians espoused meekness and humility. The pagans looked to public shame, Christians to private guilt. The pagans celebrated hierarchy, with superior and inferior people, but Christians celebrated egalitarianism. And, finally, for pagans there was greater emphasis on justice, while Christians emphasized mercy (turning the other cheek). Underneath all these values, according to Nietzsche is a kind of psychology—one dominated by resentment and guilt.

Every culture feels the call of conscience—the voice of internal self-criticism. But Western Christianity's cultural sense of guilt is comparatively extreme, and, with our culture of original sin and fallen status, we feel guilty about our very existence. In the belly of Western culture is the feeling that we're not worthy. Why is this feeling there?

All this internalized self-loathing is the cost we pay for being civilized. In a very well-organized society that protects the interests of many, we have to refrain daily from our natural instincts. We have to repress our own selfish aggressive urges all the time, and we are so accustomed to it as adults that we don't always notice it. But if I were in the habit of acting on my impulses, I would regularly kill people in front of me at coffee shops who order elaborate whipped-cream mocha concoctions. In fact, I wouldn't bother to line up in a queue, but just storm the counter and muscle people out of my way. But a small wrestling match happens inside my psyche to keep me from such natural aggression. And that's just morning coffee—think about how many times you'd like to strangle somebody on public transportation.

When aggression can't go outward, it has to go inward. So we engage in a kind of self-denial, or self-cruelty. Ultimately, this self-cruelty is necessary and good for society—I cannot unleash my murderous tendencies on the no-whip, mocha, half-decaf, latte drinkers. But my aggression doesn't disappear, it just gets beat down by my own discipline. Subsequently, I feel badly about myself, and I'm supposed to feel that way. Magnify all these internal daily struggles by a hundred, and you begin to see why Nietzsche thought we were always feeling a little guilty. Historically speaking, however, we didn't really understand this complex psychology—it was, and still is, invisible to us. We just felt badly about ourselves and slowly developed a theology that made sense out of it. God is perfect and pristine and pure, and we are sinful, unworthy maggots who defile creation by our very presence. According to Nietzsche, we have historically needed an ideal God because we've needed to be cruel to ourselves, we've needed to feel guilty.

And we've needed to feel guilty because we have instincts that cannot be discharged externally—we have to bottle them up.

Feeling unworthy is still a large part of Western religious culture, but many people, especially in multicultural urban centers, are less religious. Many still believe that God is watching them and judging them, so their feelings of guilt and moral indignation are couched in the traditional theological furniture. But increasing numbers of people, in the middle and upper classes, identify themselves as being secular or perhaps "spiritual" rather than religious. Now the secular world still has to make sense out of its own invisible, psychological drama—in particular, its feelings of guilt and indignation. Morally righteous secular causes come to the rescue: environmentalism, wage inequality, sexual orientation, and so on.[13]

Guilt creates an internal and relatively automatic way for social cooperators like us to avoid the many daily temptations to exploit the group for our own advantage. As Pascal Boyer (2001) puts it, "Guilt is a punishment we incur for cheating or generally not living up to our advertised standards of honest cooperation with others. But then a feeling of guilt is also useful if it balances the benefits of cheating, making it less tempting. Prospective guilt provides negative rewards that help us brush aside opportunities to cheat, a capacity that is crucial in organisms that constantly plan future behavior. . . ."[14]

Pre-Christian pagans were very concerned with shame and honor, but not guilt. And more importantly for us, the ancient pagan West had no significant forgiveness tradition. The version we moderns are familiar with appears to be an invention of Judeo-Christian religious cultures. Plato makes almost no mention of forgiveness, and Aristotle offers a detailed analysis of excusing and pardoning wrongs, but this is different from forgiveness.[15]

FORGIVENESS OR JUSTICE?

In the Greek tradition, the truly virtuous person (the *megalopsuchos*—great souled person) is above and beyond forgiveness. If the virtuous person has perfected herself, then she will not harm others and never need forgiveness. More importantly, Greek ethics claims that a truly virtuous person cannot be harmed by others, because her mental equanimity immunizes her from the slings and arrows of her fellow citizens.[16] People who attack you and try to do you wrong demonstrate their inferior, uncivilized nature in the attack itself. Hence the proper response to these uncivilized barbarians is contempt or moderate disdain—not forgiveness.

Aristotle discusses the act of dismissing or releasing someone from a debt, and pardoning (*sungnome*) someone for uncontrolled behavior, but these are only virtuous in specific contexts (Nicomachean Ethics, Bk.V). Excusing someone, for the Greeks, is a recognition that the offender has acted involuntarily—either because he was forced to do wrong, or he was ignorant. We can pardon "whenever someone does a wrong action because of conditions of a sort that overstrain human nature, and that no one would endure" (1110a). If I find that you missed our important meeting because you became very ill, or you were assaulted on your way, or you received inaccurate directions to our destination, then I should pardon the transgression. Moreover, I can extend my charitable attitude further if you have misbehaved because of a lapse in self-control. However, the desire that has gotten the better of you must be one that we all possess and that we also occasionally fail to control. Here the judgment must be nuanced. If you were distracted from our meeting because you were suddenly honored with an award and your pride sidetracked you, this is more excusable because the interference was from a nobler part (*thumos*) of your psyche. However, if you missed our meeting because you were passing by the brothel and stopped in for quickie, then I don't need to excuse you—because this interruption originated in the lower part (*epithumia*) of the psyche.

For the ancients, giving pardon was an acknowledgment that the offender was a person who had temporarily lost his "agency"—lost his free voluntary control. Religious forgiveness is different because it assumes that the offender voluntarily did wrong. And despite this damning responsibility, the Christian, for example, offers forgiveness anyway.[17]

The Christian gospels use a different Greek word for forgiveness than the pagan word for pardon (*sungnome*). The gospels use *aphesis*, which means "dismiss" but has a connotation like "release from bondage." And the Latin Church continues with *dimiterre* (to dismiss): *et dimitte nobis debita nostra, sicut et nos dimittimus debitoribus nostril* (And forgive us our debts, as we forgive our debtors).

My argument is that religion acts as a management system on our emotional lives—it is a far-reaching cultural regulation of our native affective instincts. This becomes easier to see when we look at the difference between religious beliefs about justice and religious beliefs about mercy or forgiveness. There are emotional engines inside the call to justice, and inside the pursuit of mercy. We need both.

The emotions of justice and mercy are channeled well by religion because religion is an imaginative system (dealing with images and stories), and it is a great activator of our imagination. Imagination (being perceptually and emotionally rooted) has unique power to activate the motivational system of human beings. Reason is good at cost/benefit calculation, and the assessment of means to ends, but affect-based imagination pushes me toward action. Sentiments, or emotions, cause disgust and outrage toward social injustices. And emotions also cause attraction toward cooperators, as well as congenial people and behaviors. In addition to motivational superiority, the imagination helps us consider strangers as family members (fictive kin). If I imagine what it is like to be beaten, or denied, or even enslaved because of the color of my skin, I enter into solidarity that may, with further cultivation, attain levels of "brotherhood."

The Christian parable of the "prodigal son" is a good example of the imaginative work of religious emotional regulation. In the Gospel of St. Luke (Luke 15), we find Jesus in the company of sinners, and the outraged Pharisees and scribes are upset that Jesus receives outcasts and even breaks bread with them. In response, Jesus tells the famous parable of a rich man with two sons. The younger son asked his father for his inheritance, and went away to another town, spending his whole fortune foolishly and "living riotously." When he had depleted his funds, he found himself friendless and starving. As the old blues song goes, "Nobody knows you when you're down and out." While contemplating stealing food from some pigs, he realizes that even the lowest servant at his father's house has enough to eat. He resolves to return to his father and ask forgiveness. "I will arise, and will go to my father, and say to him: Father, I have sinned against heaven, and before thee: I am not worthy to be called thy son: make me as one of thy hired servants. And rising up he came to his father. And when he was yet a great way off, his father saw him, and was moved with compassion, and running to him fell upon his neck, and kissed him" (verses 18–20). The father kills the fatted calf and organizes a celebration for the son who has returned.

The older brother sees this display of love and forgiveness and bristles at the injustice. Like the Pharisees judging Jesus's generous spirit toward the sinners, the brother admonishes the father for being unfair. Anger is an emotion that fuels the call for justice.

Philosopher Robert Solomon claims, "Resentment figures prominently amongst one's initial, legitimate response to unjust harm," and the thirst for justice begins with "the promptings of some basic emotions, not only sympathy and compassion but also such negative emotions as envy, jealousy, and resentment, a keen sense of having been personally cheated or neglected and the desire to get even."[18] The father replies to the angry son, "you are always with me, and all I have is yours. But it was fit that we should make merry and be glad, for this your brother was dead and is come back to life again; he was lost, and is found" (Luke 15:32).

The great Dutch painter Rembrandt van Rijn created two masterpieces around the parable of the prodigal son. Early in his career, when he was himself enjoying the taste of wealth and fame, he painted himself as the prodigal son in "The Prodigal Son in a Brothel" (1635). Laughing, with a giant beer in his hand and a woman on his lap (his model/wife Saskia), the reckless Rembrandt looks like pure egoistic hedonism.

This is the great sin of the profligate person, who breaks from the tribe to go it alone—seeking only selfish satisfactions. You can't count on this guy. He's eaten from your surplus, and now he's in the wind. In evolutionary psychology, he is called the "defector" or the "free-rider." He is the person who *could* contribute to the success of the family or the tribe, or the community, but who chooses to defect and let everyone else do the hard work required for a cooperative social contract.

The social group, whether it's the family or the regional tribe, must punish the prodigals, otherwise we'd all slouch toward self interest, then burden the rest of the hardworking cooperators, and maybe even end up as criminals or shiftless predators. Justice and its emotions seek to find the defectors, redress their exploitation of resources, and punish them (revenge and retribution are much older than rehabilitation).

Once trust had been betrayed, returning the extreme defector to society was not an option in most early societies. A compelling example of the European Renaissance-era merger of justice and mercy can be seen in the diary of Nuremburg professional executioner Franz Schmidt (1555–1634).[19] Meister Franz dutifully and carefully hung people by the neck, burned them to death, drowned them, broke them on the wheel, and decapitated them with the swift sword. The ritualized violence of public executions was itself a masterful piece of emotional regulation and moral theater. To modern sensibilities these public spectacles seem to be from a time before established legal and court justice, but they actually served to establish trust in those relatively new legal institutions. Execution simultaneously "(1) avenged victims; (2) ended the threat represented by dangerous criminals; (3) set a terrifying example; and (4) forestalled further violence at the hands of angry relatives or lynch mobs" (Harrington, p. 14). Executioners like Meister Franz were real-life assertions and manifestations of the sword of justice.

Mercy, however, was a dominant theme in Meister Franz's diary, and he was devoted to it in his daily work. He often looked for remorse and contrition in his victims, and if they acknowledged guilt and asked for forgiveness, then officiating clerics could offer absolution and redemption—but not rehabilitation, reintegration, or reconciliation. Promised clemency was to be delivered after the execution (in the world beyond), rather than before it. But Franz could and did change the form of execution in such cases, from agonizing torture methods to the quick and merciful sword strike—a change that inspired tears of gratitude from many of his victims.

In this harsh sixteenth-century world of extreme justice and unworldly redemption, we might imagine that prodigal sons and other defectors had no escape once caught. Indeed, Meister Franz had the unpleasant task of beheading a thief named Georg Schweiger, who had been prosecuted by his own father for stealing money. Even the executioner lamented the situation, but not because he had to cut the son's head off. That, after all, was just mundane justice, and Franz was simply the arm that swings the sword. Rather, as a devoutly religious man and father of four, Franz could not understand why the injured father didn't forgive his prodigal son, as in the Gospel of Luke. It seemed unnatural and un-Christian to Franz that any father could choose justice over mercy for his son.

Of course, filial forgiveness is easier to dispense than stranger forgiveness, and both are easier than forgiving one's enemies. From the anthropological point of view it seems somewhat foolish to forgive your enemies, given that everyone's survival hinges on cooperation and your enemy is not a reliable team player. Also, as Confucius incredulously once noted (in response to a pre-Christian Chinese version of pan-clemency), if you give such charity to your enemies then what special treatment have you saved for your friends?[20]

But as social groups get bigger, and more diverse (as they did during Axial Age urbanization), increased pressure on emotional tolerance is absolutely necessary. Larger regional populations must learn to pardon and excuse high degrees of irritating, offensive, and modestly unjust behavior, if they are to function at all. It is likely that copious amounts of defector behavior can be tolerated in a large-scale society, as long as the sword of justice is swinging full on the more egregious forms of defection. A religious culture that places forgiveness at the center of the virtues, may be well-poised to cooperate effectively with strangers, but the balance with justice must be maintained or the forgivers become like doormats among aggressive neighbors. Justice means that you get what you deserve, and forgiveness grants you more than you deserve. Forgiveness can be a social strategy that folds higher degrees of adaptation into reciprocal altruism. I give so that you will give (the Romans said *do ut des*), and eventually I forgive so that you will forgive.

The more powerful locus of forgiveness, however, is at the familial, personal, and psychological levels. In Rembrandt's second painting of the prodigal son story, *Return of the Prodigal Son*, he shows the moment when the father and son embrace, and it is deeply moving—harnessing the painting skill of a lifetime, given that it was one of his last paintings (c. 1668). Here we see the tattered and pathetic son kneeling in supplication as the father embraces him. There is something pitiable in the son, whose shoes and clothes are torn and filthy, and whose head seems burned and shorn by privation and misfortune. Standing to the side is the disapproving brother, who looks on with thinly veiled condemnation. You can tell that this painting is the creation of a mature Rembrandt, who has forgiven the unworthy (among his family and friends), and who has been forgiven.

Like the prodigal son, Rembrandt himself had lost his wealth, and he struggled to provide for his family. Indeed, his personal life was filled with tragedies. His wife Saskia gave birth to four children, but only one, Titus, survived. Saskia herself died young, in 1642, at the age of thirty. He had financial success, but like the prodigal son, he squandered it and had to declare bankruptcy in 1656. Rembrandt fell in love with his housekeeper, Hendrickje Stoffels, and they lived as common law husband and wife, but the local church council investigated and publically shamed her for immoral cohabitation. They had an illegitimate daughter, Cornelia. In 1663 Hendrickje herself died, leaving Rembrandt deeply bereaved. And in 1668, his beloved son Titus died, at the young age of twenty-seven. This was the same time that Rembrandt was finishing his *Return of the Prodigal Son*. He died the following year.

The religious story of the prodigal son and the imagery of artists like Rembrandt sculpt our emotions toward ethical and spiritual norms. When we hear of the profligate idiot son whoring through his inheritance, we feel like the brother—outraged, disgusted, angry, betrayed, and other emotions of justice and injustice. This has a normative effect upon us, because we simultaneously feel and judge the many harms and injuries of the defector.[21] We feel the need to avoid such behavior ourselves, and the urge to punish it in others. This is normative awareness at the gut level, not a rational cost-benefit analysis of free-rider behavior. And yet these gut emotions serve the larger social needs of our cooperative species. The emotions of anger or rage were selected for by natural selection over hundreds of thousands of years of mammal fighting. They developed to help males fight for access to females, to help mammal mothers and fathers protect their young, to help fight invaders, and so on. Those emotional adaptations remain in humans but become redirected and channeled into vigilant cultural forms—beliefs and behaviors that police threats and fight against them. Prodigal sons, and myriad other kinds of defectors, are threats to cohesion, threats to resource surplus, and even threats to themselves. Religious stories and images help shape our normative response to such threats.

The story, however, is more complicated. The fall and forgiveness of the prodigal son, like so many religious stories, requires us to alter the emotional trajectory. We may be skeptical that the son's remorse is sincere, or we may think that he will revert to his old ways, but if we are ultimately moved by his regret, it is because we, too, have had a genuine change of heart. The show or expression of regret may be fakeable, yes, but a profound change of heart is also real, because most of us have experienced it. The biblical story of the son's transformation is moving, and our empathy is stirred to feel compassion for him. So, too, a long look at the son in Rembrandt's painting is emotionally powerful, stirring feelings of pity and kindness. The righteous response of the viewer—disgust and a sense that I am not like that lowlife—is overcome by tenderness and the sense that, "there but for the grace of God go I." I am weak, too. I am an occasional defector.

The father's behavior is almost shocking because he so rapidly abandons justice in favor of love. But he is a model, an exemplar or archetype. He shows us the way to do it. We, the audience, toggle between the distrustful brother and the forgiving father. It is very difficult to reroute an emotional trajectory from angry disgust to pity and compassion. The emotions, behaviors, and beliefs have to *volte face*. We need prototype characters to show us how to achieve such emotional transformation. And religion provides those prototypes.

Stories like the prodigal son, or Jesus forgiving the adulteress (John 8), or Esau forgiving Jacob (Genesis 33) are emotionally didactic. In the early Buddhist scriptures, the Jataka Tales, we learn similar stories of forgiveness. Many children in Southeast Asia first learn the morality of Buddhism by hearing the Jataka Tales (from the *Tripitka, Khuddaka Nikaya*), which are fanciful tales about the past lives of the Buddha—when he is often incarnated as an animal.[22]

In the tale of the Golden Deer (Jataka 482), we meet the Buddha in the form of a beautiful golden deer with blue eyes. Living in the most remote parts of the forest, he taught the other animals how to avoid hunters and other harmful humans. One day, the golden deer heard the cries of a frantic man who was drowning in a rapid river, and pulled him to safety. The golden deer warmed the freezing and exhausted man, nursing him back to health. Overwhelmed by gratitude the man asked if there was anything he could do to repay the deer.

"All I ask," said the Buddha, "is that you do not tell other humans about me. If men knew of my existence, they would come to hunt me." The man vowed secrecy and returned to the city. Some time later, the queen of the kingdom dreamt of a beautiful golden deer with blue eyes, and her husband, the king, offered a great reward for any hunter that could lead him to this rare creature. When the saved man heard that he could receive a "rich village and ten wives" as a reward, he decided to break his promise to the deer and lead the king's hunting party to the rare creature.

After a complex journey, the Buddha—grazing in a quiet field—was eventually in the king's sight. The king fitted an arrow to his bow and took aim.

> "How did you find me here, mighty king?" shouted the Buddha. The king pointed to the saved man who betrayed the deer, and the Buddha scolded the traitor.
>
> "It is better," said the Buddha, "to take a log out of a flooding river, than to save an ungrateful person."

Hearing this the king was astonished, and when he learned that the saved man had betrayed the deer, he turned viciously on the man. The traitor, filled with guilt and fear, admitted his sin.

"Why should this lowest of men live any longer?" roared the king, as he aimed his arrow at the traitor. But the deer leapt between the king and the traitor, pleading for his life: "do not strike one who is already stricken." When the king saw the deer's great compassion, he was humbled and inspired.

"Well," said the king, "if *you* can forgive him, then so can I." Instead of capturing the golden deer, the king invited him to visit the palace. And while there, the deer preached the dharma of compassion to everyone in the kingdom.

This well-known Buddhist story has the imaginative charm of many Western religious and folk tales, and the ethical punch as well. But notice that we are taken through the emotional therapy of the ethical transformation. We are taken through the emotional regulation of outrage, to forgiveness, and on to magnanimity.

Imagination is a kind of embodied cognition, creating and employing the prototypes to produce adaptive emotional regulation.[23] Recall, as psychologist James Gross pointed out, the five methods of emotional regulation include a kind of cognitive reframing of our feelings. Parables help us do a virtual reality reframing of emotions—in this case, from justice outrage to compassionate forgiveness. We are rehearsing the reframing process, and learning how to regulate our emotions in service of ethics.[24] In this way, the imagination has therapeutic power, and loosens the hold of negative emotions, freeing the self for vital activity.

SOCIAL PSYCHOLOGY AND THE RESET BUTTON

Religion is part of a larger system of cultural evolution that selects for behaviors and ideas that are beneficial to the survival of the group. *Natural* selection explains why sharper canine teeth and powerful leg muscles were favored in cheetahs, but *cultural* selection explains why cultural memes such as "democracy" or "Christianity" are widespread.[25] "Memetics"—which is one school of cultural selection—argues that cultural units are like genes, in the sense that they vary, have the ability to reproduce (often via "hosts"), and are selected for or against depending on their ecological fitness. Cultural selection is also shaping even deeper cognitive and emotional dispositions, such as the human propensity to follow a leader.[26] In short, if a species survives best in cooperative relationships, then cultural and biological variations that promote cooperation will contribute to fitness.

Many primates, not just humans, engage in reconciliation or forgiveness behaviors. When two primates have a fight, they often will follow up in the next hour with affiliative or friendly grooming or touch behaviors, maybe even food sharing. Neuroscientist Robert Sapolsky points out that male baboons never reconcile, "there is nothing that looks like forgiveness in them."[27] But reconciliation behavior has been observed in over twenty-five different species. And forgiveness behavior is increased when the two animals share longer history together. "There is a pattern that looks perfectly human, which is that not everybody reconciles with each other, but some pairings are more likely to reconcile. What we are seeing is that the more valuable your relationship with the other animal, the more likely you are to make up afterwards."

The larger tribal society of primates, and especially human primates, functions better when its inner squabbles are minimized and negative emotions are directed outside the in-group. Forgiveness helps this happen, because it reduces in-group anger, the thirst for vengeance, and the in-group grudge; all of which reduce cooperative efficiency. A religious "reset button" in the form of public and private atonement, apology and forgiveness is a way to reintegrate those salvageable free-riders and defectors. In this way the community strengthens itself by repairing injuries. Absolution improves the community, not by cutting off the irredeemable free-rider, but by recovering the redeemable cases. This makes "the team" stronger and more able to contend with competitors, so religious forgiveness may have evolved in the suite of cooperative social strategies. Natural selection may have shaped the emotions of mercy, by giving the merciful more opportunities for successful reproduction, and sexual selection may have spread mercy, if females found it an attractive trait. Why a disposition to forgive might be attractive in a mate should be obvious to anyone who's been married. Moreover, cultural selection has its own causal pathways, and educating offspring to engage in forgiveness strengthens in-group cohesion (although, ironically, it may also increase out-group enmity).

The smaller society—the original society—is the family. Here, too, and maybe especially here, forgiveness is an adaptive survival strategy. A series of psychological studies by Frank Fincham and Steven Beach reveal that a married couple's longevity and ability to resolve conflicts are improved by increased forgiveness practices.[28] Studying both American and British couples, the researchers found that family forgiveness had two components; a reduction of negative emotion (i.e., revenge and avoidance feelings) in the harmed spouse, and increase in positive or benevolent feelings toward the harm-doer. These two changes are often very difficult to complete, in part because gendered styles of communication differ (e.g., women are less likely to avoid difficult and painful conversations and confrontations, while men are more likely to withdraw). These difficult demand–withdraw cycles can reduce forgiveness opportunities. Equally important, the injured spouse has a perspective that requires her to cancel a bigger debt than the one perceived or acknowledged by the transgressing spouse. And this creates fresh trouble, when the transgressor thinks the other is dramatizing or overblowing the infraction ("what's the big deal?"), which, in turn, leads to further escalation of injury and negative emotion.

Forgiveness helps spouses stay healthy as a social unit, but it does not come easily. Religion is helpful in inspiring, reminding, and facilitating the difficult work of forgiveness. And not just marriage benefits; the mental, emotional, and social health of children is impacted greatly by family forgiveness or its lack. The family is the original arena in which children learn how to forgive. The cultural transmission of pro-social forgiveness happens *unconsciously* as parents unwittingly demonstrate the behavior, and it happens *consciously* as the stories, images, maxims, and didactic techniques are applied. Historically speaking, these stories and images have been religious.

Granted, forgiveness helps to improve social cooperation, even in the microsociety of the family, but how does it "reset" the emotional life of individuals who have suffered substantial tragedy? The Stanford Forgiveness Projects are a series of workshops that help people begin the process of forgiveness, especially when the injuries have been extreme.[29] They have worked with mothers from both sides of the Northern Ireland conflict who lost sons, and found that forgiveness exercises and therapies reduced reported stress levels by 50 percent, reduced reported depression by 40 percent, and reduced reported anger by 23 percent. Subsequent workshops have been conducted with victims of financial disasters, and victims of the World Trade Center attacks of 9/11.

The Stanford Forgiveness Projects use the same kind of emotionally powerful strategies as religion (e.g., guided imagery, narrative, and body movement therapy) to walk patients through a nine-step sequence. I'll only mention the most relevant steps for our discussion. The third step: "Forgiveness does not necessarily mean reconciliation with the person that hurt you, or condoning of their action. What you are after is to find peace." Step four: "Recognize that your primary distress is coming from the hurt feelings, thoughts and physical upset you are suffering now, not what offended you or hurt you two minutes ago or ten years ago." And finally, step five: "At the moment you feel upset practice a simple stress management technique to soothe your body's flight or fight response" (Luskin, p. 211).

These steps are difficult to fulfill, but people who were debilitated by anger, revenge fantasy, depression, and stress report improved psychological, social, and physical health after forgiving their wrongdoers. In some extreme cases, forgiving your wrongdoer is the only way to rejoin the world and stop the slide into dysfunction. Psychologist Nikki Hawkins led a team to investigate the emotional responses of the students and parents of the Columbine High School massacre.[30]

Recall that in 1999, two deranged students shot and killed twelve fellow students and one teacher, and wounded twenty-one others, at Columbine in Colorado. Amazingly, the psychologists discovered that within one week of the shootings, over half the Columbine students and parents they surveyed were already trying to forgive the assailants. That is a stunning fact, when we consider the natural rage, fury, and impulse for revenge that must be activated in such mass shooting events. In a subsequent study, the same team of psychologists studied forgiveness tendencies in the aftermath of the September 11, 2001 tragedy.[31]

The psychologists interviewed hundreds of college students and early adolescents three to six weeks after 9/11. Interestingly, they found that people who could not make up their minds as to whether they would forgive the attackers, were the ones who reported the highest levels of psychological turmoil, whereas both the forgivers and those who decided to refuse to forgive were more psychologically stabilized. It's unclear why this correlation exists, but it hints at an important point. In the face of potentially debilitating depression or rage, perhaps the highly adaptive survival response of forgiveness is effective because of the "closure" factor. And perhaps a definitive decision to refuse forgiveness has its own sort of calming closure. Ambivalence, then, might be a greater source of stress than conviction—wherever that conviction settles. This makes sense when we realize that placing terrible events into a meaningful frame (e.g., religious or otherwise) brings cognitive and emotional closure through a sense of purpose.

A very interesting data point for us, however, is that refusal to forgive the 9/11 assailants correlated with less religiousness. Religious people tended to report more desire to forgive, or perhaps could not bring themselves to reject the value of forgiveness even in the case of a terrorist attack.

More studies need to be done, of course, but this is a tantalizing correlation. Religious people are more willing to forgive, even in extreme cases. Of course, this will not impress the critic of religion, who can reasonably challenge the overly ambitious cheek-turning of the devotee. Maybe we shouldn't forgive some people. Also, the data may be capturing the periphery of the injured and not actual families of those killed—because, presumably, they may be unlikely to fill out surveys so quickly after their loss. But the empirical study does confirm our long-held assumption that religious people try more than others to overcome their grudges. When a religious person feels deeply wronged, they have a cognitive and emotional strategy (more habitual than conscious) to let go of the wrong and reset the game or struggle of life. The habit is codified in a typical scriptural passage:

> Repay no one evil for evil, but give thought to do what is honorable in the sight of all. If possible, so far as it depends on you, live peaceably with all. Beloved, never avenge yourselves, but leave it to the wrath of God, for it is written, "Vengeance is mine, I will repay, says the Lord." To the contrary, "if your enemy is hungry, feed him; if he is thirsty, give him something to drink; for by so doing you will heap burning coals on his head." Do not be overcome by evil, but overcome evil with good. (Romans 12:17–21)

Of course, it's true that some religious people, like members of the Westboro Baptist Church, are vengeful grudge holders, but these pockets of pathology are small. Atheist critics of religion are fond of holding up these antisocial groups (e.g., Westboro Baptist Church) as indicative of religion, but they are smaller than they seem. The Westboro church is well known because the media has celebrated their weirdness, but there are only forty members of that bizarre parish. Their renown is outsized and they reveal little to nothing about mainstream religion, where mercy is a coin of the realm. We'll return to vengeful religion in the chapter on anger.

Consider the challenges of close-contact group conflict. For most Americans, the war on terror is remote. Unlike in places such as Syria, Turkey, Nigeria, or Iraq, Americans can hate, hold grudges, or forgive at a relative distance. But what is it like to know that your neighbor—the one who lives down the street and whom you see regularly at market—is the person who killed your family member? This seemingly unbearable situation is one that many people endure, in places such as South Africa, Palestine, Cambodia, Rwanda, and Sarajevo, to name a few.

Ethnic groups and tribes that have violent history remain hostile long after the warfare or violence has stopped. They may not be able to reconcile fully, but forgiveness returns some social stability. One of the most horrific tribal slaughters in recent memory occurred in Rwanda, between the Tutsis and the Hutus. I spent time in Rwanda in 2010 and was astounded (as I had been in Cambodia and Vietnam) by the resilience, dignity, and genuine warmth of the people. It is humbling to meet people who have suffered so dramatically. It inspires us to overcome our own relatively minor problems and to appreciate the heroism and grace that emerge spontaneously under such pressure. But make no mistake, Rwanda is still a land of nightmares—terrible dreams and memories—haunting almost everyone you encounter. A visit to the Kigali Genocide Memorial Center will give you a few souvenir nightmares of your own.

I became friends with a man named John, who had lost most of his family during the genocide. He had gone to study in Uganda in the early 1990s and became trapped there during the complex civil war. Eventually, he was forced to fight in the Ugandan army and saw many horrors of his own. When he returned home after the genocide, he found his parents and siblings had been killed. His old rival neighbors were living in his childhood home.

With the help of his military connections, John retook his own property and slowly rebuilt a life for himself—eventually marrying and starting a family. When I asked him, one day, if he was Tutsi or Hutu, he laughed and said, "I cannot tell you that, my friend. It is against the law to reveal my ethnicity to you." Why is it now forbidden to declare one's tribe in Rwanda?

Between April and July of 1994, an estimated 800,000 Rwandans brutally murdered each other, often cutting each other down with machetes. The United Nations failed to give its own commander the manpower and approval to mitigate the disaster, and the wider world stood by while the slaughter took place. Majority Hutus were attacking minority Tutsis—trying to wipe them off the earth. The violence targeted Tutsis, but Hutus killed many other Hutus as well. American pundits chalked up the disaster to inevitable tribal warfare.

There were indeed old tensions between the tribes. Minority Tutsis had ruled over majority Hutus for centuries before German and then Belgian colonialism. During the colonial period (1890s–1950s), Tutsis remained in power, both facilitating and benefitting from colonial interests. As independence unfolded, in the late 1950s and early 1960s, Hutu power grew and eventually replaced the traditional Tutsi monarchy with a Hutu republic. The new Hutu republic immediately began persecuting Tutsis.

In the 1970s, Hutu general Juvenal Habyarimana seized power and increased the campaign of revenge and degradation toward the Tutsis, fear-mongering the majority into paranoia about Tutsi plans to enslave Hutus. None of this typical "strong man" political manipulation would have been possible if the Belgians had not previously dramatized and exacerbated tribal differences—forcing everyone to carry separate tribal ID cards.

Divide and conquer techniques proved so effective during colonial rule, that Habyarimana and his allies continued the practice, introducing mass media publications and radio broadcasts that demonized Tutsis as "cockroaches." The infamous "Hutu 10 Commandments" propaganda article was published in the anti-Tutsi newspaper *Kangura* in 1990. It lists a frightening set of hateful rules that fueled the eventual genocide, including the warning to never trust a Tutsi woman (do not marry across tribal lines), and the command "The Hutu should stop having mercy on the Tutsi."

In the early 1990s, the government began stockpiling weapons and training killing militias to wipe out the "scheming" Tutsi "threat" walking among them. Neighbors eyed neighbors suspiciously and Hutus listened to unfounded radio conspiracy theories about Tutsis torturing and killing the Hutu president of Burundi. Then, when distrust was at a fever pitch, Habyarimana's plane was mysteriously shot down in April 1994, and violence exploded around the country—setting off 100 days of horrifying genocidal bloodshed. When I asked my friend John how neighbors could so viciously kill neighbors, often raping and torturing them, he said, "the people were brainwashed. The people could not see the humanity in their enemies—they saw them as monsters or demons."

Psychologists Ervin Staub and Laurie Anne Pearlman have studied and even helped foster forgiveness in postgenocide Rwanda.[32] They developed a model in which trained facilitators worked with groups of Hutus and Tutsis, educating them about the causes and effects of genocide. People who participated in these programs showed fewer trauma symptoms when studied two months later, and they reported a more positive orientation toward and "readiness to reconcile" with the members of other tribes.

The general approach of this method is to engender a climate for forgiveness and reconciliation by exploring the causes of social violence. Facilitators explore the social history of tribal conflict, the competition for resources (e.g., food, shelter, jobs, property), and the cultural machinations of demonization. Rwandans are invited to see their own trauma as a species of this larger social phenomenon, in hopes that this will demystify such radical violence and place Hutu and Tutsi behavior back in the realm of human behavior, albeit terrible behavior.

Anthropologist Jared Diamond summarized a compelling Malthusian interpretation of the Rwandan genocide. The violence takes its start from the fact that population growth increased more rapidly than food production in the postcolonial era.[33] From the 1960s to the late 1980s populations spiked, as did short-term agricultural practices that ultimately eroded topsoil and compromised irrigation. This led to famines in the late 1980s, early 1990s. Larger farms had off-farm incomes that allowed them to buy up smaller farms, and radically increase the divide between haves and have-nots. All this led to a social context of hunger, suspicion, and desperation—perfect chaos into which old ethnic differences could be introduced as simplistic subterfuges for more complex economic ecological problems. When the genocide broke out in 1994, many killings failed to fit into the ethnic interpretation of the conflict, but did conform to the economic interpretation. Professor Diamond quotes sociologists C. Andre and J. Platteau as saying, "The 1994 events provided a unique opportunity to settle scores, or to reshuffle land properties, even among Hutu villagers. . . . It is not rare, even today, to hear Rwandans argue that a war is necessary to wipe out an excess of population and bring numbers into line with the available resources" (p. 326).

Through group education sessions, but especially national radio programs, psychologists Staub and Pearlman exposed Rwandans to these naturalistic explanations of tribal violence. The researchers suggest that such education helps toward reconciliation, stating "understanding the roots of violence between groups was of great interest to participants. It seemed to have special value in contributing to healing and to greater openness by members of the two groups toward each other, as well as in giving rise to the motivation to prevent new violence."[34]

The Enlightenment fan inside me cries out for this sort of thing to be true. The sleep of reason produces monsters (as Francisco Goya reminds us), so turning on the light of education should clear away the violent monsters of superstition and prejudice. Unfortunately, the empirical evidence that education increases forgiveness and reduces violence is somewhat thin.[35] On further reflection, it's not even clear how this can reliably work, if the causes of such violence are ecological overload and basic-needs frustration. A clear-eyed understanding of *why* I'm starving is not going to stop me from starving or stop me from untoward means of survival.

An alternative approach to reconciling and healing group animosity after injury is more commonly found in religion. One of the most important promoters of reconciliation is the feeling and conviction that you and your enemy are members of some superordinate group. You are not just Hutus or Tutsis, but Rwandans. You are not just Confederates or Yankees, but Americans. You are not just Jews or Christians, but Judeo-Christians. However artificial some of these fictive kin groups may be, they tend to blur the us vs. them distinction and reduce animosity in the newly expanded intragroup dynamic. These are forms of emotional regulation, not theories about the hidden causes of events.

As we've already pointed out, religion can be quite tribal, but it is often idealistic about our common human bond. The Quran states, "And hold fast, all together, by the rope of Allah and be not divided; and remember the favor of Allah which He bestowed upon you when you were enemies and He united your hearts in love, so that by His grace you became as brothers" (Chapter 3, Verse 103). The New Testament and the Buddhist Sutras, for example, also are devoted to breaking down ethnic and class differences to find a "brotherhood of man." Researchers Michael Wohl and Nyla Branscombe have experimental data that verifies the importance of this mindset for forgiveness, reconciliation, and subsequent cooperation.

Wohl and Branscombe looked at ingredients that improve or hinder forgiveness; in particular, they studied the North American Jewish community and their emotional reactions to the Holocaust and the Palestinian–Israeli conflict.[36] The researchers found different moods of forgiveness depending upon how the subjects were first primed. Jewish subjects who were first reminded of Holocaust history were more likely to forgive their in-group's contemporary actions against another out-group (e.g., Israeli activities against Palestinians) and more likely to see contemporary out-groups as more threatening. Unsurprisingly, memories of past injuries are usually preventative to contemporary forgiveness and reconciliation.

However, if the Jewish subjects were primed to feel like part of a superordinate group with Germans, for example, then they showed a greater willingness to forgive the historical perpetrator group. Jewish subjects read articles that described the Holocaust as an event in which humans victimized other humans. The subjects were subsequently divided into two groups with one group asked to explicitly identify as either Jewish or German (all of them were Jewish) and the other group was asked to make no such identification. In the consequent testing, the group that was asked to explicitly identify their ethnicity showed less likelihood to forgive Germans (i.e., Nazis, descendants of Nazis, and miscellaneous Germans) than the test group that identified themselves as human. The subjects who categorized themselves as humans, rather than as Jews, also showed more interest in social mingling with Germans and German culture.

My point is not that science cannot tell us a unifying story about our common human ancestry and the ethical implications of our shared descent. My point is that religion can do it better, because it can *show* us (not just tell us of) this solidarity. Religion can get at the emotional cores that help transform a "them" to an "us" or a mood of vengeance to one of forgiveness. Art, too, of course, can give me a virtual reality in which I feel what it's like to be a slave, or a Jewish person in a concentration camp, or a Tutsi, or whatever, but religion mixes the imaginative, the emotional, and the metaphysical.

One of the surprising things about forgiveness—one that underscores its adaptive significance—is that it often reverses our expectations of cause and effect. We usually expect that an apology from the perpetrator comes first and causes or elicits the forgiveness response. But while that certainly happens, it is quite often the reverse. The injured party expressly forgives the perpetrator first, and this act of mercy elicits contrition in the perpetrator—the harm-doer acknowledges her actions, finds empathy with those she hurt, and expresses apology and regret. So forgiveness is not just an emotional relief and liberation for the individual, but also a serviceable means of social group repair.

MOVING ON, *WITHOUT* TRUTH OR RECONCILIATION

Very often in life there is no apology. There is no acknowledgment, regret, or reconciliation. In Cambodia, Rwanda, U.S. civil rights conflict, Nazi Germany, Syria, South Africa, and so on, the balancing of the scales of justice never actually comes. The wrongs are not righted, and sometimes the wrongs are not even admitted or conceded. Hell, even in our marriages, the scales never really balance.

Given that over half of all marriages end in divorce, marriage forms an important vector for the battle between forgiveness and grudge. The stakes are high, because the animosity spills over to the children, as well as wider circles of family and friends. Some couples cannot forgive each other, and some things may be unforgivable. On the other hand, some spouses who stay together perfect the art of saying "it's my fault, I'm sorry" even when that's not the case. It is very common for couples who break up to feel varying levels of injury and betrayal. Most people taste anger in high doses, but some people remain angry for decades after. Other people manage to let go of the injuries and remember the positive elements of the relationship.

At some point in your life—and it's different for everyone—you begin to realize that if you wait for the wrongdoers to own up and make amends before you forgive and move on, then you will *never* move on. Because they are not coming, they are not owning up. They are dead, or unrepentant, or disinterested, or confused, or whatever. So now what?

It is unlike a philosopher to argue for *health* over *truth*, but that is not going to stop me. Forgiveness, in some cases, is a great survival mechanism, and not as a simple psychological sop. Letting go of extreme injuries and debtors is an existential choice that gives one a new ground project or orientation in life. Being the "injured" or the "victim" in life can be debilitating, as we've already seen, but it also can be an attachment, a habit, and an addiction. It can ensure that there is no "moving on."

It would be great if people cleared the slate with me, when they wronged me. Then we could mutually gaze upon the glistening truth of my injury and their culpability. But it almost never happens, and my survival, healing, closure, and flourishing cannot be held hostage to this rare event.

The Buddha loved truth, knowledge, and justice as much as any philosopher, but he recognized how Truth (with a capital "T") is sometimes a luxury we cannot afford. He was a pragmatist. When his friends kept pressing him about metaphysical questions regarding the infinity of the universe or the immortality of the soul, he responded that these are impossible to answer definitively, and they tend to distract us from the present moment and the overcoming of suffering. He calls these "*avyakata* questions," or unanswerable questions. The Buddha says that we cannot wait for all the theoretical issues to be resolved before we act or commit. It would be great if we could refrain from acting until we had the very best description of things available, but we can't.

> It is as if a man were pierced by a poison arrow, and his friends and relations called in a surgeon, but the injured man said: I will not have this arrow pulled out until I know who the man is that has wounded me; whether he is a noble, a prince, a citizen, or a servant; or whether he is tall or short, or of medium height. Truly such a man would die, before he could adequately learn all this. (*Cula-Malunkyovada sutta, Majjhima Nikaya* 63)

Just as I have to try the pragmatism of Buddhist liberation without solving all the metaphysical mysteries, I often must decide to forgive someone before my wrongdoer acknowledges the truth of his sin. Forgiveness is a way of taking the poison arrow out of my body.

Besides habituating us to the practice of clemency, religion offers another strange consolation. It says there is truth and justice out there, but you can't really access it fully or bring it about fully. Trust that things will ultimately balance, even if they don't seem to do so in your lifetime. Scores will be settled, so you can unburden yourself of that job. God or karma will settle those scores.

Is it possible that this leads some people to accommodate earthly injustice? Quite possibly, yes. Thomas Paine thought there was too much forgiveness in Christianity, and it sank humans to the level of spaniels (*Age of Reason*, Pt. II, Sec. 20), while Malcom X famously said that Christianity's focus on forgiveness had failed the black race because it taught them to tolerate the injustice of slavery. I'm sure this is true in some cases, but it is also wishful thinking to imagine that people who are suffering can fix every injustice with reason, science, democracy, and some mythical, nemocentric calculus of impartiality. Work for justice, yes, but religious people also sprinkle in high doses of mercy while they work.

In closing, it is worth reviewing the many benefits of forgiveness. The person who forgives often experiences a positive change in affect and this aids psychological healing after injury. Forgiving someone also restores a victim's sense of personal power, agency, and existential mission. As Daniel McIntosh puts it, "forgiveness may be a way of regaining control over a situation and its emotional aftermath when no direct action is possible."[37] Additionally, forgiveness may sometimes bring about reconciliation between the victim and the offender. And forgiveness may help reduce intergroup conflict at higher social levels, such as tribe and state.

My argument is not that forgiveness is *always* the better approach to life. Incest survivors, victims of parental abuse, rape victims, and so on, may find it impossible to forgive, and it is not for me to lecture them about the benefits of forgiveness. A life of anger or outrage may be personally meaningful, and may even produce social and legal policy changes. But if it is possible to forgive, then the benefits (personal and societal) are undeniable. Research results compiled by the American Psychological Association United Nations report (2006) summarize empirical research: forgiveness interventions lead to improved affect, lowered rates of psychiatric illness, lower physiological stress responses, and restoration of relationship closeness.

Forgiveness may not always be the preferable life choice and social norm. But cooperative societies (and even families) that engage in some form of forgiveness can more easily rededicate themselves to the ongoing challenges of living in a hostile world. You are not, however, a better person in some absolute sense because you chose to forgive your transgressor. I'll let the priests sell that message. I'm describing the psychological, social, and existential benefits of emotional management through forgiveness, but there are many legitimate reasons why some people refuse such benefits. Some people, faced with the choice of forgiving the murderer or being eaten alive with rage, will choose the latter. It is not my view that they are wrong. Count Ugolino, gnawing on Ruggieri's head for eternity in Dante's *Inferno,* is not violating some absolute ethics, in my view. He is instead choosing an emotional life that many of us cannot sustain and need to lay down. Thankfully, religion gives us a way to lay down such a burden.

CHAPTER 4

Mental Training

Peace, Resilience, and Sacrifice

Reckon the days in which you have not been angry. I used to be angry every day; now every other day; then every third and fourth day; and if you miss it so long as thirty days, offer a sacrifice of thanksgiving to God.

—Epictetus

Resolutely train yourself to attain peace.

—Buddha (*Utthana Sutta*)

Fear not, for I am with you; be not dismayed, for I am your God; I will strengthen you, I will help you, I will uphold you with my righteous right hand.

—Isaiah 41:10

Do not be anxious about anything, but in everything by prayer and supplication with thanksgiving let your requests be made known to God. And the peace of God, which surpasses all understanding, will guard your hearts and your minds in Christ Jesus.

—Philippians 4:6

In addition to ritual, theology, service, and so on, most religions have a contemplative branch. Sometimes the contemplative branch is removed from the life and domain of householders and laypersons, thriving instead in monastic communities or isolated small groups. Sometimes contemplation is just a prominent aspect of the everyday mainstream religion, such as Christian prayer or some forms of meditation.

Saint Anthony of the Desert (c. 251–356) often is referred to as the "father of monks," having created a desert monastic tradition in Egypt that drew Christian ascetics away from urban centers. His famous fight with demons in the desert also laid the groundwork for all subsequent thinking about demons and demonic possession.[1]

Questing after spiritual purification, Anthony left the pleasures of domestic life and moved to live in a tomb outside his village, where he was attacked by a "multitude of demons" who sliced him into a bloody mess. "For he affirmed that the torture had been so excessive that no blows inflicted by man could ever have caused him such torment."[2]

However, Anthony assured us, most demons have no real power in the physical world. They only *seem* to be causally efficacious. The trick is to acknowledge that you are having a frightening experience, but to realize that what frightens you is like a hallucination rather than a material creature. In fact, reading St. Anthony is like reading an early self-help treatise for schizophrenics. He engages in a kind of mental training, albeit an extreme form, trying to reduce negative thoughts and feelings, and increase positive ones.

Although some isolated religious contemplation can develop into hallucination and detachment from reality, most of it is healthy introspection. The Catholic tradition refers to it as *ruminatio* or pondering. But rumination without focus or direction can be disturbing, and the purpose of most religious pondering is peace of mind. Preventing rumination from spiraling into anxiety is accomplished by the use of *lectio divina*, a Benedictine technique of slow scripture reading and contemplation. Similarly, in Buddhist meditation, the mind is focused (during the first step of mindfulness) on a devotional object, or a candle, or one's breath. The goal in these traditions is to quiet the mind.

In this chapter I want to consider two forms of mental training ubiquitous in religion. Most religious people do not learn the activities of prayer, meditation, contemplation, as "mental training" per se. For example, the monotheist usually sees prayer as a form of communication with the divine, but I want to argue that this is not its true function. Instead, the two major functions of prayer, *ruminatio*, and meditation are (a) peace of mind or equanimity and (b) resilience training.

PEACE OF MIND

In prescientific cultures the mind is often understood in terms of metaphors and analogies, and truth be told even contemporary neuroscience is chock-full of metaphors (e.g., hot cognition, reptilian complex, circuitry). But one of the main metaphors of mind, especially strong in Asian cultures, is the pond, or lake, or stream of water. When the pond is disturbed, by winds on the surface or currents underneath, the water becomes muddy, confused, unclear. When the pond is calm and there is no agitation, the waters become crystal clear and pure. Objects in the water can be clearly discerned and seen for what they are. External forces can easily disturb our clarity of perception and understanding, and these forces can then control or beguile us.

Hinduism and Buddhism, for example, have different meditation techniques (and metaphysics), but they share some goals of introspection. In particular, they seek to cleanse the mind of bad thinking and harmful emotions. Calming the mind does two important things. It reduces stress and is therefore an important technique in emotional management, and it gives one clearer insight into reality. Calming the mind has psychological and epistemological benefits.

The adaptive aspects of mental peace are almost too obvious to point out. Stress is helpful when we are in a fight-or-flight scenario. When our resting state of homeostasis is disturbed (via alarming sensory signals, or pain, or fear, etc.) our hypothalamus secretes corticotropin-releasing hormones. This begins the stress response cascade—from hypothalamus to pituitary gland, to adrenal gland and cortisol production, which puts the whole body/brain on high alert, sending energy (glucose) to vital areas. But our mind is like a muscle, and when the threat diminishes, the mind needs relaxation from its unique flexion tension. The body returns to a state of homeostatic equilibrium, and the mind, too, is liberated from the domination of fear and action.

This liberation is physiologically adaptive because it helps the immune system do its important work. Too much stress (cortisol) reduces our T-cells (a form of white blood cell) and reduces our overall health. Chronic stress causes or exacerbates dozens of illnesses, including hypertension, heart attack, stroke, and infertility. But peace of mind is also psychologically adaptive, reducing anxiety, headaches, and depression. Moreover, it is philosophically adaptive in the sense that we can think better when the mind is rested and undistracted. We can better grasp means versus ends relations, cost-benefit relations, and we can better prioritize values and predict and project responses. If philosophers are conceptual engineers, then peace of mind can create a clear mental workspace for such engineering.

On top of all this, a cooler disposition and "grace under pressure" are socially adaptive for such a cooperative species as *Homo sapiens*. The ability to cool down one's anger is important in tight-knit hunter-gatherer groups, but also in Holocene agricultural groups, and right down to today's crowded urban environments. A recent study shows that police officers trained for eight weeks in mindfulness meditation showed decreased levels of stress and anger.[3] Many law enforcement professionals attempt to manage their stress through unhealthy pain relievers, such as alcohol, but meditative techniques reduced their post-shift emotional distress and reduced angry responses in volatile on-the-clock scenarios.

Meditation is a significant aspect of Buddhism, but it is often mistaken for a simple relaxation exercise or it is mixed up with other forms of contemplation. The Buddhist practice of *sati* (mindfulness), for example, is not the same as *samadhi* (concentration). The practice of meditation (bringing the mind into the present moment) needs some detailing because it's not just a spiritual technology aimed at the goal of freedom—it is also *the thing itself* (freedom). And crucial to understanding Buddhist meditation is knowing that it can be attained during the most active athletic, artistic, or creative pursuits. Cooking, serving tea, drawing, folding your laundry, and every other mundane activity can be transformed into mindful experience. So, peace of mind does not need to be correlated with sedentary inactivity.

In the *Samyutta Nikaya* (35.206), the Buddha offers a simile of "The Six Animals." Imagine, he says, that your six senses (the mind is considered a sense in Buddhism) are like six different animals: a snake, crocodile, bird, dog, hyena, and monkey. Imagine now that each animal is bound on its own rope-leash, but all of the ropes are tied together in a central knot. Because each of these animals has its own respective habitat, they will all pull, crawl, or fly toward that habitat home. The crocodile will struggle to get to the water, the bird to the air, the monkey to the forest, and so on. But when the animals become exhausted and can no longer struggle, they will submit and surrender to whichever animal happens to be strongest on that day. This chaos, according to the Buddha, is what it's like to live *without* mindfulness. Our senses are drawn toward their particular pleasures, and we haphazardly pursue whatever is momentarily strongest. We are locked in an internal struggle—a roped-up, six-animal tug of war.

The solution, according to the Buddha, is to live in the present without attachment and slavery to sensual and intellectual cravings. One should, Buddha suggests, take one's six animals and tether them to a strong stake or pole (i.e., the practice of mindfulness). In this way, they will still struggle for their respective pleasures, but they will grow tired and then stand, sit, or lie down right there next to the stake. The discipline and restraint of mindfulness brings tranquility or equanimity.

Recall that the Buddha had lived as a wealthy hedonist and as a poor ascetic, but neither lifestyle had given him peace of mind and freedom from suffering. He vowed to engage in intensive mental contemplation in order to break through to a cure. Sitting under the Bodhi tree, the Buddha used his meditation skills to enter into deeper and deeper trance states (*jhanas*). He had learned these techniques from Hindu ascetics during his days of wandering, and properly speaking, *jhana* concentration (samadhi) is a pre-Buddhist form of mental training. The Buddha, however, became a master of samadhi, and found that he could move through different trance states with relative ease. First, sitting quietly and focusing on the breath as it moves in and out, the Buddha was able to quiet the mind and body. In this jhana, one detaches from the usual sense-desires and moves inward to watch the bubbling flow of thought itself. This first jhana is accompanied by feelings of delight and pleasure. From here, one moves to the second jhana, which is the cessation of thought itself. The constant discourse inside our mind, running like an incessant commentary on all experience, is finally silenced. When the inner monologue finally quiets, one has arrived in the second jhana. This trance state is still accompanied by a refined sense of delight and joy. But now, one is able to move to an even deeper level of concentration. In the third jhana, the more active feeling of joy (*piti*)—which is like a form of rapture, evaporates and leaves behind only the awareness of happiness (*sukha*). Finally, even this sukha passes away, and in the fourth jhana, only the purest equanimity, empty awareness, remains. The mind has been utterly cleansed.

Samadhi meditation is a prized form of mental training in Hinduism and Buddhism because it gives greater powers of concentration to the practitioner. It also reveals the deficiency or conventionality of the usual subject–object distinction. In ordinary consciousness, we are always separate from the object of our experience—separated by words and labels (symbols and signs), separated by mental representations (ideas), and even separated by sensual representations (sense data impressions). Jhana meditation empties the mind of its usual representational activity and gives the practitioner an awareness that is supposedly beyond the usual subject–object duality.

For all those good achievements, however, jhana meditation was not the break-through technique for the Buddha. The problem with jhana meditation, according to the Buddha, is that it does not have the practical insight (*vipassana*) to overcome the problem of suffering in our daily lives. Jhana meditation is a great head-trip, which allows the practitioner to clear out a great deal of the mind's content, leaving the *form* of consciousness; but we need something else, according to the Buddha, to help find peace in our day-to-day lives.

Under the Bodhi tree, the Buddha switched from jhana meditation (samadhi) to his unique technique of mindfulness (*sati*). Mindfulness is a meditation on the impermanence of all things (*anicca*), but it is a systematic method. It proceeds sequentially through four domains; mindfulness of body (*kayanupassana*), mindfulness of feeling and sensation (*vedanupassana*), mindfulness of our conscious thinking patterns (*cittanupassana*), and mindfulness of our "mind objects" (i.e., our beliefs and ideas) (*dhammanupasanna*).

Each domain of mindfulness must be meditated in two modes, *internal* and *external*. For example, my body must be contemplated from the *inside*—I must become more aware of it in the present moment (its weight, shape, movement, and my own ability to calm or agitate the whole body). I must become mindful of the body's ever-changing aspect. But then, I must contemplate bodies generally (the external modality) by reflecting on their common nature. And what I find is that all bodies, my own and everyone else's, are slowly decomposing sacks of flesh, tissues, organs, and so on. The Buddha frequently describes the body as a repulsive "bag, with openings at both ends, filled with impurities." This is not because he hates the body per se, but rather because he wants to detach from the normal clinging attitude that we usually have toward our bodies.

Here we see an important point about Buddhism, and an important point about my overall defense of religion. The Western fascination with Buddhism is long, dating back to the Romantics and Transcendentalists, and up through the Beats, Hippies, and so on. And Buddhist mindfulness is presently enjoying great popularity in the West. There is a growing movement in the United States and Europe, for example, to introduce mindful meditation in primary schools, prisons, and workplaces. This movement has been welcomed in some quarters and reviled in others. But much of Buddhist meditation has been stripped of its original metaphysical content and turned into something more vague and explicitly secular. Mindfulness is now just a quieting of the mind, without any beliefs, commitments, or insights into reality per se. Western mindfulness practitioners want to get "in the zone" or "in the flow" of their activity or thinking, but nothing else (no constraining ideas, beliefs, or feelings) should contaminate their state of mental cleanliness. This may be a good thing as mindfulness spreads around the world and attains therapeutic respectability, and it's probably also an inevitable result of the influence of Zen on our encounter with Buddhism.[4] But I have been arguing that religion has adaptive benefits for emotional management and it's important to appreciate that many of those benefits come from seeing the world in a specific way, not just from making the mind a better formal processor.

Buddhism is not just being mindful about whatever comes into your cognitive interface (although that can be helpful). It is being mindful *that*.

And the *that* is pretty specific, and constitutes the metaphysical aspects of Buddhism. As we saw, in Chapter 2 for example, Buddhism sees the soul as figmentary and unreal, so a lot of mindfulness is devoted to reminding us that we are impermanent.

Impermanence and *interconnectedness* are overused words. Most people nod their heads when they hear them, but for Buddhism they are foundational ideas that provide core values and cognitive/emotional tendencies. For classical Buddhism, there is no eternal human soul (*Atman*). The Buddha points out, in the *Potthapada Sutta*, that a man who believes he has a soul is like a man who is madly in love with a woman whom he has never seen, or otherwise experienced, and about whom he knows absolutely nothing. In other words, he's in love with a fiction. Belief in the permanence of my own ego is a mind-game, according to the Buddha. But worse, it is a dangerous game, because it continues to create two worlds—this mundane, imperfect, and impermanent one, and the next perfect and permanent one (e.g., the idealism of the *Bhagavad Gita* and the *New Testament*). Buddhism seeks to reconcile the radical divide of two worlds, a divide that leads people to devalue flesh and blood in favor of figmentary perfection. When there is no next world, then *this* world becomes sacred.

In Buddhism, there are levels of reality. The top level is pretty much the world we see around us, the phenomenal world. Our day-to-day experiential world is made up of individual beings who seem separate or individuated from one another. These beings seem relatively the same over time but differ from one another. If we go down beneath this conventional layer of reality, however, we find a deeper layer in which each being is only a momentary confluence of the five aggregate forces (*khandas*). The idea of compositional levels here is not much different from what we already accept from the physical sciences, just not as reductionist (e.g., consciousness is irreducible in Buddhism). We are accustomed, for example, to seeing that biological organisms are composed of smaller and less visible chemical interactions, while those chemical interactions are themselves composed of atomic and subatomic interactions. And, in Buddhism, one goes deeper (as seen in the *Abhidhamma* scriptures), to discover that beneath the stratum of the five aggregates, there are more fundamental elements of mind and body—almost like atoms of consciousness (and below this, *emptiness*).

Emptiness (*sunyata*) is a crucial idea in Mahayana Buddhism. The *Diamond Sutra* (*Vajracchedika Prajnaparamita sutra*) closes with the following lines:

> All composed things are like a dream,
> a phantom, a drop of dew, a flash of lightning.

That is how to meditate on them,
that is how to observe them.

Emptiness becomes a major theme in later Buddhism, and reminds us that religions are metaphysically diverse. Almost every other religious and philosophical system (East and West) has attempted to ground the experiential world on some more durable eternal foundation. Monotheism, for example, assumes a deeper divine reality beyond this mortal coil. Buddhism is a rare exception to this tendency.

The idea that reality is empty dominates later Chinese and Tibetan Buddhism, even though it has roots in Indian Buddhism. Indian philosophers like Nagarjuna (c. 150–250 CE) argued that all dichotomies of thinking (e.g., us or them, good or bad, being or not-being) are illusions of the conventional mind. But this had special resonance for Chinese philosophers and artists, whose indigenous Daoism also celebrated a deeper unity beneath the opposites of yin and yang.[5]

My point is that the adaptive peace of mind and psychological freedom that come from Buddhist meditation come from the ability to contemplate the ephemerality of reality—including the temporariness of my pain (and pleasure). Liberation from suffering and stress follows upon the realization that "this too shall pass." Anxiety and addiction are reduced when we cease to cling to things and experiences. Clearing the "mind pond" allows us to see the true impermanence of things, but it is the truth of impermanence that grounds our liberation. And on this view of nirvana (*nibbana*), we still feel pain, pleasure, occasional anxiety, and so on, but constant reminders of impermanence (through meditation and cultural images, etc.) stop us from being dominated by desire. So the point of meditation is not just better concentration (cutting through distractions), but concentration on the right thing (ephemerality). The Buddhist is cleansing her mind in order to see the truths of the Dharma better, not just so her mind is more fit. This reveals the metaphysical core of Buddhism and shows that it is not just a thinking technique, easily abstracted for insertion into the secular projects of the West. Yes, its metaphysical views are accidentally consilient with some of contemporary science (e.g., its pragmatic rejection of souls, essences), but that is just a happy accident and does not explain its longstanding adaptive value.

To appreciate how the perspective of impermanence can have liberating effects, consider our own contemporary culture. We are obsessed with body image. We are surrounded by pictures of perfectly toned hard bodies on TV, the Internet, magazines, and so on, and the reigning question of pop-culture seems to be, "Am I desirable?" Young girls become bulimic and anorexic over this obsession. Young and not-so-young men are getting "thigh implants" and "pectoral implants" because their hours at the gym have failed to give them the comic-book bodies they're after. Older folks are having themselves injected regularly with botulism (Botox) in order to arrest the inevitable facial droop of aging. Skin is sliced, diced, grafted, and fat is sucked out, while bones are broken and reset; all in pursuit of the urgent question, "Am I hot?"

This is not just a Western phenomenon. South Korea, for example, tops many lists for plastic surgeries, as women have their eyes widened, noses enlarged, skin bleached, and every other kind of surgical enhancement. Nor is this tendency new or purely modern. The Buddha didn't know anything about sci-fi technologies for prolonging the inevitable, but he understood very well how human *ego* is tightly bound up and concerned with the body. Mindful meditation is designed to detach our *ego* from the body and to see it for what it is—an impermanent composite thing that cannot avoid eventual breakdown. According to the *Mahasatipatthana sutta*, a Buddhist should look at his body in a clinical, detached way. "Just as if a skilled butcher, having slaughtered a cow, were to sit with the carcass divided into portions, so a monk reviews his own body . . . in terms of its elements." My body is made up of chemicals, like everything else, and these are capable of rearrangement into new forms, or eventual decay. "Again, a monk, as if he were to see a corpse in a charnel-ground, thrown aside, eaten by crows, hawks or vultures, by dogs or jackals, or various other creatures, compares his own body with that, thinking: 'This body is of the same nature, it will become like that, it is not exempt from that fate.'"

How does this help with suffering? Isn't it just depressing to focus on my slow decomposition? At first it might seem like adding insult to injury, but meditating on your own impermanence is the way to liberate yourself from a common delusion. We suffer greatly, Buddha thinks, because we want our bodies to last forever and always be beautiful, but they cannot. We cling to our bodies because we are all craving for immortality. In doing so, we make the error of thinking that an inherently impermanent thing will last—a philosophical mistake in thinking. And we succumb to an unhealthy fantasy—a craving that we will live forever.

Japanese Buddhist aesthetics crystallize the feeling of impermanence in the phrase *mono no aware* which means, roughly, the wistful sense of impermanence, or the appreciation of the ephemeral aspect of things. The Zen pottery tradition *kintsugi*, which repairs broken ceramics with thick and unapologetic resin marks, captures the Buddhist love of flaws, and impermanence. In this aesthetic tradition, sometimes called *wabi sabi*, the pristine and perfect object is less beautiful than the broken.

That day under the Bodhi tree, the Buddha expanded this rigorous mindful technique into domains besides the body. Our subjective *feelings* of pain and pleasure are also objects of our ego-craving tendencies. We seek to hold on to those feelings of bliss that come with intense pleasures such as sex, food, drink, and even aesthetic pleasures. But we must, according to the Buddha, get a reality-check about these transient joys. Accept them for what they are, and even enjoy them. But don't obsessively chase after them in a state of denial about their fleeting nature. And just like one's feelings, one's *mental tendencies* must be analyzed and corrected—after all, the mind has narcissistic tendencies and ego-serving ways of operating. Each of us has his own particular neurosis and must engage in a detached and systemic meditation on his own unhealthy thinking patterns. And lastly, our beliefs, ideologies, and *ideas*, can also fall prey to the clinging and attachment that mar other aspects of the human experience. Many of us cause tremendous misery to ourselves and others by our dogmatic allegiance to our beliefs. We make the same mistake—thinking that our ideas are perfect and permanent principles. We try to protect our pure incorruptible beliefs, and we suffer when things change and the beliefs no longer seem coherent.

My grandmother, for example, was so attached to her Catholicism (and her wounded pride), that when her own brother left the priesthood to marry a woman and be happy, she concocted a story and sustained it for decades. Because he moved out of state, she could tell friends and even relatives that he was doing the Lord's work as a missionary in Africa. She would not recognize his new family or otherwise interact with him anymore. That is a sad sacrifice of the natural filial bonds on the altar of dogma. And yes, there are many religious extremists who make such lamentable sacrifices, but they do not represent the moderate majority of believers. One can see that radical Islam's suicide bombers seem to be neurotically attached to their beliefs about Islam—how else could they place those principles over the value of the flesh and blood that they leave in the streets and marketplaces? Buddhism suggests that a more realistic understanding of *belief* itself—one that's more flexible, revisable, and capable of evolution—will save us from the deep disappointments of punctured naivete and the consequent evil that we often enact on others. Experience should teach theory, not the other way around.

I've suggested that *what* we concentrate on (e.g., impermanence) affects the stress reduction and addiction reduction of Buddhist religion. The fact that Christianity and Islam also emphasize the ephemerality of this mortal coil, in an attempt to get us beyond egoistic hedonism, only strengthens my overall argument that adaptive mental training redirects desire.

Never mind that monotheism reasserts permanent bliss in the afterlife and Buddhism doesn't; both traditions converge in a campaign against superficiality. Both traditions remind the believer that "this too shall pass." But I also don't want to give short shrift to the empty mind itself—or to the offline mind.

Christian prayer, Buddhist meditation, and even Islamic Sufi whirling, all endeavor to take the mind offline for a little bit. Religion has a history of redirecting the mind away from the utilitarian aspects of life. Our mental lives are largely consumed by work, parenting, and otherwise provisioning ourselves and our families. These utilitarian demands were even tougher for our ancestors, who had little in the way of a social welfare safety net. Amidst this world of struggle, religion offered (as part of its overall cultural structure) the chance to stop, rest, and turn the mind inward. Yes, monks and nuns have always walked away from the rat race, but householders and laypeople also could find temporary respite in religion.

The Sabbath (from the Hebrew *sabbat,* "to rest") is an obvious way that Jews, and Christians, take time out from utilitarian life. Of course, a day of rest does not just benefit the body, but also refreshes the mind. It offers the possibility of decoupling one's cognitive patterns from pragmatic survival pursuits, and it allows the emotional mind to return to homeostatic levels of calibration. It should not surprise us to discover that there are Sabbaths or days of rest in many religious traditions, including Buddhism, Cherokee culture, and Zoroastrianism, as well as Islam's celebration of Friday rest, *jumu'ah*. Moreover, many religions use nonutilitarian time frames to redirect the minds of followers to prosocial patterns. These longer stretches of nonutilitarian time, such as Catholic Lent, Muslim Ramadan, and Buddhist rains–retreats, follow the ecological contours of weather in their historic locations—and have ascetic aspects of fasting and self-denial—but they are also about "the things that really matter." These nonutilitarian respites are ostensibly about subservience to God, but their actual function is the strengthening of family and cultural ties, and the decoupling of mind from profit.

In agricultural societies (all of us since c. 10,000 BC), the rainy season has shaped the cultural life of human beings. Civilization itself is the result of the Neolithic agricultural revolution, and a cereal belt (e.g., wheat, barley, lentil, rice) that fed the Axial Age cultures from China to Rome. Or as in Egypt and elsewhere, civilization grew around the fertility of great rivers, such as the Nile or the Mekong. Religion helped to structure the emotional and cognitive niche of human downtime. For example, Southeast Asia is debilitated for three months during the monsoon season—it has been this way for thousands of years. Buddhism was born and first transmitted during these rainy seasons, and today it is fostered and flourishes during monsoon season.[6] Every Thai man, for example, is expected to take a temporary ordination when he is a young man and go live as a monk during the rainy season, learning and ruminating (*ruminatio*) on the dharma. This gives his parents good karma merit, but also structures his cognition and emotions for dealing with the difficulties of adult life as a householder and parent. Christian Lent is also correlated with the leanest time of food surplus in Mediterranean and European agricultural societies, and it can be reasonably argued that ascetic Lenten practices structure hunger and emotional stress into endurable prosocial sacrifices, rather than self-interested exploitation when times are hard. The way religion reinforces difficult selfless emotions and behaviors will be examined shortly, but let's return to the issue of adaptive peace of mind.

There is a connection, I'm arguing, between these religious cultural structures of nonutilitarian downtime, and successful adaptive psychology. Prayer that seeks to change the world or shape the future is not a good example of the peace of mind tradition. If I pray for a new car, a good crop, a beautiful wife, or even world peace, I am still extending the wanting mind. In praying to beseech or implore the gods, I am only extending the desire psychology of the utilitarian mind. But prayer that simply contemplates an ideal, or expresses gratitude, or just observes without judgment is similar to the meditation of the East.

The Thai monk Buddhadasa Bikkhu (1906–1993) nicely articulates the attainability of the clear-pond mind. A cleansed mind is not remote nor is it only attainable to monks and mendicants. Nibbana itself is an attainable state for most of us, albeit accidental and short-lived. The training of Buddhism is to make nibbana more accessible, more regularly. Nibbana is a multiuse term in Buddhism. Sometimes it's used to mean a dramatic culmination of freedom that occurs to monks after years of solitary practice, but more commonly and more importantly it's used to describe a cooling or an absence of craving (and consequently a cessation of suffering). Nibbana, in this sense, is something that anyone can increase through effort, and benefit from tremendously. There is nothing abstract or mysterious about cooling off our boiling manic dispositions. Buddhadasa Bhikkhu, for example, points out that everyone has a few moments of nibbana in the morning after a restful sleep. "When you awaken, you usually continue in this state of calm, even while talking, thinking or doing anything at all. You are usually not possessed by love, hate, greed, anger, passion or the feeling of 'me and mine.'" Mindful Buddhists can keep much of that negative egotism at bay throughout the day, while the rest of us quickly become filled with poisonous feelings.

Relaxing the judgmental utilitarian mind is relevant for psychological health, but it also pays epistemic (knowledge) dividends. The director of Stanford's Center for Compassion and Altruism Research and Education, Dr. Emma Seppala, has shown that meditation has the power to increase our attention spans and our perceptual awareness, as well as our compassion.[7] Meditation also shifts our attention from what philosopher Martin Heidegger called "ready-to-hand" consciousness, to "present-to-hand" consciousness. The tool I'm using, say a hammer, is a utilitarian extension of my hand while I am hammering nails (ready-to-hand mode), but it switches to becoming a thing in its own right—independent of me, with features that I had not attended to—when I examine it or contemplate it (present-to-hand mode). All of us do this switching when some utilitarian object we're using suddenly breaks or fails, and we turn to contemplate it anew. These various ways of operating in the world deliver different insights and knowledge. The contemplative moment does not just rest the mind for further utilitarian exercise. It also furnishes us with fine-grained information about the world and fresh perspectives. This applies not just to objects like hammers, but to people, too.

We tend to use other human beings as tools—or as means to ends. But the contemplative mode usually requires us to treat them as ends in themselves. Moments of downtime reflection furnish us with the mental space to explore the motives, values, and beliefs of other people, enriching our humanity. An anonymous quote floating around on the web captures the point succinctly: "People were created to be loved. Things were created to be used. The world is in chaos because things are being loved, and people are being used."

Consider how the *!Kung* peoples of Africa engage in an evening tradition of "firelight talk" that gives them some break from the utilitarian mode of daily problem solving. Firelight talk is an important informal institution—like religious downtime—that structures emotions and fosters cognitive complexity. As anthropologist Polly Wiessner (2014) points out, night activities around a common fire steer the whole group away from daytime tensions, and toward prosocial bonding activities, such as songs, dancing, and storytelling. These observable traditions today may be ancient traditions that developed during the rise of Pleistocene hearth culture. "Night talk plays an important role in evoking higher orders of theory of mind via the imagination, conveying attributes of people in broad networks (virtual communities), and transmitting the 'big picture' of cultural institutions that generate regularity of behavior, cooperation, and trust at the regional level". So, in addition to the natural emotional bonding that occurs during firelight social traditions, the practice also creates a space for slower-paced reflections that better appreciate or consider the thoughts and emotions of agents who are not immediately present. This is a kind of cultural expansion and enrichment of theory of mind (our ability to attribute mind to other agents). And such informal institutions are helpful in the expansion and enrichment of human cooperation, so they are highly adaptive.

Neuroscience also confirms that two conscious states correlate with utilitarian and contemplative mind. Since the development of electroencephalogram (EEG) technology, in the 1920s, we've seen evidence that the brain has a Default Mode Network or DMN.[8] This is the brain phase that we slip into once we stop attending to specific things or tasks in the external world. It consists of medial or middle brain regions, such as the medial prefrontal cortex (mPFC), the posterior cingulate cortex (PCC), the hippocampus (in the medial temporal lobe), and the amygdala (in the medial temporal lobe). This brain system is active when we are in wakeful rest, like mind-wandering or daydreaming, mild introspection, and other nondirectional or low-attention states of mind. As a default system, it characterizes our *goal-irrelevant* frame of mind. And it contrasts strongly with the Task Positive Network or TPN, which consists of more peripheral brain regions: lateral prefrontal cortex (lPFC), the anterior cingulate cortex (ACC), the insula, and the somatosensory cortex. The TPN underscores our focused attention and goal-directed activities—everything from concentrating on a chess game, or analyzing a mechanical problem, to baiting a fishhook or solving a math problem.

The long-standing correlation of meditation states, flow, and creativity would seem to align such forms of consciousness with the DMN, because that network is detached from the usual goals of waking task orientation. Dr. Heather Berlin, for example, suggests that the flow state of free associations is indicative of the DMN, and we find such experience in dreams, daydreaming, and meditation.[9] We may find that contemplation, in certain forms of prayer and meditation, releases the mind from the usual tyranny of calculation and judgment. I have been suggesting that such release has therapeutic benefits regardless of the content of those ruminations, but also certain content (e.g., contemplation of impermanence) is potentially value-added content. Certain aspects of religion (e.g., prayers, retreats, days of rest, festivals) encourage mental vacations to the DMN. Some creativity theorists (Asma 2017) argue that a loosening of executive self-control (located in the frontal lobes) can allow the free flow of associations that tend to generate creative imagination.[10] Because creative thinking is largely adaptive, it seems reasonable to suggest that creativity-inducing religious traditions would be enhanced by cultural selection.

Somewhat surprising, however, is that the opposite seems to be true of Buddhist meditation.[11] That is to say, Buddhist meditation does not activate the default mode (DMN), but the task positive network (TPN). Yale psychiatric professor Judson Brewer and colleagues (2011) have studied the practitioners of several different meditation traditions and found that their DMN becomes deactivated or down-tuned in meditation (and even at baseline rest).[12] In fact, contrary to long-standing assumptions, meditators show the opposite of "self reduction"—revealing, instead, increased self-monitoring and cognitive control. Some kinds of meditation then are not vacations to the mind-wandering state of the default mode network (DMN), but strenuous, top-down, vigilant thinking.

At first this seems paradoxical because we think of the meditator as free from self-consciousness, but it actually takes a fair share of one's executive control to keep the mind from tilting toward the past or the future. Meditators are becoming more in control of their inner lives, not less so. A possible resolution to the seeming paradox is that mindful meditation is an intensive concentration on the experience of the present moment, but without the traditional desires and emotional attachments. If the meditator concentrates on the human body before him, for example, he must divorce all the affective coding that usually comes with that perception. In my usual daily mindset, I see a beautiful woman's body and I am automatically charged with some affect or emotional attraction. But imagine if I could contemplate that body (i.e., its forms, functions, and history) without feeling attracted or repulsed, or any other emotionally based judgment. As we pointed out in Chapter 1, our minds appear to have two different aspects, an indicative function and an imperative one. The mind-brain itself has two mental pathways—dorsal and ventral, cold and hot, indicative and imperative. We briefly considered an experience such as fear of a predator—part cognitive and part emotional—to see the two-faced aspect of our perception, partly *imperative* (e.g., I should run away) and partly *indicative* (e.g., that creature is a snake). The same duality marks the positive experience of a beautiful woman, or luxury item, or whatever. The Buddhist meditators (and other religious contemplatives) may be using their Task Positive Network to strip away the affective (imperative) aspects of their experience—seeing the object simply as an object with no other intrinsic value than the kind we supply. Philosophers call this the object qua object.[13]

As to why such purely indicative thinking might be beneficial or adaptive, I offer two reasons. One, seeing an object (or an idea, or a feeling) as a naked datum—which is how master meditators see them—can reveal important information and features of those realities. Detaching our subjective agendas from things may give us helpful access to the real causes of phenomena. When I detach my ego-bruises from my perception of the bully at work, I begin to see that his own history causes his hostility. Secondly, detaching my desires from an object allows me to replace an unhealthy attachment with a healthier one. Many Buddhists and Western monotheists agree that emotional addictions to behaviors and things can be *trained off* of negative or harmful objects and *trained on* to positive things. For example, meditation and prayer can help the believer remove her own desires from the equation and recognize that her pleasures (internal endorphins, endogenous opioids, etc.) can be trained off drink and drugs and trained onto exercise and social behavior. The goal for the Tibetan monk might be to divorce his mind entirely from desire, but the rest of us can employ meditation and prayer to get a little more control of our impulses.

Occasionally trying to let go of our emotional tethers to the world, through religious contemplation, is an important aspect of emotional intelligence. It is how humans, unlike most other animals, can actually condition or recondition themselves.

My argument has been that religion contains cultural structures that enshrine and celebrate some important adaptive psychological–philosophical states: respite from utilitarian mind, objective contemplation, awareness of impermanence, and creative imagination.

It might be argued that economically based leisure affords a similar freedom from rat-race mind and qualifies as a secular surrogate for religious contemplation. The logic here is that wealth also removes us from the utilitarian world of rat-race mind (or as Buddhists call it "monkey-mind"). It does this, supposedly, by freeing the rich from survival obsessions. Unfortunately, the wealthy (e.g., the Kardashians, the Trumps, most people on the *Forbes*' "Rich List") seem to "suffer" badly—in the Buddhist sense of craving—from obscene "first-world" problems. They do not appear to be good examples of clear-pond mind, because leisure itself does not quiet desire. Witness the bald egotism and hedonism of the leisured class, and it becomes clear that wealth can't buy peace of mind. The level of narcissism in our wealthy celebrities is enough to make the ancient Roman emperors appear temperate and selfless.

Finally, we need to consider some of the enemies of contemplation. My suggestion in this section has been that cognitive-emotional downtime has been adaptive from the Pleistocene to the present. But we may be living in the most distracting era of human history. Even the Pope had to issue a warning to cloistered contemplatives, in July 2016, to guard against the subtle temptations of digital culture.[14] Smart phones, Wi-Fi access, computers, digital gaming, and mass media are all waiting outside the monastery, like a new species of tempting demon outside St. Anthony's cell. *Ruminatio* is under siege.

Americans work hard and, of course, they play hard. But playing hard is not downtime from monkey-mind. Increasingly, Americans prefer their play in the *virtual* world rather than the real world. Americans don't vacation travel, for example, with any of the same frequency as the citizens of other developed nations. When it comes to leisure, we're not very interested in the real world (unless it's fabricated "reality TV"), and we prefer the imaginative realms of Hollywood movies, television, video games, and virtual realities. Many Americans would prefer a simulated "Paris" (maybe at Disneyland or Vegas) to the real Paris, France.

One wonders whether popular culture, the crème de la crème of escapism, isn't contributing to more suffering—by promising something it cannot deliver; namely, happiness. Have our cushy American lives, our prosperity and privilege, led us to produce a culture of banal trivia? Today's young American is a pastiche of company slogans, predigested musical clichés, movie one-liners, and consumer cravings. Mass media entertainment can be a thin gruel. And Baby Boomers also seem to be living in a fog of mediated dramas and narratives created by pop-culture industries. Some Americans seem unable to relate to each other, or themselves, without the mediation of *People* magazine, *Entertainment Tonight*, and a horde of reality show shrews. And increasingly the "news" is just a summary of other shows (like upcoming award shows) that celebrate . . . um, *other* shows. The simulacrum of mass media and entertainment is not even trying to mirror reality anymore—it's just a simulation of itself.

As disturbing as it may be to contemplate the effect of this petty chaff on the *consumer's* psyche, it's even more troubling to examine the *producer's* relentless agenda. Increasingly, industry seems to be weaving together the pop-culture threads so we can more efficiently consume the related products. Websites now "integrate" product advertising into the actual news content of their articles. And laser-like marketing displays our own idiosyncratic tastes before us every time we log on to a device—beckoning us to more consumption. Additionally, the fictional entertainment products are tightly woven together now, to increase consumer behavior. For example, blockbuster Hollywood movies are recreated comic books, and along with your Spiderman, X-Men, Hulk, Superman, and Batman movies all your favorite pop singers have contributed to the soundtrack. And a Superman fashion line is rolling out for teens, while a breakfast cereal line rolls out for kids.

All this is symptomatic of a relatively new cultural category—it's the consumer culture of the *cool*. The people on TV, in movies, in pop music—they all have it, and many Americans want it. "Cool" is what's left to sell to people when they already have everything else. And it does double duty by distracting us, even when we don't have everything we need.

Contemplatives have a different kind of "cool" than consumers—one that's a little closer to the root meaning of the word. Their minds have a quiet, detached, low-temperature way about them. Pop-culture and mass media entertainment seem dead set on preventing mindful contemplation—on stopping reflection, sedating awareness, and numbing compassion. But mindfulness contemplation can still be cultivated even amidst the shrill blast of mass media. We don't have to go off to live in a hut in order to get inner peace, and we don't have to deny the obvious pleasures of leisure (in moderation), but we do have to explicitly cultivate greater peace of mind. Religion provides structures that foster such cultivation.

DEVOTION: RESILIENCE AND SACRIFICE

The evolution of human morality is a complex and contentious topic. Some researchers argue that strong reciprocity (i.e., altruism) emerges as a feature of human genetic endowment, while others argue that the development of big-brained rationality gives us cooperative ethics. Still others argue that the expansion of empathy lets morality scale up to larger social levels, so that humans can live in bigger tribes and eventually in cities.

While evolutionists from Darwin to E. O. Wilson have argued that religion plays a role in social coercion, social allegiance, and cooperation, I want to focus on the lower level of emotional management that lives inside the nation-state social reality. In particular, I want to look at the relationship between religion and human impulse control, or delayed gratification. But whereas most social theorists, from Plato in *The Republic* to Freud in *Civilization and Its Discontents*, consider the question of how a citizenry of strangers comes to act for one another's interests, I will concentrate on self-control at the level of family. After all, most state or city-level cooperation will be evolutionarily descended from filial teamwork. Contrary to the confusions of Marxism, the nuclear family is not a recent invention of capitalism, but indeed the ancient "elemental social unit."[15] The earliest forms of devotion are not ideological, but personal. How does religion help us adapt to family social life?

There are many threats to social cohesion and survival of a group, but two related challenges stand out: the problem of hedonism and the problem of non-kin competition. These are both forms of free-riding on the backs of others—trying to acquire maximum benefits for minimum costs. But I will use the problem of hedonism to refer to the unique temptations facing small bands of hunter-gatherers or extended families. And I'll refer to the problem of non-kin competition as a difficulty emerging during the Holocene era, when we became an agricultural and then urban species. Even though life in small bands preceded urban life, both problems are alive and well in our contemporary lives today. Readers of this book live simultaneously in small-scale kin groups, which are nested within large-scale nation states.

The hedonism problem is a question. Why should I, as a member of a family, behave in selfless ways (e.g., provisioning, feeding, sharing food, helping group defense, teaching), when they cost me vital calories and frankly feel painful? Why not pursue my own pleasures exclusively?

In *The Republic*, Plato tells the story of a simple man named Gyges who discovers a mystical ring that makes him invisible when he turns it on his finger. The ring removes the possibility of any detection and punishment, so the ring bearer—originally a decent fellow—degenerates into a life of indulgent vice. He sets about sleeping with the queen, murdering the king, and taking over the kingdom.

Allegorically speaking, the father of every nuclear family is a potential Gyges. He can easily act with impunity, abusing his family for his own hedonistic pleasures. He may not have a ring, but—to the same effect—he is bigger and stronger than his wife and children and may escape small-scale social justice altogether. Sad to say, some fathers are indeed ruling their families as selfish hedonistic despots, but not most fathers. Most fathers behave exactly the opposite of the loathsome hedonist. They wear themselves out and grind themselves to nothing in order to provide for their families. They are all give, and no take. Obviously, the same is true of mothers, but everyone knows that already and I'm focusing on the father because, statistically speaking, he is physically stronger and more easily positioned to abuse power. The evolution of humans from Homo erectus to Homo sapiens is, in part, the domestication of males and females to family life.[16]

Plato's melodramatic thought-experiment of "the ring" (so loved by J. R. R. Tolkien) scales up to the city and state, too. The prediction that "power corrupts" was something I witnessed regularly while living in Cambodia. Living in Cambodia was like having the ring, in the sense that very few laws constrained the prosperous residents—this went for police, military, and politicians but also the average expatriate resident—who could, if he desired, float above the usual legal and ethical constraints of civilization. If one should be unfortunate enough to cross over a legal line somewhere and have someone notice or care, the offense was easily remedied by a small bribe. There was a general culture of impunity that allowed the powerful, the modestly rich, and the criminal elements to act in any way they wished, with no real danger of justice. Anyone living above the poverty line in Cambodia experiences the lure of temptations, in a world where desires and cravings (the chief enemies of altruistic cooperation) are easily indulged. Buddhism has its work cut out for it in Cambodia. Hedonism is readily available, so overcoming one's cravings can be like trying to "cool off" (nibbana) in the middle of a firestorm.

This brings us to the second threat to social cohesion: Why negate my own desires, when I'm living among anonymous strangers? The problem of non-kin competition is unique to large-scale societies, such as those of modern life. I live in Chicago, with 3 million other people. I've also lived in Beijing (11 million), and Shanghai (14 million). Why should I cooperate with people in these cities, whom I'm never going to see again? In a small group I might cooperate with you because I will later need your help, or I might otherwise "pay" for my antisocial behavior because I regularly encounter injured parties. When we scale up groups to urban size, however, we continue to need extensive cooperation, but the temptation to free-ride on anonymous suckers is even greater.

From Karl Marx to Richard Dawkins and Sam Harris, most critics have focused on this large-scale level of religious social control. The history of religion is filled with giant institutions that seek to frighten the vice out of their parishioners, and funnel resources up to the clerical elites. Using Dostoyevsky's phrase, religion uses "miracle, mystery and authority" to control the masses. No student of history can doubt the truth of this indictment, and the misery it caused to people cannot be ignored. High-population urban living, however, requires some modification of our natural competitive urges to pursue the immediate benefits for our family alone. Institutions, such as church, law, education, or property rights become ways to protect humans from their own short-sighted cravings. Our deep instincts to raid the food storage sites or deceive a neighbor for our own short-term advantage are overcome by institutions (e.g., religion) that ensure we all survive the harsh winter vis-à-vis food surplus and community cooperation. They frequently do this indirectly by making us beholden to an invisible police force, such as karma or divine justice. But the institution only has power to the extent that it taps into the personal or family-level emotional life.

Fear is an emotion that elites can manipulate easily for the purposes of social cohesion, as well as exploitation, of course. Christianity can demonize Jews and Muslims as infidels, for example, and instigate violence against the other. Islam does the same, and in the case of radical Islam we find fear and anger concentrated against Western liberalism. But fear as a motivation for ethical behavior is a more common mechanism in large-scale cooperative societies, where strangers must observe duties and obligations that keep the peace. According to this model, people are good to one another because it is a necessary evil, and they would rather be free-riders, taking the spoils whenever possible (see Thrasymachus's and Glaucon's arguments in Books I and II of Plato's *Republic*). As I've said, this can be a lamentable oppressive dynamic, but it is also highly effective at helping a large society maintain cooperative relations inside its borders.

However, the common critique of religion as top-down institutional manipulation is missing the heart of religious life. At the local, rather than city or nation-state level, religion offers more bottom-up emotional management. In baptisms, coming-of-age ceremonies, marriage ceremonies, funerals, and other social rituals, small religious communities band together and create emotional ties that can be depended upon when economic and psychological hard times inevitably come along. But the stories and parables of religion also serve as emotional guides to keep devotees from sliding into the hedonism problem.[17]

Religion helps manage emotions and desires such that families can be successful elemental units. Human culture—and religion has been the lion's share of culture—helps children deny their own hedonistic impulses—through delayed gratification, and the substitution of social pleasures for merely sensual pleasures. Mainstream religious culture teaches us from a young age to sacrifice for others (e.g., share and care) and to take emotional pleasure from such selfless activities. The first letter of Paul to the Corinthians, in the Bible, could be modified slightly and fit comfortably into most religious scriptures:

> If I had the gift of prophecy, and if I understood all of God's secret plans and possessed all knowledge, and if I had such faith that I could move mountains, but didn't love others, I would be nothing. If I gave everything I have to the poor and even sacrificed my body, I could boast about it; but if I didn't love others, I would have gained nothing. Love is patient and kind. Love is not jealous or boastful or proud. (1 Corinthians 13:2–4)

Adaptive cost-benefit calculation and even a sense of obligation are not quite enough, as religion pushes one to have sincere feelings of charity, care, or love. Such feelings are less vulnerable to the breakdowns and failures of rational ethics and begrudging devotion. Someone who loves her family will be a better protector and provider than someone who merely recognizes a cost-benefit advantage to familial cooperation. Evolution selects for emotional equipment, as well as cognitive and physical equipment.

In addition to religion helping acculturate children to prosocial feelings and actions, it also helps parents resign themselves to twenty years of relentless calorie expenditure and resource provisioning. Yes, parenting is wonderful, but only the most deluded fail to see that it is the most exhausting enterprise of life. Culture (religion) is a centripetal force that helps rededicate the family and resist the centrifugal forces of selfish hedonism (and free-riding). The emotional logic is this: If Jesus can hang on the cross and die for us, I can surely give up my drunkenness, my sexual craving, my gluttony, my selfish vices, etc., for the sake of my family. If the Bodhisattva can cut his own throat and lay down to feed his blood to a starving animal (Prince Sattva, Jataka Tales), then I guess I can take that extra job to send my child to school, and so on.

Terrible parables contradict my generalization. Abraham going to sacrifice his son—or God sacrificing his son Jesus for that matter—makes filial devotion appear subservient to otherworldly devotion. But closer examination of such cases reveals that devotion to an invisible super-God is also tied to more mundane social goods. The lesson is not to forget about your family, but to expand your family to a larger unit. Abraham, after all, becomes patriarch of the whole tribe of chosen people.[18] And even the hapless Job gets a bigger family after he loses his smaller family. "Go forth and multiply" is a constant expansionist addendum to the more radical devotion stories.[19] "Behold, children are a heritage from the Lord, the fruit of the womb a reward. Like arrows in the hand of a warrior are the children of one's youth. Blessed is the man who fills his quiver with them! He shall not be put to shame when he speaks with his enemies in the gate" (Psalms 127:3–5).

Pauline Christianity is a good example of the cultural management of kin emotions to larger social groups (fictive kin). Note the careful familial language, which turns slaves into sons: "But when the fullness of time had come, God sent forth his Son, born of woman, born under the law, to redeem those who were under the law, so that we might receive adoption as sons. And because you are sons, God has sent the Spirit of his Son into our hearts, crying, 'Abba! Father!' So you are no longer a slave, but a son, and if a son, then an heir through God" (Galatians 4:4–7).

For the average devotee, learning extreme sacrifice stories and taking inspiration from them prepares one for lesser sacrifices that come with daily family life. By analogy, training for the Olympics indirectly makes you a much better athlete at your local sports gym, even if you never make the Olympic team. Macrocosmic or deity devotion strengthens microcosmic or familial devotion. This is as true today as it was during the Axial Age.

Although devotion to the invisible divine can strengthen the emotional grit needed for more proximate familial devotion, we should not ignore the obvious way such cosmic devotion can destroy families. An extremist Muslim woman typifies the problem in her account of jihad for ISIS's propaganda magazine *Dabiq*. Raised in Finland, the young mother converted to Islam and moved to the Middle East with her husband to live under the ISIS-based Caliphate.

> [U]nless you're living here you don't realize what kind of life you had before. The life here is so much more pure. When you're in Dar al-Kufr (the lands of disbelief) you're exposing yourself and your children to so much filth and corruption. You make it easy for Satan to lead you astray. Here you're living a pure life, and your children are being raised with plenty of good influence around them. They don't need to be ashamed of their religion. They are free to be proud of it and are given the proper creed right from the start. After four months of us being here, my son was martyred, and this was yet another blessing. Every time I think about it, I wonder to myself, "If I stayed in Dar al-Kufr what kind of end would he have had? What would have happened to him?" Alhamdulillah, he was saved from all that, and what could be better than him being killed for the cause of Allah? Obviously, it's not easy, but I ask Allah to allow us to join him. (*Dabiq*, issue 15, 2016)

The almost cavalier mention of her son's death is alarming, and reveals a careful psychological deflection of any culpability for her and her religious beliefs. The fact that extreme devotion to an intangible force is partly responsible for the death of her very tangible son reveals the greatest threat of extremist religion—namely, its ability to deprioritize one's natural devotions.

Saudi-based Wahhabism, Christian fundamentalism, and Gita-based Hinduism all cause misery in this way. Each of these obsess on an afterlife paradise and devalue the flesh and blood of this world. So much misery is caused by this move, but importantly, it is not the interpretation of the vast majority of mainstream religious people, who temper their theology through the lens of family ties. Moderate mainstream religious people tend toward pragmatism and prioritize this world, with supplemental appeals to a transcendent realm. And even the extremists, like the ISIS mother, find it almost impossible—once affiliated with kin bonds—to let them fall away amidst the light of some beatific vision. Close attention to her *Dabiq* lunacy reveals that she, like other jihadis, has not forsaken familial love, but reinterpreted it such that her loved one is not really dead (fully terminated) but living on in paradise. In other words, even the abstract love of a deity is tied to a notion—albeit a twisted one in this case—of familial flourishing (posthumously). It is as if extremist religion can only break familial bonds by promising to restore them (even stronger) at some future posthumous time. Such is the strength of kin bonds.

Despite the excesses of otherworldly forms of devotion, the main share of devotion and sacrifice is directed back at the mundane members of kith and kin. Virtue evolved as a value system in the earliest cultures. But this difficult level of devotion is uniquely facilitated by religion and not just secular, rational calculation. As early as the Shang dynasty in China (1554–1045 BCE) oracle bones discuss a new kind of power, namely virtue (*de*). Paradoxically, you get de by sacrificing for others (i.e., family). The more you give to your family (or collective), the more you get de, or virtue. In this early form, virtue is a kind of moral power or charisma. If you are sincerely altruistic, Heaven (*Tian*) bestows de on you. This is an illustrative case of developing emotional modernity. The gods, or heaven, recognize your difficult impulse control, charity, and delayed gratification, and reward you by making you a new kind of "big man" or "chief." You acquire power and prestige by sacrificing.[20] And, according to the Zhou dynasty culture, if you sustain sincere virtue, you can pass it down to your son. Virtue is a kind of magical currency, bringing real advantages.

The advantages of virtue accrue to the individual and the community over the long term, even if virtue costs the individual in the short term. The virtuous religious person is a kind of hero or big-man, but as others emulate him and relate to each other in magnanimous fashion, trust grows in the community. More than a cognitive gamble, trust is a feeling—it is affectively or emotionally rooted. Trust is part of the emotional niche that helps communities transact trade, justice, education, war, and almost everything else. So, against the *institutional model* of cooperation, so popular among social scientists who study large-scale nation states, the *virtue model* of cooperation makes sense of the small-scale communities in which humans have evolved. Religion should not be understood primarily as a large-scale institution, although it has such manifestations. Rather, it is a proximate set of stories and rituals that sculpt emotions into habitual value patterns.[21]

Most scholars of religion, even those who recognize the emotional dimensions, tend to think of virtues (e.g., gratitude, temperance, honesty) as "signals" that we broadcast to others to increase cooperation among individuals.[22] The argument is that "strengths of character" (virtues) facilitate cooperation and therefore contribute to our biological fitness. Because cooperation increases our survival rate and our ability to produce and raise progeny, gene-culture evolution selects for such signal mechanisms of cooperation. This may be true, but I am pointing out an important amendment. It is not just the signal that is selected for, but the emotional source of the signal. The affective sources of care, love, and devotion are animal or mammalian in origin (underwritten by oxytocin, vasopressin, dopamine, etc.) but exquisitely tuned in human cultures. A reliable signal for trustworthiness is helpful, but the emotional bonds beneath trust cannot be easily faked and provide the truly robust foundation for community. The emotional community is the bottom-up cause of successful cooperation.

Put forthrightly, mainstream moderate religion helps individuals love their families more. No doubt individuals who have had experience with abusive families and extremist religions will object to this characterization, but I submit that such exceptions are rare when compared with the scale of mainstream religiosity. The routine piety of an ordinary peaceful Muslim, for example, stands in marked contrast to the extremist version of Islam. Such moderates spend their days like moderate Christians or Buddhists, by working for their children's health and education, tending to the elderly and sick in their community, counting their blessings or marking their gratitude with prayer and devotional acts, and generally helping rather than abusing others.[23] Their religion infuses and inspires all this prosocial activity, in part, because everything is God's work and garners respect, and, in part, because empathy and compassion have been dialed up by constant cultural reminders of our essential solidarity.

"We must respect the other fellow's religion," H. L. Mencken famously said, "but only in the sense and to the extent that we respect his theory that his wife is beautiful and his children smart."[24] This hilarious quote brings us to our ongoing question of why we need religion. Granted religion helps quiet the mind, fosters devotion, and ameliorates the hedonism problem, but why religion and not simply secular psychology and philosophy to the rescue? One answer is just historically descriptive; religion has done this adaptive management of emotions for thousands of years before secular alternatives were viable.[25] But the other answer is more complex and interesting. I want to suggest that special benefits accompany metaphysical commitments (so dominant in religion) that do not accompany purely secular alternatives.

There are a few ways to read Mencken's famous quote. People are highly biased and their conviction about their religion is as subjective and slanted as their other idiosyncratic tastes. Because "love is blind" we know that affection can transform a homely or ugly person into a thing of beauty. So, too, a dumb ideology can look brilliant and true if it arrives at the right time and in the right way. As such, Mencken's quote is a funny dig on religion and the believer's fundamental confusion about reality. We must acknowledge that there is no objective truth to the believer's religious claims. And this is where the new atheists and other critics of religion get very excited—as well they should. Poking holes in creationist "fact" claims or Mujahideen zealotry is important work and needs doing. Unfortunately, the necessary critique of these religious overreaches also distracts us from a deeper notion of subjective truth.

There is a more charitable and complex reading of Mencken's acerbic quote. I submit that there is a deep and powerful subjective truth to a man's belief that his wife is beautiful and his children intelligent. And obviously the same is true of a woman's beliefs about her spouse and children. Such beliefs are defining aspects of a man's life, and the fact that they are biased does not render them flimsy, or trivial, or dismissible. The same is true of his religious commitments, as they give scope, and focus, and purpose to his existence. As we mentioned in our Introduction, the philosopher Bernard Williams refers to these deep convictions as "ground projects" to distinguish them from other kinds of cost-benefit utilitarian calculations. If all our commitments were cost-benefit judgments, then we would trade-up to a new wife as soon as we encountered a better looking or smarter alternative. Most of us don't do this, in part because emotions have a strategic role to play in our lives.

In his book *Passions Within Reason*, economist Robert H. Frank argues that emotions play an underappreciated role in our decision-making. They often seem irrational on a simple cost-benefit model of *Homo economicus*, but make deeper sense in long-term adaptation. Love, for example, glues together a partnership like no rational calculation can. A purely rational person would dump her partner as soon as a better one came along, but emotional attachment gives greater long-term union to partnerships. As Frank puts it, "Those sensible about love are incapable of it." Love is, among other things, a commitment mechanism that keeps humans in cooperative relations, thereby increasing their survival chances.

Properly speaking, a man's belief that his wife is beautiful and his God exists is not a belief at all, but a feeling, or an affective commitment. This—affective commitment —is what I mean by subjective truth. Your spouse, kids, and gods, are the emotionally laden ground projects that make you who you are. But your ground projects are more than feelings, too, because they are also imperative behaviors. Loving my son is not just an idea or even a feeling, but also a lifetime of high-stakes actions that seek to provision him properly. This stuff is way more powerful than many of our competing objective truth claims (e.g., Was there a Noah's ark?; Did God speak to Muhammad?). Indeed, as we saw in Chapter 2, George Orwell argued these biased commitments of loyalty and love were the things that made us human, and it might be better to be loyal than to be objectively correct.

In the domain of religion and amorous commitment, our emotions and beliefs converge into a primitive theory about how to live well. We often call these values and trivialize them by equating them with matters of taste. But these deep values (part belief, feeling, and action) are not arbitrary. They are adaptations, in the personal sense of responses to environmental challenges (including social environment) and in the group sense of widely replicated cultural values that contribute to fitness.

Religious values are a lot like family values. They only make sense as commitments to specific people, not in general or abstract terms. I don't love dads; I love my dad. I don't love gods; I love my god. And values are pragmatic commitments, in the broadest sense of that term. The lover and the devotee don't care whether their belief/commitment is corroborated by some nemocentric investigation of the facts. Indeed, it's hard to imagine how such an investigation could proceed. They commit to people they feel strongly about, or share blood or history with, or from whom they take inspiration. And it means less than zero to them if you point out that their beloved idea or spouse is objectively ugly or dubious. So, it is no trivial thing that a man believes his wife is beautiful and children smart. We disrespect it at our own peril.

It is common to think of knowledge as an unbiased neutral grasp of objective facts, while feeling-based values are unreliable appraisals based on subjective biases. But recent arguments by cognitive scientist Donald D. Hoffman suggest that there is no unbiased neutral grasp on reality, because our sensory and cognitive equipment evolved to improve survival, not truth-tracking.[26] Darwinian evolution builds minds that work serviceably well in their environment. Our senses and cognitive capacities were shaped in order to solve survival problems, and we assume that the best way to solve such problems is to get the most accurate and detailed grasp on reality. But such a grasp is not really necessary for survival. Dr. Hoffman summarizes this idea with the theorem: "According to evolution by natural selection, an organism that sees reality as it is will never be more fit than an organism of equal complexity that sees none of reality but is just tuned to fitness."[27] For example, there are physical wave forms, particles, microorganisms, and other properties of reality that we are not evolved to experience directly because they do not help a middle-sized organism such as a human survive better. The regularity of our experience, and the reliability of our predictions, lead us to confidently assume our theories and perceptions grasp some aspects of reality, but much of reality is hidden from us because natural selection (safeguarding fitness) has no reason to tune us to every frequency of reality.

This is relevant for my argument because it throws doubt on the clean distinction between facts and values that many critics of religion assume. In fact, it reverses the age-old assumption of secular rationalists that science and reason ascertain true facts, while religion (and emotion) only serve our therapeutic needs at best and only persist as useful fictions. The indirect realism argument of Hoffman, and the Pragmatists before him, suggests that it's useful fictions all the way down. That is to say, even our scientific empirical knowledge is the result of data from capacities that were tuned for fitness (successful reproduction), rather than for objectivity.

Even charitable critics like Stephen Jay Gould famously split human concern into two domains: facts and values—with science generating the former and religion generating the latter.[28] But even this conciliatory move—designed to let each domain exist independently—is incorrect. Our values and our science are both rooted in the Darwinian imperative of survival, and a unbiased god's-eye perspective on reality is a pipe dream. The proponent of scientism laughs at religion as a merely helpful ideology, but precisely speaking so is secularism and every other epistemic endeavor, because all of them are ultimately downstream of fitness pressures. This frightens the rationalist, because he thought he had a hygienic escape from bias and the "merely therapeutic," but the operating system of the human mind is already deeply biased for maximizing reproductive success (for primates in Pleistocene and now Holocene environments). Religious values are not outliers, but age-old adaptations. Science is better at describing and predicting nature, but it is just another adaptation (albeit impressive). My argument is that religion is better at describing and managing the emotional inner life, and it is an equal player in the adaptive game.

This Darwinian view of the mind as a fitness tracker rather than a truth tracker underlies the distinction we drew in Chapter 1 about hot cognition and cold cognition. Recall that the cold cognition system of the brain is well suited to the *indicative* detached description of the world (science), whereas the hot cognition system functions as an *imperative* action-oriented problem solver. Cold cognition is associated more with neocortex processing and hot cognition with emotional limbic system activity. As we pointed out, the religious person is living more in the imperative world than in the indicative. We are all living in both worlds, but one is usually more dominant. For religious people, the world is drama first and physics second. Their world is already populated with good guys and bad guys, fates, destinies, sacred missions, and other theatrical features. For the secularist, the indicative mode is more dominant, and the material system of impersonal laws is primary. From the secular perspective, norms, values, and the imperative life generally should follow the contours of objective description. Things are reversed for the believer. For him, because he believes his wife is beautiful, she is. Any external evaluation of that belief must consider whether it improves or diminishes fitness.

How do metaphysical commitments—such as, I have a soul, or all things are impermanent, or God exists—play an especially powerful role in the adaptive aspects of religion? We've already discussed the way that religious stories and rituals structure prosocial emotions because they draw upon the imagination, which is uniquely adept at triggering and directing affects and feelings. The vivid story of Jesus hanging on the cross acts like inspirational nourishment, helping people get through moments or even years of self-sacrifice. A famous Buddhist Jataka Tale tells how the Buddha realized he was born into a life that would lead to bad karma, so as a baby he decided to pretend he was a paralyzed deaf-mute (thereby escaping the bad fruits of karma). Though in reality able-bodied, he remained utterly motionless through many painful experiences over the course of twenty years. It is an outsized inspirational story of virtuosic impulse-control and self-discipline. Moreover, rituals are forms of mind/body training, where believers habituate themselves to altruism, self-control, and reduced hedonism.[29] But metaphysics lends exceptional force to the cultures of selflessness.

As I argued in the previous section, the metaphysical idea "this world is impermanent" helps people restore some peace of mind and reduce anxiety. Other similarly metaphysical ideas (e.g., there is a hell) motivate prosocial behaviors by structuring emotions such as fear. Metaphysical commitments are more compelling than sheer logic in overriding natural egoism (overcoming selfishness to provision one's family and to inspire altruistic cooperation). Metaphysical narratives trump powerful antisocial drives (e.g., lust and anger).

Anthropologist Marvin Harris analyzed the prohibition of pork in Judaism and Islam, and found that a metaphysical commitment—God doesn't want you to eat ruminants with cloven-hooves—amplifies a very adaptive set of behaviors. On the face of it, prohibiting pig meat is illogical and bizarre, but many people have pointed out how the religious injunction masks an adaptive health concern about trichinosis and other diseases among "unclean" animals. Harris examines this carefully in his book *Good to Eat* and finds that the disease argument is not really tenable. Undercooked pork does indeed contribute to trichinosis, but undercooked beef gives rise to giant tapeworms, and brucellosis and anthrax can be transmitted from cattle, sheep, and goats. The real reason for a pork taboo, Harris argues, is that pigs are incredibly desirable from a nutritional point of view (dense in needed fats and proteins) but incredibly dangerous to domesticate in the habitat of the Middle East. In the arid deserts of the region, pigs become competitors with humans for food supplies—namely, underground nutrient storage organs such as tubers. Humans need tubers to survive when resources are scarce, and pigs will decimate the tuber supplies. So, a religious injunction was necessary to stop the people of this region from swine-herding, thereby saving them from themselves. For the Israelites and other nomadic Semitic peoples, swine-herding would be highly tempting but a kind of long-term ecological suicide.

Whether the underlying justification for pork prohibition is trichinosis prevention or Harris's ecological preservation of food resources, the same basic truth applies. Metaphysical ideas—in this case God's dietary demands—amplify adaptive behaviors when rational cost-benefit calculations are not enough to override really tempting actions. As Harris succinctly puts it, "religions gain strength when they help people make decisions which are in accord with their preexisting useful practices, but which are not so completely self-evident as to preclude doubts and temptations."[30]

Metaphysical commitments that God exists and has a plan for us are common in Axial Age religions, and they are alive and well. These *strong* cases of metaphysical influence can be contrasted with the more moderate or weaker versions. Comedian Jim Gaffigan, in an interview with Terry Gross for National Public Radio's *Fresh Air*, articulates a common and more modern version of the "metaphysical amplification" argument when he explains that belief in God reduces his natural egotism. Gaffigan says, "my faith kind of keeps me in touch with the idea that I'm not in control of things. When I'm in touch with the idea that there is a higher power and there [are] other factors at work, it kind of quells my narcissism, and a lot of the teachings really kind of keep me grounded."[31]

It might be suggested that metaphysics has no power to motivate ethical behavior or prosocial behavior. Christians and Hindus, after all, believe that another permanent world where the soul travels gives them motivation to treat people ethically, whereas Buddhists think rejection of the soul and the next world gives motivation to treat people ethically. To the outsider looking in, almost any metaphysics can be paired successfully with any ethical norms, so we might conclude that metaphysics does not entail (logically or historically) any definite ethical system. This would be true if culture worked like a rational syllogism, but that is not the way with culture. Culture is primarily associational. It does its work by habitual repetition, not logic. The Hindu metaphysics of permanent *atman* (soul) traveling around *samsara* (the wheel of becoming) motivates and amplifies prosocial behavior because Brahministic culture has conditioned the link. The same is true of Christian pairing of metaphysics and ethics, and Islamic pairing, and Jewish pairing. A logic can always be teased out (e.g., Buddhist rejection of a transcendent world leads them to seek greater amelioration for suffering in *this* world), but logic is not how most religious people, or cultures generally, structure adaptive behavior.

My argument is not that a specific metaphysics motivates prosocial behavior, but rather that many kinds of culturally enforced metaphysics work as amplifiers for ethical behavior. Some notion that an ultimate reality lies underneath the phenomenal reality of daily experience is highly effective in steering humans away from short-term immediate fixations and toward long-term benefits (via impulse control). These are forms of emotional management that we might call grit, or perseverance, and play a major role is sacrifice and service.

In the first part of this chapter, I showed how some religious technologies, like prayer and meditation, served to decrease stress and increase equanimity. In this second part, I have been showing how another emotional management by religion, this time emotional energy, is being used to motivate us against temptation and egoism. Many of the heroes of religion are cartoonish examples of good versus bad, but many of them are psychologically subtle—showing the attractiveness of sadistic enjoyment and the need to overcome it with altruism; showing the ease and ubiquity of jealousy and the need to overcome it in oneself. These are ostensibly morality tales, but any anthropologist can see that they are norms of prosocial cooperation and group survival, in the face of free-rider temptation.

CHAPTER 5

Ecstasy, Joy, and Play

So, taking pity on this suffering that is natural to the human race, the gods have ordained the cycle of festivals as times of rest from labor. They have given as fellow celebrants the Muses, with their leader Apollo, and Dionysius—in order that these divinities might set humans right again. Thus men are sustained by their festivals in the company of gods.

—Plato, *Laws*

Christmas is joy, religious joy, an inner joy of light and peace.

—Pope Francis

A joy there is that is not granted to the godless, but to those only who worship you without looking for reward, because you yourself are their joy. This is the happy life and this alone: to rejoice in you, about you and because of you. This is the life of happiness, and it is not to be found anywhere else.

—Augustine

Our mouths were filled with laughter, our tongues with songs of joy. Then it was said among the nations, "The Lord has done great things for them." The Lord has done great things for us, and we are filled with joy.

—Psalms 126:2–3

Writer Simon Barnes traveled all over the globe, covering cricket and soccer but also wildlife and environmental issues for *The Times*. His writing has a knack for finding an uplifting spiritual note in a mundane event, whether in far-flung regions like India and Africa, or merely Norfolk. While in Africa he describes how a giraffe slowly entered the light of his campfire, tiptoeing gently through camp without much regard for the humans. Watching the giant lanky animal "as it snacked daintily on leaves," Barnes felt "an almost religious joy: and like many religious experiences, it comes from a sense of our own smallness."[1]

The sacred depths of nature commonly elicit the joyful wonder that many of us recognize—theists and atheists alike. Influential agnostics Stephen Jay Gould (in *Natural History* magazine) and Ursula Goodenough (1998) echo Darwin's godless appreciation of nature's wonder in the final page of the *Origin of Species*.[2] Evolution is a nonmiraculous view of life, but, as Darwin says: "There is grandeur in this view of life, with its several powers, having been originally breathed into a few forms or into one; and that, whilst this planet has gone cycling on according to the fixed law of gravity, from so simple a beginning endless forms most beautiful and most wonderful have been, and are being, evolved" (1859 edition; p. 490).

Wonder and awe before Nature seem almost inevitable for us humans. But the religious believer adds some other ingredient to this wonder and awe, and not just the belief in a creator God—because many religions do not posit such a creator. For lack of a better term, I'll call this other ingredient "transcendental everydayness."[3] But this is not transcendental in the sense that another realm exists beyond this one. It is not the usual dualistic metaphysics of another more perfect divine reality beyond our shadow world of appearances. That's too metaphysical for transcendental everydayness.

What does it mean to be "transcendental" without traditional metaphysics? We need to rethink the term while still preserving its recognizable meaning. To transcend means to go beyond some limit, but that activity need not be connected to a supernatural metaphysics. If I have an ecstatic experience (from the Latin *ex stasis*, "to go out of one's place"), I do not transcend to an unworldly divine realm. I transcend my usual egoistic perspective and see things in a fresh way (in a "disinterested" way, to use an old Enlightenment term). Religion helps give us this unselfish perspective, this sense of awe and reverence. Because there is no distinction between the hidden and the manifest in Buddhism, for example, one only needs to attend (in a mindful way) to a bit of mundane experience in order to let the sublime aspect shine through. The Western tradition of hermeticism, too, is filled with transcendental everydayness because it sees our body, our behaviors, and our arts and alchemies as microcosms of the macrocosm.[4]

Aldous Huxley expresses this idea, which I'm calling "transcendental everydayness," in his novel *Point Counterpoint*. One of the characters says, "The whole story of the universe is implicit in any part of it. The meditative eye can look through any single object and see, as through a window, the entire cosmos. Make the smell of roast duck in an old kitchen diaphanous and you will have a glimpse of everything, from the spiral nebulae to Mozart's music and the stigmata of St. Francis of Assisi. The artistic problem is to produce diaphanousness in spots so as to reveal only the most humanly significant of distant vistas behind the near familiar object."[5]

The transcendent is not something that lives beyond the here and now, not something that we will meet in the future after death. It is the perfectly brewed cup of coffee on a crisp autumn morning. It is the sense of connection that comes suddenly in the middle of a card game with your father; or the terrible yank on your heartstrings when you hear the stories of heroism during the 9/11 tragedy; or the shock of unexpectedly playing out a beautiful solo on your musical instrument; or the full sweaty weight of your lover's body on top of you.

Actually, it's not quite accurate to say, as I did before, that the believer *adds* this ingredient to nature, because more precisely the atheist *subtracts* transcendental everydayness from his experience. As the sociologist Emile Durkheim (1858–1917) pointed out, the notion of "supernatural" as distinct from natural is a relatively modern invention. It arose largely in distinction to the "mechanization of the world picture" during the scientific revolution (in the seventeenth century).[6] Before then, *everything* was supernatural. In many parts of the world it is still so. Most people reading this book live comfortably in the de-sacralized world of impersonal laws of nature, but this is a very recent and provincial worldview being that most of human history has experienced nature as a capricious tumult of invisible agencies.

The joy of seeing nature as a unified holistic system of meaning is powerful but fairly abstract and philosophical. The devotee needs something more substantial, and gets it in religion. She needs joy here and now amidst personal suffering. Cosmic interconnection is not helping much when her child contracts a disease, when her downsizing company lets her go, when her marriage falls apart, when she can't pay bills.

One of the unique aspects of religion is the way it encourages joy amidst the hardships of life. It is a mistake for critics to accuse religion of postponing joy until the beatific vision after death. Yes, for Christians, the suffering of this life will be compensated in the next life, but the daily teaching and consolation of religion—its stronger attraction—is to find some joy in today, or in this week.

In my home of Chicago, for example, we have double the murder rate of New York City. In some neighborhoods, shootings are not just daily, but hourly. Living in these neighborhoods is tantamount to living in a war zone. And yet, remarkably, the tears of loss, and cries of fear and anger, are occasionally—indeed regularly—broken by laughter, play, and joy. The Black churches in these neighborhoods are not simply anesthetizing the parish with stories of posthumous justice and reunion, but also applying more immediate medicine. The positive emotion of joy comes in the form of collective social bonding, through liturgy, song, dance, meals, and so on. And beyond the positivity-injection of Sunday service and festivals, the message of daily grace can be taken back home to sustain the believer through the difficult week ahead. As African American writer Tomi Obaro puts it, "The gravitational pull of the black church, its significance on the culture of black life cannot be denied. It is a lodestar, and, for better and for worse, we live under it."[7]

Just as the epigraphs at the beginning of this chapter celebrate elusive positive moments in troubled environs, so, too, Chicago native Chance the Rapper writes lyrics that merge God and spirituality into the daily life of the streets. In his 2016 mixtape, *Coloring Book*, Chance encourages listeners to notice the divinity in everyday interactions. Heaven and hell are not abstract metaphysical realities, as much as observable certainties. He raps: "*Heads bowed, hands clutched, bottles gone, Heavens up. Smiles come through, though my eyes might cry.*"

Salvation is a this-worldly process. Chance the Rapper reminds his listeners that seeing "the hood" spiritually is potentially empowering because it generates more love, and inspiration. The "hell" of violence in some neighborhoods also is easily infused with the hell of despair. He raps: "I don't make songs for free, I make 'em for freedom/Don't believe in kings, believe in the kingdom." Seeing one's rough neighborhood as a potential (and sometimes actual) kingdom of justice, joy, and hope is a way of counteracting the troubles all around you. It doesn't change crime statistics directly and immediately, but strengthens the believer directly for such pragmatic battles ahead. More importantly, it reminds believers to taste the sweetness amidst the otherwise bitter flavors of life—not just for some future application of social justice, but also for this moment now.

A Buddhist parable captures this unique existential joy. A man crossing a meadow was startled by an approaching tiger, which suddenly gave chase. Running as fast as he could, he came to a cliff edge and had nowhere left to run. Grabbing a vine, he scurried over the edge of the cliff and climbed slowly downward to get away from the clawing tiger above him. Here, he hung suspended, safely out of reach of the tiger. But shortly, he looked down below him and saw that another hungry tiger had arrived and was now waiting for him to descend. When things could not seem worse, he observed a mouse arrive a few yards above him and start to chew through his lifesaving rope vine. "The man saw a luscious strawberry near him. Grasping the vine with one hand, he plucked the strawberry with the other. How sweet it tasted!"[8]

That's it. That's how the parable ends. In part, this is an allegory about cultivating mindfulness of the present moment in between the suffering bookends of life and death. It's not about simply enduring strife, but finding what longtime Google engineer Chade-Meng Tan calls "thin slices of joy" all around us. Tan, whose affectionate title at Google was "Jolly Good Fellow," argues that small joyful events can build up—if you learn to attend to them—into a force of inspiration and strength. Simple enjoyments, like coming out of the cold to a warm fire, or eating something delicious, or getting a text from an old friend, can be momentary. But the more you attend to them and register them consciously, picking them out for special awareness, the more you familiarize the mind with joy. Thin slices of joy occur everywhere in our daily life. Tan suggests that once you start noticing them, you eventually find that joy is always available. It becomes something you can count on.[9]

PLAY

We all know that positive emotions are quite different from negative ones, because they feel very different. But, because we're too close to our own feelings, we may not have noticed an additional feature of this difference. Negative emotions act like warning lights and focus our attention on a specific problem, initiating a solution sequence of behaviors. Fear, for example, launches us into action, focusing our attention on the unfamiliar sound in the basement, or the dubious character approaching fast, or the looming political climate of fascism. Positive emotions, however, arise in nonthreatening, safer situations. They don't usually require or initiate specific action pattern responses. For example, the joy of a musical concert, or fine meal, or having drinks with friends gives us an aimless activation—we are aroused, but contented with the activity and we are not pushed into a specific action response.

The fact that fear motivates escape behavior, and anger sparks attack, means that such negative emotions are adaptive and can evolve via natural selection. But positive emotions are either vague (as in contentment) or immobilizing in their intensity (as in sexual orgasm, religious ecstasy, or even being tickled). It's harder to see the adaptive significance of feelings that have indeterminate action responses. Perhaps such positive emotions are just nonadaptive "gifts" of the mammalian nervous system, and looking for their utility is barking up the wrong tree. Of course, even if joy and other positive emotions are "spandrels" (byproducts) of natural selection for sensitive nervous systems, they can become targets of direct selection at a later phase of evolution. Some psychologists have argued that positive emotions help us build up a cache of personal resources—physical, intellectual, and social.[10]

Positive emotions tend to broaden our focus rather than narrow it, in contrast to negative affects. In cases of joy, pride, hope, awe, gratitude, love, and play generally, we open up to the world. "This broadening," according to psychologist Jonathan Haidt, "counteracts the narrowing effect that negative emotions typically have, and it makes a person more open to new ideas, new relationships, and new possibilities."[11] From this more open interaction with the world, we inevitably pick up new personal resources—new friendships/alliances, new skills, new understanding of others and ourselves. In this way, positive emotions have indirect benefits because they relax our narrowing anxieties and fears, and give us the energy for exploration and experiment. Play, for example, is both intrinsically pleasurable, but also extrinsically useful as a kind of "practice" or low-stakes rehearsal and investigation.

Philosopher Baruch Spinoza (1632–1677) argued that experiencing moderate joy revitalized the body and the mind, and that such positive affects can clear away negative emotions, giving us greater energy.

> I say it is the part of a wise man to refresh and recreate himself with moderate and pleasant food and drink, and also with perfumes, with the soft beauty of growing plants, with dress, with music, with many sports, with theatres, and the like, such as every man may make use of without injury to his neighbor. For the human body is composed of very numerous parts, of diverse nature, which continually stand in need of fresh and varied nourishment, so that the whole body may be equally capable of performing all the actions, which follow from the necessity of its own nature; and, consequently, so that the mind may also be equally capable of understanding many things simultaneously.[12]

If positive effects, like joy, give us greater overall vitality, then it is no longer difficult to see the adaptive value of such feelings. Indeed, what could be more adaptive? For Spinoza and the Buddha, the beneficial aspects of joy actually underpin the spiritual imperative to meet hate with love. "He who lives according to the guidance of reason strives, as far as he can, to repay the other's hate, anger, and disdain toward him, with love or nobility" (*Ethics* IV.46). To hate someone is to imagine him, incorrectly, as the cause of one's sadness. And, making this mistake, we will be tempted to remove or destroy that person. But this is like confusing a symptom with a disease. And Spinoza, like the Buddha, adds that a kind and noble person will be more joyful (because joy is a harmonic state of the healthy psyche), so such a person will be more powerful and effective in pursuit of his goals.

Plato goes a step further, in the *Laws*, and argues that joyful play is the best model for how to live. People think war is serious, Plato admonishes, but there is no culture or play in war, and these are some of the highest expressions of humanity—and therefore the most serious. We should focus more on play because it is intrinsically good, but also—if need be—it is the best preparation for serious competitions of all kinds, including war. "Hence all must live in peace as well as they possibly can. What, then, is the right way of living? Life must be lived as play. Playing certain games, making sacrifices, singing and dancing, and then a man will be able to propitiate the gods, and defend himself against his enemies and win in the contest" (7.796).

All mammals play, as far as we know. Juvenile apes, dolphins, dogs, and even rats enjoy play. It's the way animals figure out how to work their bodies—their powers and limitations— and it's how they practice for the adult world of social hierarchy, threat, and competition. Play is adaptive behavior. Neuroscientist and "rat-tickler" Jaak Panksepp is famous for detailing how rats play, and amazingly how they even "laugh" (with 50 kilohertz ultrasonic chirps). Play is underwritten by an innate brain system, where rough-and-tumble play is motivated and anticipated by spikes in dopamine, while the play itself seems to release pleasurable opioids and oxytocin.[13]

Play is an old-brain mammal system (centralized in the thalamus). That is to say, it did not emerge with the sophisticated, big, human neocortex. Dr. Panksepp recounts that removing a rat's neocortex does not compromise its desire for play—it still seeks out and enjoys play with other rats. In fact, rats also have particular areas of skin, "tickle skin," which conduct specialized signals to the brain, indicating and activating social play.

In the centuries leading up to anatomically modern Homo sapiens, our ancestors developed some cultural technologies that allowed kids to play much more. Biologist Sarah Hrdy argues that our ancestors created a new kind of parenting or child-rearing, one that enlisted grandmothers, aunts, uncles, cousins, and older siblings (collectively known as alloparents).[14] Unlike chimps who are raised almost exclusively by their mothers, we received much more care and protection from our increasingly stable and prosperous extended kin group. This set the stage for intensive learning—rich childhoods, wherein kids experimented with diverse tools and techniques. Philosopher Kim Sterelny claims that this period of human evolution is marked by an expansion of "apprentice" childhoods, and notes that information transmission (e.g., hunting and gathering skills) would be accompanied by emotional changes toward greater docility, patience, and empathy.[15]

This kind of safe, experimental childhood was an "enchanted garden" compared with the nasty, brutish, and short lives of *Australopithecines* and early *Homo erectus*. Biologist Eva Jablonka argues that, in this relatively protected space, hominin children had extended exercise of imaginative play.[16] And unlike apes and other mammals, our ancestors did more than tackle each other and wrestle around. Our ancestors imitated other animals, people, and things. Impersonation is actually a huge leap for imagination and our species. Fantasy is something in which every young child can engage. Two-year-olds can imitate dogs and doctors, build skyscrapers from blocks, and imitate tool use. They thrive on fantasy imagination.

Mythology and early religion are products of the imagination. Even if you believe that your religion is true, you must concede the vast role that imaginative storytelling and artistry play in giving us the flesh and blood of our respective faiths. Even Jesus, Muhammad, and Buddha were great storytellers who fashioned parables to convey meaning and significance to devotees. Cultural historian Johan Huizinga puts the case more forcefully, when he says, "In all the wild imaginings of mythology a fanciful spirit is playing on the borderline between jest and earnest." Myth and ritual are some of the earliest forces of civilized life because they help produce order, law, commerce, art, craft, and wisdom. "All," Huizinga suggests, "are rooted in the primeval soil of play."[17]

Religious festivals have been some of the oldest and most pervasive forms of collective human celebration. Some might be resistant to calling religious festivals "play," but from the previous discussion we can recognize that play is serious business, too. Important social bonding, positive psychology, and the entrenchment of meaning and purpose occur in festivals, such as Day of the Dead, Vesak Day, Christmas, Diwali, Holi, Eid al-Adha, Hanukkah, and nondenominational neo-pagan festivals like Burning Man.

It may be difficult for contemporaries to appreciate the dramatic and totalizing aspects of religious festivals, given that our recent culture has grown around the pleasures of consumption and comfort. Our religious festivals have become managed and condensed into short, convenient holidays that do not otherwise interrupt the goals of consumerism. But in other parts of the world, and within certain U.S. subcultures today, one finds exhausting multiday festivals that involve food, drink, song, dance, sleep deprivation, body ornamentation, large-scale collective devotional art projects, and, in short, intense psychological transformation. Extreme capitalist cultures, such as the United States and contemporary China, have lost these inconvenient transformative festivals, and tried to replace them with secular rituals of shopping, sport, and music or food festivals. These secular festivals are perfectly fine, and they capture some of the important emotional management that religion offers, but they truncate, dilute, and control. Big religious festivals, on the other hand, cannot be controlled so much as undergone. There is a Dionysian aspect to religious festivals—the play is not merely fun (sometimes it isn't, because it's occasionally boring, irritating, confusing, etc.), but rather it is "broadening," in the sense that psychologist Jonathan Haidt mentioned earlier. The festival is a celebration, not a specific task. And that is its great difference from routine life. In addition, the religious festival brings several generations together to experience each other in a structured event, but with a collective agreement to bracket-out utilitarian agendas (e.g., work, money, or personal advantage).

Of course, we now live in very pluralistic urban societies containing several religious traditions, but religious festivals are still ways in which social divisions are overcome and mended. Historically, conflicting groups within a city could come together in religious festivals. Many religious festivals (e.g., Sinulog-Santo Nino or the Feast of San Gennaro) even have ways for subgroups to compete with each other (by making parade statues and effigies of the Virgin Mary or Ganesh, or dance competitions, or even body mortifications), but then they also affirm the group's common solidarity and union.

Being induced and ritually required to play or celebrate may not sound like a successful recipe for fun. But most people who undergo such ritual celebrations—even the long inconvenient ones (perhaps especially those) are bolstered by them. They are bolstered in the sense of positive emotion, but not just pleasure. The religious celebration fosters positive affect, but they are not purely hedonistic experiences—even Bacchanalian revelry had higher goals than sheer pleasure. Instead, they are "eudaemonic" experiences—to use the technical term. Eudaemonia is the Greek word for "happiness," or more accurately, "human flourishing." Aristotle makes it the central concept in his ethical philosophy, suggesting that we are all trying to attain this "blessed life" of happiness, but we frequently make mistakes about the proper means to our goal. We think hedonistic pleasure will get us happiness, but Aristotle follows his teacher Plato, who suggests that chasing pleasure is like trying to fill a bottomless cup with water. Then maybe honor will bring us happiness? Or wealth? But Aristotle thinks honor requires too much acknowledgment from other people, and wealth is unreliable.

Eudaemonia is a little like athletic training, in the sense of "no pain, no gain." We cannot expect to be truly happy unless we actualize our potential. And we cannot actualize our potential unless we are challenged or inconvenienced. Here, the Stoics offer a similar insight, when Seneca says, "You are unfortunate in my judgment, for you have never been unfortunate.

You have passed through life with no antagonist to face you; no one will know what you were capable of, not even you yourself" (On Providence, iii. 14–iv. 4). We'll have more to say on this in the following chapter, when we consider some of the negative aspects of religious zeal. But for now, we see that there is nothing wrong with being uncomfortable or inconvenienced in religious festivals. Comfort is not an important ingredient in happiness. The commonly agreed upon crucial ingredient in human happiness is friendship or strong social bonds. A recent Niagara of longitudinal happiness studies (e.g., the Harvard Grant Study) all confirm that the most important element in a good life (eudaemonia) is close social ties—ties that bind. These are not digital Facebook friends nor are they needy faraway strangers, but robust proximate relationships—and these bonds are created and sustained by our very finite resource of emotional care. As Graham Greene reminds us: "one can't love humanity, one can only love people." Religious festivals put us in proximate relation to these other people (not abstractions like "humanity"), and forge and strengthen positive emotions with them. But the ritualized nature of religious festivals also requires large groups of people to collectively practice inhibitory control or self-regulation together. This is a challenging but powerfully bonding experience, too. It is collective actualizing of potential.

The Dalai Lama and affective neuroscientist Dr. Richard Davidson have been collaborating for over a decade to study positive psychology. We understand quite a bit about the pathological psyche, but less about the happy or eudaemonic psyche. The Dalai Lama challenged the neuroscience community, in 2005, to turn their fMRI machines on fulfilled and happy people to see how humans can better actualize their potential.

One of Davidson's discoveries is that specific behavioral habits can produce neurological effects that produce or at least correlate strongly with well-being (eudaemonia). His obvious case is that even limited meditation practices produce measureable changes (albeit small) in our neuroplastic system and our psychological mood. But he also found that spending ten minutes every day compiling a "gratitude list" generates beneficial brain changes as well.[18] Repetition of these behaviors gives immediate positive emotion, but also slowly creates stable personality traits (with neural underpinnings). Presumably such changes help people meet adversity better, or at least recover better after adversity (resilience).[19]

Play functions the same way. Being a spontaneously playful person, or practicing playfulness, may be creating a reliable personality resource within us. But it is difficult to be playful when life's slings and arrows are coming at you relentlessly. Neuroscientists Stephen Siviy and Jaak Panksepp's work with mammals proves what we've all known personally; stress kills playfulness. But if play is a kind of antidote to stress, and stress is preventing play, then we are in a catch-22. The solution, however, is to mix with other people who are playing, even for a brief interaction. Siviy and Panksepp have shown that stressed rats increase their playfulness as soon as they are placed with other less-stressed rats. Play is contagious.[20] I submit that religious festivals are, in part, a culturally structured form of this collective play—collective joy.

Religion was one of the earliest areas of play in human evolution. It is not often considered in this way, because the serious sacrificial aspects crowd out the playful when we analyze it. But play is a fundamental form of creativity or improvisation, and it consists of taking representations (either symbols or simulations) out of their natural context, and mashing them up with other such decontextualized representations. The children playing "cops and robbers" are taking chunks of narrative scripts (from television, movies, other kids' behavior, stories, books, etc.) and re-enacting them in jumbled order, and hybrid mash-up style. So, too, the cave painters of the Upper Paleolithic era are using "representations" or images—decoupled from direct perception—as the raw elements to mix and mingle into a new narrative, via the imagination.

Imaginative play is not some latecomer in the evolution of mind, but an early human aptitude for responding to the changing environment. Play has an emotional component that attracts us, but it also brings together innovative cognitive options for us. Religion is one of the most productive systems of such composition and playful imagination. It uses symbols to reclassify reality and give us a "second universe" inside our mind's eye. It reminds us of this virtual world with routine rituals, but it retains its playful dimension in the re-creating festivals, the practical applications of moral rules, and, of course, the artwork of religion (from Michelangelo's *Pieta*, to Bach's *Mass in B minor*, to Chance the Rapper's *Coloring Book*).[21]

Consider that a team of Hollywood writers and special-effects artists could never invent anything as fantastic as the Indian *Ramayana* (composed between 200 BCE and 200 CE). Through kidnapping, Rama (an incarnation of Vishnu) loses his beautiful wife Sita to the evil god Ravana (who has ten heads). What follows is a strange story in which Rama enlists the monkey god, Hanuman, and the king of monkeys, Sugriva, to fight evil Ravana and his monster minions. Hanuman has the ability to jump from one side of the planet to the other, which he uses to great effect—grabbing a whole mountain of the Himalayas, for example, to bring back medicinal herbs. After fourteen years of warfare, Rama wins back Sita by shooting Ravana's multiple heads with arrows. But Rama's unfounded suspicions about his wife's fidelity cause her to be swallowed up by the earth (burned up, in some versions), and so Sita and Rama (who truly love each other) are tragically separated forever.

As if the *Ramayana* was not imaginative enough, Khmer culture has also mixed the characters together with other Hindu stories from the *Puranas*, and the resulting mash-up can be seen all over Southeast Asia. The popular scene has Vishnu transformed into a giant turtle, helping Hanuman (monkey god) and Ravana use a huge cobra (*naga*) to churn up an ocean of milk. By twisting the naga through the milky sea (a metaphor of lactation and semen), they create foam that spits forth beautiful dancing maidens called *apsaras*, and the overall motive for this cosmic churning is to froth up the elixir of life itself.

From this, and many other examples, we can see that there is indeed play in religion. The reader's own religion is undoubtedly filled with similarly beautiful and strange stories, but we are too close to them to see their creativity. Only in the "other" culture's religion does the imaginative aspect announce itself clearly.

MEANINGFUL CONJURING

Recent scientific approaches to religion have tried to understand the unique counterfactual entities and beliefs of religion. Familiarity often conceals the weirdness of religious beliefs. An invisible man living in the sky (but also everywhere) had a son with a human mother, and the offspring was part human and part god. This offspring was also the father God himself. The offspring willfully allowed other humans to persecute and kill him, in order to save other humans. But he stopped being dead three days later, visited friends in a different physical form, and eventually went to live in the invisible realm with (and as) his father. We will all meet him after we die, if we are good people, and being near him will give us the best happiness possible forever and ever. Amen.

That is strange, by every measure. The magical thinking involved requires many violations of regular everyday cognition—violations that don't help us think about everyday experience. Perhaps our "thinking wires" get "crossed," so to speak, and this produces the strange entities and narratives of religion. Maybe religion is a result of cognitive glitches. Or maybe the glitches started magical thinking, and the subsequent usefulness of magical thinking snowballed into our magnificent spiritual traditions.

In what sense is religion a byproduct of mind or cognition? Several recent evolutionary anthropologists and the Cultural Evolution of Religion Research Consortium (at University of British Columbia), have argued that religion emerges out of cognitive precursors (or preadaptations), such as folk-physics, theory of mind, categorical schemas, innate essentialism, and so on.[22] If our folk taxonomic mental categories carve the world into basic domains, like animate and inanimate, or more complex schema, like animal, artifact, and human, then occasional category mismatches can spark unique cognitive arousal, producing supernatural counterintuition.

Artifacts that are thought to speak, or dead creatures that are thought to live again, consist in relatively simple category transpositions or violations. A talisman, for example, is a physical object that can "hear" your wishes and influence the world toward those ends. It is an inanimate object blended with agency properties usually reserved for creatures. Religions around the world contain similar category violations, and this suggests that innate cognitive architecture can, with slight distortions, produce the paradoxical entities of religion (i.e., animistic river spirits, virgin mothers, resurrected messiahs, invisible men, etc.).[23]

Similarly, our ability to "read" other minds (called "theory of mind") is a cognitive ability that evolved to help us understand what our fellow tribal members might do next. We don't literally read minds, of course, but infer inner intentions and goals in our friends and foes by watching their behaviors and projecting intentionality. It is a psychological ability to project a different mind (with different information, beliefs, and desires) into another person's head. Normal kids develop this ability somewhere around age three or four, but before this benchmark, kids do not understand that other people have private minds separate from their own. An older child can deceive her friend because she comes to understand that her friend has different headspace, different access to information—and such information can be manipulated. It's currently a great debate whether other mammals have *theory of mind*. Having sophisticated language allows humans to engage in elaborate transmissions (deceptive or honest) between other minds.

Once the "theory of mind mechanism" evolved or came online (probably during the Pleistocene), it enabled our ancestors to project mind to nonpersons as well—any natural object or even artifact. These false-positive attributions of mind generate the thick world of invisible agents that religious people believe to be everywhere in nature. In these ways, it is thought, religion emerges as an exaptation or byproduct of other cognitive adaptations for navigating the world. This analysis gives us the mechanical prerequisites of religious thinking but not the meaning or function of such magical thinking.

In the same way that cognitive preadaptations (i.e., domain categories, etc.) preceded religion proper and enabled the many functions of religion, even more so did the emotional precursors feed into imaginative supernatural systems. Jared Diamond (1997) argues that the main functions of religion include explanation of nature; political obedience (especially in the Holocene); the teaching of moral precepts (important in large-scale stranger societies); and finally, justification for wars (i.e., murder is wrong inside our community, but not against heathens/pagans). We've already seen, however, that religion has many additional functions, loosely housed under the umbrella of emotional management. Indeed, even the functions on Diamond's list are largely facilitated by religion's ability to harness and exploit our affective systems.

Concepts have affective or emotional content. From our trivial concepts, such as "dog," to our sublime concepts, such as "God," we have feelings that associate (either weakly or strongly) with our cognitive contents. In fact, William James (1879) noticed that a concept only has essential or defining properties in light of the goals or purposes we are pursuing, and the same holds true in supernatural concepts. "What now is a *conception*? It is a *teleological instrument*. It is a partial aspect of a thing which *for our purpose* we regard as its essential aspect, as the representative of the entire thing." "But," he continues, "the essence, the ground of conception, varies with the end we have in view."[24]

It is not enough, as the cognitive scientists suggest, that a conceptual domain, such as "inanimate object," gets a binary switch from "unconscious" to "conscious," and suddenly produces a religious supernatural entity (e.g., a talisman or a totem). We must remember that the content of these cognitive categories—which often dictate metaphysical commitments—contain emotional tone from the low-level approach/avoid feelings to high-level layers of ennui, angst, and wonder. When we conceptualize God or spirits or other features of religious cognition, those concepts are infused with FEAR, or CARE, or ANGER, and complex mixtures of these systems. Thinking about God is not primarily an amodal inferential processing of symbols. If the cognitive science approach to religious concepts focused more on developmental learning, it would appreciate the sensory-motor-affective dimensions of our supernatural commitments. By analogy, experiential associations inform whether a child sees his father as a frightening threat, or a benevolent force (or some specific mix of the two). Experiential associations with religious representations are less direct, but no less emotional. Put differently, it is only because we are afraid of the spirits or love the spirits that they mean anything at all to us. On that emotional foundation, most of the adaptive aspects of religion are built.

So, how do cognitive mismatches become more than just cognitive glitches? Given that the mind engages in all manner of magical mash-ups (e.g., elephant-headed demigods, replicating fishes and loaves, resurrected dead, invisible persons), how can such imaginative conjuring be meaningful? This has always been a challenge for religion, because the mash-ups of magical thinking are not corroborated or verified in daily experience, but the challenge is particularly keen for those of us living in the age of science. The secularist rejects the challenge altogether and solves the issue summarily with a denunciation of all magical thinking. In what follows, I want to offer an example of *meaningful conjuring*—in particular, the emotional and existential benefits of "soul talk."

Recent surveys of religious affiliation reveal that organized religion is disappearing among the millennial generation (i.e., those born between 1981 and 1996).[25] But *spirituality* is alive and well. Young Americans are unhappy with the hypocrisy and hierarchy of institutional religion, but they are not unhappy with metaphysics. They believe in all manner of spooky divine vapors, God particles, reincarnation, astral projections, heaven, auras, ghosts—and above all, the soul.

As a philosophy professor, I get unprecedented access to the spiritual beliefs of young Americans, who otherwise keep their metaphysical commitments quite private. For example, every semester I am repeatedly informed, by confident students, that "noetic science" has "proven" the existence of the soul. It was on a TV science show, I am assured.

Since the early 1900s, a handful of marginal experimenters have tried to weigh the soul—by arranging dying people on scales and taking their weight before and after the moment of death. Nothing even vaguely suggestive was discovered by that experimental approach, except a very high degree of wishful thinking. One humorous and underreported "finding," made by an Oregon sheep rancher and earnest amateur scientist, was the discovery that sheep actually gain a little weight as they die. It's hard to know where to start with all this.

Even if we could show that some energy was leaving our bodies at the moment of death, it can't really be a surprise, given that thermodynamics tells us that energy is always being exchanged through physical systems. When I die, the slowing of my thermodynamic processes will become irreversible; my local entropy will increase. When I die, my energy will go on. But, of course, we can't get too excited by that fact, since we're talking only about heat and the chemical transformation of my decaying flesh, taken up and conserved in new organisms and physical systems. The conservation of energy doesn't give us any conservation of consciousness or any continuation of personal identity. And personal continuity is the hope for most soul proponents.

But if we could set aside all the problems with these badly controlled and executed experiments—if we could create highly precise measurements—we would still have the more challenging issue of coherence. Most people's concept of the soul includes the idea that it is incorporeal or immaterial (this is how the religious traditions have conceptualized it). So, how then could an incorporeal entity have any weight or mass or volume, that is, any of the spatial properties we assign to matter? Thinking that the soul has weight seems like a category mistake—like saying the number 4 weighs 30 pounds, or the color blue smells bad. Weighing the soul, or searching for the soul in the brain, seems like a similar mistake.

Science seems entirely justified in its soul skepticism. But if such speculative metaphysics is bracketed out of science, then what is left of the soul issue? What remains of soul talk? Is it merely folk language that has been replaced by more accurate descriptions of the human experience?

One response is for believers to rush headlong into a faith-based rejection of rationality and just hold fast to the traditional soul idea; another is to give it a New Age paint job with quantum-energy talk. Many millennials are very enticed by that response, partly because they see no other avenue for preserving their meaningful soul language. But I want to argue for an alternative, nonmetaphysical, way to retain the soul, even if it is a feature of imaginative conjuring.

Instead of asking whether we can verify the soul's existence—find some empirical evidence for it—I suggest a Wittgensteinian approach. Following the Austrian philosopher, we can ask: How do people actually talk about the soul? How is soul talk used in ordinary language? And here, we find that the soul is alive and well in certain kinds of expressive language. When you look at actual soul talk, you find the following kinds of expressions: "He is my soul mate," or "She really sold her soul," or "That's good soul food," or "This nature hike is good for my soul," or "She is an old soul," or "James Brown has soul," or "The soul reincarnates," or "Her soul is in heaven now."

Those expressions share little similarity. Like Wittgenstein's famous example of diverse "games," they probably represent a *family resemblance* of meanings rather than a common essential definition. Notice, for example, that only the last two expressions have any metaphysical connotations.

More importantly, however, the expressions are not really propositions about the world. They express emotional attitudes and resemble other kinds of imperative or aspirational speech, such as, "You go, girl!" or "Don't do that," or "Have a nice trip," or "I got soul, and I'm superbad." When I say, "You've got soul," it's not a description of some factual state of affairs; rather, it is an evaluation. It expresses as much about the subject as the object referenced. We cannot expunge the subjective expressive/evaluative properties from the sentence and arrive at some testable proposition (as in science). Saying "James Brown has soul" is nothing like saying "The cat is on the mat," or "Water freezes at 32 degrees," or "The hippocampus plays a large role in memory." Those are all testable propositions.

Soul talk is expressive in the same way as other nondescriptive utterances, such as "Oh my God," or "Ouch," or "Yuck," or (with head nodding to music) "Yeah, that's funky." There is no clear referent for those. They don't seem to refer to or represent anything—they seem somehow prerepresentational (or presentational). Soul talk, like other emotive talk, bears little relation to the goals of scientific language and probably can't be assessed with that language. Like other expressive forms, soul talk in ordinary folk language won't have much theoretical interest, because it is rarely, if ever, trying to explain a phenomenon. In the same way that a poem is not trying to explain a phenomenon, soul talk is equally uninterested in induction, hypothesis, prediction, and corroboration. Instead, soul talk tries to express our hopes and aspirations ("I hope I see my family again in the afterlife"), or to identify inspiration ("This song really speaks to my soul"), or to express feelings deeper than friendship ("I've finally found my soul mate"), or to scare people into doing something ("Your soul will burn in hellfire"), and so on.

Moreover, the meaning of soul talk should not be searched for in the correspondence theory of truth. When I try to establish the meaning and the truth of the proposition "The cat is on the mat," I attempt to find a correspondence between my word "cat" and the actual feline animal, and my word "on" and the actual spatial relation of said cat to mat, and so on. I'm looking for a correspondence between propositions and the external world. In that way, I can verify the meaning and truth of my proposition.

But the sentences "James Brown has soul" and "My soul is anchored in the Lord" rely on a very different system of meaning—they don't correspond to anything particularly. Instead, they take their meaning from a coherence they have with other terms, concepts, values, connotations, emotions, and associations. "This song has soul" means: This music restores us, this music has integrity, there's something authentic and natural in its style, this music contains strong emotion, the repetition is hypnotic or ecstatic, there are elements of the African-American experience in this music and these lyrics, this song draws on gospel and R&B genres, this song is so funky you can smell it, and so on. That is the matrix of connotations that make up the context of soul talk—and the soul talk is coherent to the extent that it coheres in some way with all these other experiences and meanings. In that sense, the soul is meaningful to many of us without any scientific verification of its existence.

That is not the same as just having faith in the soul despite a lack of evidence. I'm not suggesting that familiar view. What I'm suggesting is more sly—the soul can be deeply meaningful whether it exists or not, and it can be deeply meaningful even if you disbelieve in its literal, metaphysical existence. That is not the usefulness of fictions and delusions. It's the usefulness of an expressive folk language (imperative) that can't be replaced by a scientific language (indicative).

So why is soul talk still meaningful, and why can't it be replaced? If we think about the human being, we can analyze ourselves into various parts and functions: the body, cognition, emotions, memory, perception, and so on. And we can make many impressive scientific claims about those parts and functions. Modern medicine is a testament to the genius of methodological materialism and a mechanical approach to the human being. But in this matrix of human thoughts, feelings, and experiences, we also find forms of awareness and activity that call out for a different language. The kinds of awareness I'm thinking of might be described as affective and aesthetic—feelings of ecstasy, feelings for the beautiful or the sublime, poignant stirrings that might be labeled transcendent—or, negatively, feelings of horror or dread. And the kinds of activities I'm trying to isolate might be creative acts (playing music, writing poetry, handcrafting furniture, serving tea while a Zen master whacks you with a stick) as well as ethical activities (acts of altruism, self-sacrifice). It's hard to see how a purely descriptive scientific language can find good traction in those domains, but an alternative language exists and has existed for a long time (in religion). Soul talk is a part of that successful expressive language.

Philosophers such as Wittgenstein, Heidegger, and Kenneth Burke even went so far as to suggest that language is originally expressive, rhetorical, and dramatic, and only derivatively descriptive, scientific, and explanatory. If that is true, then soul talk is a part of that primordial language, not reducible to ignorance.

Wittgenstein's focus on ordinary language shows where we can preserve intelligent soul talk but avoid common category mistakes and tendencies toward reification. We can "debug" soul talk. We can detach it from its now unwarranted metaphysical history—and we see this already in ordinary language when we say, "That singer has soul" or "This nature hike is good for my soul."

Our tendency, however, to turn this soul language into metaphysics is strong—Wittgenstein said that sometimes "language goes on holiday," and that we have to coax it back to its useful, functional meaning. Just as we don't hear a smell or taste a color, we also don't literally "live after death," or have a "soul mate." Those are perfectly good metaphorical uses of language, but they shouldn't be confused with literal descriptive uses of language. When I say, for example, "My soul will go on," I'm probably really saying, "I hope I live more." And when we've arrived at that naked expression of subjective yearning, then we've probably reached the end of our analysis. We're done understanding it.

The problem with some religious and New Age soul talk is that it exports the soul concept from the domain of subjective expression to the domain of objective fact, where it can have no empirical corroboration. That is the main category mistake. Many atheists, like Richard Dawkins, criticize soul believers as dimwits. But everybody makes category mistakes, and everybody confuses subjective yearning and hope with objective matters of fact. Even the phrase "He is a dimwit" is just an expressive claim masquerading as a descriptive claim. Emotive evaluation is our native language, and science is our second language.

Once we take the metaphysics out of the language of soul, we begin to see how the soul is used in social contexts of ordinary language. When a minister tells parents at their son's funeral that they will see their son again, and his soul is in a better place, I cannot dismiss it or heap scorn on it. If we agnostics hear this language as a description of reality, then we're bound to be irritated by the issue of truant evidence and the lack of warrant. But if we hear it as emotive hope, then our objections fall away. American millennials are right to want to hold on to this language. Metaphysics aside, the minister's language seems to suggest that there are emotions so deep and bonds so strong that not even death should end them. That is a beautiful sentiment no matter what you think of the soul.

This case of meaningful conjuring reveals that magical thinking contains cognitive glitches, but these only grow, develop, and persist because our emotional lives make good use of them. For example, it is the larger emotional narrative of the saint overcoming temptation, or the martyr enduring pain, or the posthumous reunion with the loved one, that makes magical beings (cognitive mash-ups) interesting and valuable, not the other way around.

SEXUAL COMMUNION AND RELIGION

Lust is the main driver of sexual communion—that unique form of ecstasy that motivates many humans. The felt psychology of lust is familiar enough to all of us, and the adaptive value of lust is also clear—given that reproduction is the engine of evolution. But the affective neuroscience of lust is only now emerging and promises new insights. And considering the evolution of lust is also helpful in understanding the way that religion turns it from a cultural liability to an asset.

Religion manages lust. Freud argued that libidinal erotic drives (eros) are manipulated by culture toward the construction of civilization. Religion is part of this transformation of lust energy into creative energy, producing art, science, and politics. This hydraulic view of psychological energy suggests that sexual desire does not simply dissipate upon frustration, but rather reroutes into alternative pathways (sometimes constructive, and sometimes destructive). Putting Freud aside, this is the same basic assumption of most ascetic religious traditions (from Hinduism to Christianity), in their denial of the pleasures of the flesh for the sake of piety.

Religion can redirect the lust impulse or reconfigure it, such that lust does not pursue every attractive sex partner (arguably, its default orientation). Instead, religion—the vast majority of which is socially conservative—requires monogamy or some similarly constrained libidinal pathway. It does this emotional management by threats, as when religion designates extramarital sex as a punishable sin, and by rewards, as when it promises posthumous ecstasies for disciplined sacrifice in this lifetime.

From an anthropological viewpoint, constrained sexuality has been an important ingredient in the development of successful cooperative collectives. There are occasionally thriving "free love" utopias (e.g., Oneida stirpiculture, hippie communes), but they don't last long. We'll see that the only primates who have effectively built sexual promiscuity into a stable social strategy are the bonobos (*Pan paniscus*). Humans have done better when sexual desire is structured in the service of nuclear families, which are the elemental units of human social life (Johnson and Earle, 2000).

So, one of the principal ways that religion manages lust is by structuring its acceptable targets (i.e., spouses) and expressions (consensual sex). It also sometimes reinterprets sexual ecstasy as a form of transcendent communication (e.g., Tantric Hinduism and Buddhism). This is also implied in the Platonic idea that erotic drive can be repurposed to go beyond the mundane beautiful body to the *Form* of Beauty itself (see Plato's *Phaedrus*).[26] And to some extent it is entailed in the free exchange of sexual and religious description in St. Teresa of Avila's writings. Let us look more closely at the inevitability of lust. What is it? And how is it culturally managed?

Ethologists who study animal behavior increasingly accept the idea that *fear* keeps animals away from predators, *lust* draws them toward each other, *panic* motivates their social solidarity, and *care* glues their parent–offspring bonds. Just like us, they have an inner life because it helps them navigate their outer life. Spending time on the Serengeti makes you think a lot about the inner life of animals, and on a recent safari to Tanzania and Rwanda I watched the mammal emotions in action.

One scorching hot afternoon, we came upon a huge male lion in his mating ritual with a female. With stealthy off-road driving, we crept within a few meters of their love nest. They had detached themselves from the larger pride and were engaging in the standard three-day romp. When the female is in estrus, or on heat, the male will spend the first day mounting her every 10 minutes, like clockwork. On the second day, they mate every 15 minutes, and on the third day, every 30 minutes. In between these quick sex sessions, the two laze about sleeping in the high grass. The male mounts the female from behind and engages in light neck-biting until he achieves a roaring *petite mort*. None of this is cute or cuddly or tender. In fact, in many cases, the male lion has put the female on estrus by killing her cubs. Killing the babies of a previous romance will stop the lactating of the mother and put her back in estrus, so the new male can replace the previous genetic line with his own.

Lions, our guide informed us, do not have sex for pleasure. Other animals do, but lion sex, at least from my perspective in the safari truck, looked perfunctory, utilitarian, and grudgingly purposeful. It is sex at its adaptational no-frills finest: chemically triggered, involuntarily acted, immediately forgotten.

Lust behaviors are easily identifiable: genital arousal, pursuit of copulation mounting, mouth open, teeth bared, neck biting, vocalization, submission and dominance displays, and so on. In the same way that our fear system or bonding system is rooted in a specific brain circuit, lust is also a unique brain pathway in mammals, extending through the hypothalamus, ventral striatum, and insular cortex. In lust, norepinephrine and dopamine increase, serotonin drops, and androgens—such as testosterone—fuel both male and female sexual drive. Lust is a different circuit from attachment bonding, or CARE.

Lust is an affective system shared by many vertebrates, but it often operates in a mechanical way. Female estrus triggers chemical and physical changes that draw males to copulation. Like moths to flames, males perceive the chemical changes in females, then libido ignites and copulation follows in short order. When you filter this emotional energy through different prisms of primate culture, however, you get unique sexual customs.

The genital area of female chimpanzees, who become sexually mature around eight years of age, swells up and changes color. This signal initiates attention from many males, who attempt mating. Females copulate around eight times a day, often with different males, and this may be an unconscious strategy to keep males calm and nonaggressive (because male orgasms increase the quieting chemistry of oxytocin). But a pattern of possession quickly develops. Male chimpanzees use three strategies to establish ownership over the female and subsequent offspring. A male might start a dedicated bodyguard routine, fighting off competitors, or, if the number of males is too large, then two males will establish a coalition—sharing the copulations. Or finally, a male might sequester the female, taking her away from the group (by persuasion or force) to copulate privately for a period of days.[27] Chimpanzee paternity is important and infanticide might become a default solution, but such aggression is usually averted by these various sequester techniques. And the fact that most males in groups are brothers may also reduce the paternity aggression considerably, leaving most in-group aggression for issues of mating access rather than paternity.

Obviously, humans have evolved a more byzantine sexual culture than chimpanzees, but fundamentally there are similar emotional brain and body systems at work. Presumably, early human sexuality operated along the lines of other primate strategies, but which one or even combination is unclear. Were our early lust adventures more like chimpanzees, bonobos, or gorillas? Data from most gorilla populations, for example, reveal that they have a single male mating system (i.e., groups contain only one fully mature male, who serves as silverback leader for many years). The gorilla's evolved anatomy reinforces the mating system (and vice versa), because the male is so much larger than the female (i.e., gorillas may be the most sexually dimorphic primate).[28]

Bonobos and chimpanzees are both members of the genus *Pan* and probably split around 1 million years ago. Bonobos, which were not even discovered until 1929, are smaller than chimpanzees, matriarchal, less sexually dimorphic, display less aggression, live in a rich diet environment, and engage in almost constant sexual activity. Males copulate with females, but males also engage in genital manipulations (or penis fencing) and females do genital-genital rubbing techniques.

Lust has evolved from pure procreation to other functions, but bonobo sex is not just fun and games. The sexual activity intensifies whenever potential conflicts arise, like food sharing. In the same scenarios where chimpanzees and humans will fight and display aggression—namely, competition for resources—bonobos will mount each other and restore the peace with doses of sexual ecstasy. As Frans de Waal has noted, bonobos are the hippies of the primate kingdom.[29]

The larger size of human men suggests that testosterone-fueled competition (as in chimpanzees) sculpted our sexual dimorphism. The larger size of *Homo* males makes a matriarchy somewhat doubtful—matriarchal female hyenas, for example, are 9 percent larger than males.[30] Still, an early human matriarchy is not unthinkable, given that dominant bonobo females are still slightly smaller than males. So, it is presently unclear whether we originally had alpha-male harems (gorillas), roaming bands-of-brothers (chimpanzees), or some other primate procreation system. Nonetheless, out of one or more of these procreative strategies, emerged a unique form of pair-bonding cooperation. Humans began to live in marriage-like social structures.

A recent genetic argument places the human shift from polygyny to monogamy as recent as 18,000 years ago.[31] Analysis of female mitochondrial and Y-chromosome DNA reveals that the number of reproductive females increased significantly in conjunction with Homo sapiens' migration out of Africa, but diverse male contributions did not increase until much later (c. 18,000 years ago). One explanation is that prior to 18,000 years ago, many women would have been reproducing with the same few men.[32]

Ultimately, it doesn't matter for our purposes whether human social life was comprised of fewer men with multiple females and broods, or modern monogamy. What matters is domesticated (emotionally modulated) males, who are cooperatively feeding and protecting females and needy offspring. Female primates don't hang around males that don't take care of them. For example, primate studies of gorilla social groups reveal that the level of silverback tolerance for and affiliation with infants and juveniles in his group strongly influences the degree to which females stay in his troop (Harcourt and Stewart, 2007).

Unlike chimpanzee parents—where mothers do the rearing almost exclusively—human fathers contribute significantly. Just like other primates, women are trying to maximize their genetic investment and mate with the fittest candidates. Females try to "choose wisely" through sexual selection techniques (e.g., performance displays), but they also hedge their bets with optimized deceptive copulations (common in primates and humans alike). In some cases, men attempt various vigilance strategies on specific women—guarding them and provisioning them—and in other cases, males simply play the odds, broadly investing fertilization, but not much else.

Since the Holocene period (starting around 12,000 years ago), options for humans have settled into relatively formalized monogamous patterns of reciprocal long-term partnerships. Because kin expansions, through marriage partnerships, have benefited group survival, and such pairings are susceptible to breakdown from deception, sexual mores have become fairly conservative in most human societies. Sex and lust have been channeled and transformed by the survival benefits of social emotions like loyalty. For humans, sex has been decoupled technically from reproduction and we've turned lust into a connoisseur recreation. The pleasures of lust, which motivate procreation, have been exapted by culture, but they remain tethered to their origins. Human lust, which doesn't need to wait for estrus triggers, has nonetheless been culturally constrained by the demands of survival partnerships, especially when we compare it with bonobo sexuality.

When primate lust meets top-down, competition cultures, it produces chimpanzee-like social intelligence. The major contributing factor to these cultural structures is simply access to resources. If food is scarce, then males are competitive for females, and lust tends to be channeled into a hierarchical social system, with despotic sexual politics. If food is plentiful, as in the case of bonobos, then competition reduces, and lust can channel into sexual "egalitarianism." Because female bonobos are sexually receptive to all, males do not compete like chimpanzees (de Waal, 2001). In addition to keeping the peace, radical promiscuity solves the paternity problem shrewdly by confusing it beyond any possible tracking.[33] If every offspring could be yours, then you are less likely to harm any of them.[34]

The innate sexual drive is a relative constant in primate physiology and psychology, but the expression of that force is flexible. Free love and bohemian philosophies have long held out the hope for human sexual liberation, for example, but bonobos appear to have us beat. Humans have decoupled sex from procreation, but we look like amateurs next to the bonobos. Their lust circuit has been untethered from one or even a few mates, and subsequently diversified and expanded into all manner of social grooming. So, similar emotional urges that drive procreation can become platforms for the emergence of unique social behaviors.

For human beings, religion became the central cultural mechanism that directed lust, and other emotions, into adaptive behaviors. We are the most cooperative primate, and that cooperation is possible, in part, because sexual desire is managed—it does not (usually) disrupt our network of social allies.

Critics of religion are quick to point out the historically oppressive aspects of sexual management. There is good reason to criticize Christian homophobia, for example, or Islamic adultery laws, because the condemnations and punishments are too severe and many lives have been ruined by overzealous morality hygiene. But the overriding logic of religious sexual management is positive and adaptive—it seeks, for example, to convert the lothario into the family man. The rigidity and zealotry of sexual management is related to the difficulty of the task—sexual desire is incredibly strong and leads many otherwise clear-thinking people into behaviors that destroy the nuclear family's cooperative alliance. It's not trivial that the Greeks considered erotic desire to be a form of madness.[35]

Any parent can attest to the fact that raising children is the hardest thing you'll ever do in life. It takes a lot of calories to raise a child. Sustaining this high level of energy investment for many years—while hedonistic opportunities siren-call us from all directions—is a Herculean labor. Culture, in the form of religion, lends assistance in this heroic struggle. Lust management is necessary to protect the elemental social unit of family. If fathers are betraying their wives (or vice versa) and the infidelity is detected, it destroys or reduces trust between spouse allies. For those families who are not wealthy (i.e., most families) such infidelity also takes some resources away from the nuclear unit and gives them to outsiders (e.g., expensive gifts for the paramour, or just time and energy away from childrearing and spousal social grooming).

Sexual loyalty for women is prized because it solves our paternity question. Men are more likely to invest decades of time, energy, and wealth in their own offspring, but an opportunistic female can easily hide true paternity (in the days before DNA tests). Once the believer internalizes them, however, religious norms of sexual loyalty help strengthen the reliability of spousal trust and this creates a stronger team for the difficult childrearing work. The critic of religion might object that *reason* alone is enough to convince humans to override their short-term hedonistic desires in favor of long-term benefits of healthy children, but that article of faith has not yet been demonstrated in history or in psychology.

How exactly does religion do this helpful work? The simplest form of emotional management for sexual monogamy is the threat of severe punishment (e.g., damnation), and, of course, religion has made full use of this strategy. The underlying mechanism of religious influence is *associationism*—the way mental processing is shaped by the association of one mental state with a succeeding state. If religion habitually associates extramarital sex with hellfire, then a disincentive connotation emerges in the mind of the tempted. But religious associationism works in the positive realm of rewards, too, and many parables, images, and teachings emphasize the rich compensations of familial loyalty. Religion aims to assist in the transformation of lust to love.

Recent neuroscience work is beginning to reveal how the distinct brain systems of lust and love are related. Brain scans were compared as people looked at pictures of erotic images versus pictures of loved ones. Distinct areas can be isolated for lust and love, but also a shared matrix of regions (in the striatum, thalamus, hippocampus, anterior cingulate cortex, etc.). Lust activates more subcortical or ancient brain regions, while love recruits more frontal, cognitive parts of the brain. The insula, in particular, seems like a meeting place or switching station between lust and love, given that the posterior is activated during lust and the anterior during love. Ultimately it is a shared system, where the raw ingredients (lust) are refined and restructured by higher cognition and habit. This refinement moves the early animal attractions of sexual conquest into the later phase of love emotions and cognitions, including the desire to protect, nurture, and serve the loved one. Neuroscientists like Stephanie Cacioppo suggest that love "might grow out of and is a more abstract representation of the pleasant sensorimotor experiences that characterize desire."[36]

Habituation can turn a blind desire into a focused, sustained project. Basic emotional ingredients, like LUST and CARE, require cultural work to rise to the level of love. And religion helps this elevation process by repetition of associations. We are repeatedly taught (e.g., 1 Corinthians 7, or *brahmacharya* in Hinduism and Buddhism) that sex inside marriage is good, but sex outside marriage is not. And the pleasures of sexuality are celebrated if, and only if, they are associated with the fertility and fecundity of family and tribe (e.g., the *yoni* and *lingam* cultures of Asia).

Finally, certain forms of mysticism have sought to frame sex as a communication with the divine. Mystical traditions are not mainstream and do not express the same values as lay householder traditions, but they are worth noting because they sometimes celebrate sexuality as a spiritual state. More often than not, desire has been characterized as an obstacle to, rather than a vehicle for, spiritual enlightenment.

Asceticism seeks to mortify the flesh so that the spiritual dimension of the devotee will be purified or freed—even if only temporarily. For example, according to St. Augustine—who asked god to make him "chaste" but not just yet—the erotic drives are great obstacles to virtue. It is this basic presupposition, of the human soul as divided against itself, that leads the Eastern Yogi to starve himself and deprive himself of sleep, and the Western priest and nun to refuse themselves erotic pleasures. To indulge the body, according to this tradition, is to give in to the "dark side." The early Christian presbyter Origen (184–254 CE)—who, incidentally, knew the Platonic dialogues by heart—not only pronounced that his own body was *alien* to him, but also had himself castrated as a young man so that he might, without scandal, become a scripture teacher for females.

In contrast, Tantric Buddhism extends certain features of early dharma to arrive at a spiritual sexuality. To understand this Buddhist perspective on erotic desire and love, we have to remember the Buddha's *Middle-Way* teaching (Majjhimāpaṭipadā). Sex is neither inherently wicked, as the ascetics argue, nor is it the summit of life, as the hedonists suggest. Instead, it is intrinsically neutral. It is only our psychological attachment to sex that renders it harmful. If sex is a transcendent act that destroys the ego temporarily in the "little death" or orgasm, then why not make use of it as a kind of meditation?

This idea, admittedly not a mainstream Buddhist doctrine, is nonetheless a very old Tantric tradition. But in 1970 Tibetan master Chogyam Trungpa moved to the States and began opening meditation centers, eventually creating Naropa University in Colorado. Trungpa's unorthodox Buddhism appealed to beatniks like Allen Ginsberg, who ended up teaching at Naropa. Far from the moral version of Buddhism, Trungpa introduced an almost Dionysian element—a Buddhist monk who got drunk regularly, ate meat, and encouraged naked parties. The goal of this chaos was to break down the mind's urge to classify, organize, discriminate, and judge. The craziness of Trungpa was to shock people out of their preconceptions, get them to accept the present moment (which has no intrinsic moral structure), and to de-center the ego.

Ecstasy-seeking artists, from Jim Morrison to Kurt Cobain, have sought to unleash the Dionysian detonation. Whether it's sex, drugs, rock 'n' roll, or meditation, the goal is to go behind phenomena, to go beyond the dominion of forms, and experience the aboriginal ecstasy. That act, of exploding the ego-consciousness and even entity-consciousness, is thought to have a rejuvenating effect on us when we return to mundane consciousness. Conservative religion is suspicious of ego reduction through intoxication, and with good reason. But the ecstasy traditions have sought a rapprochement between the body and spirituality, by focusing on the positive aspects of losing one's ego—by whatever means available.

All of this is very complicated down on the ground, where diverse cultures—grown by accretion, rather than logic—have celebrated and denigrated sexuality in unpredictable ways. When I was studying Vajrayana Buddhism in Bhutan, I learned of the widespread worship of the "Diving Madman." His real name was Drukpa Kunley (1455–1529), and he brought the "crazy methods" of Buddhism from Tibet to Bhutan, creating scandal and eventually great devotion. The recent case of Chogyam Trungpa, which I mentioned earlier, is just a latter-day instance of this ancient "crazy" tradition.

Kunley, the original "madman," is represented all over Bhutan as a penis and testes. Imagine the rude bathroom etchings of the average middle-school boys' bathroom lovingly painted on the walls of temples, farmhouses, businesses, and even government buildings. Ejaculating penises, eight feet tall, grace the sides of many homes; carved phalluses hang from the four corners of temples, while smaller wooden ones are used in blessings (tapped on the head). Even water fountains are carved as spouting penises.

The Divine Madman is considered the saint of fertility, and his penis is known as the "thunderbolt of flaming wisdom." In his lifetime, he supposedly brought many women to "enlightenment" through sex, and showed that celibacy is not necessary for spiritual awakening. Today, however, his temple (Chimi Lhakhang in Punakha) is a pilgrimage destination for young lovers who seek good fortune in fertility.

The ubiquity of ejaculating penises throughout Bhutan might give the reader the impression that Bhutan (and Tibet) are permissive bastions of free-love promiscuity and hippie erotic abandon. This is decidedly not the case. Bhutan is an otherwise sexually modest culture, and the phallic culture is turned toward the successes of the nuclear family. Women and men on the streets wear very modest traditional clothing that covers their whole bodies, and Bhutanese-produced TV cannot even show an amorous couple kiss directly.

Sexual imagery abounds in Vajrayana Buddhism, but not as an invitation to hedonism. It serves instead as a symbol of fertility specifically, and *power* generally. *Yab-yum* sculptures and paintings portray various multilimbed deities in the act of coitus, and they populate temples all over Bhutan, Tibet, and India. Specific interpretations of them vary slightly, but most agree that they represent the interpenetration of compassion and wisdom—the two main ingredients for enlightenment. The purpose is not to celebrate sex per se, but to celebrate potency (of which sex is but one kind), because potency is needed for the local struggles of life (e.g., marriage, work, children) and the cosmic struggles (i.e., enlightenment and the liberation of all sentient beings). Once seen in its cultural context, the eroticized tantric tradition still falls within the larger cultural project of adaptive group success (fertility and familial performance).

In sum, religion seeks to transform sexual joy and ecstasy from selfish hedonism and utilitarian functionalism to sacred practice. What this means literally is not as important as what it means behaviorally. Indeed, calling sex or anything else "sacred" is a sticky wicket, as Emile Durkheim acknowledges in his famous "Definitions of Religious Phenomena and of Religion" (Chapter One), from *The Elementary Forms of Religious Life* (1912). We have a sense, Durkheim acknowledges, that sacred things are closer to ultimate reality, and that they are higher than merely profane entities. But their metaphysical status is almost inexpressible.

Never mind about metaphysics. Sacred acts and behaviors are also thought to be *transformative* for the character of those involved, and in this sense sex is part of the pursuit of the good. Sanctified sex (in marriage) is supposed to transform and improve the very character of the partners, and indirectly strengthen the nuclear team by buttressing the parental partnership. The meaning of sexual behavior is changed from egoistic pleasure to a source of vitality for further service (ostensibly to God, but really to family). Disciplined sexuality gives strength, and strength is needed in a hostile world.

My argument here is not that religion is correct and that you, dear reader, should only have sex inside marriage. Indeed, my own views on this are irredeemably impious. But rather, I am endeavoring to show the positively adaptive aspect of sexual conservatism, in a climate where it is either slavishly followed by the dogmatic believer, or mercilessly lampooned by the skeptic—neither group bothering to understand it. It is, in short, cultural management of potentially destabilizing emotion—in service of collective cooperation. And that is partly how Homo sapiens survived.

COSMIC JOY

The critic of religion might well ask why religious joy is needed. Why not just joy? If positive emotion is adaptive, then why not just foster cultural mechanisms, such as art and entertainment, to help us cope with the various slings and arrows?

In large part, I agree that many secular forms of ecstasy, joy, and play can act as buffers against suffering. Peter Watson, in his book *The Age of Atheism*, celebrates the possibility that religion has largely been replaced by better secular therapies. Taking his start from Nietzsche's famous "God is dead" pronouncement, Watson shows how the twentieth century tried to answer Nietzsche's subsequent questions: "How shall we comfort ourselves?" and "What sacred games shall we have to invent?" The inevitable yearning for transcendence is its own kind of eternal recurrence, and the secular age has not escaped it.

Watson's story is about how prosperous Western people no longer live in the "enchanted garden" of religious metaphysics, but must try to feed their residual divine yearning with secular alternatives: science, art, New Age actualization, sex, drugs, and rock 'n'roll. We twentieth-century capitalists have been on a quest to find ecstasy in every domain except traditional religious territory. Watson, like most twenty-first-century atheists is way past the Nietzsche-era lament about God's death, and instead celebrates this secular cultural movement (the psychologizing of theology), seeing it as more mature and realistic.

After Darwin, Nietzsche, Freud, and quantum mechanics, we had to learn to live with open-ended cosmological uncertainties and real mortality (instead of the death-denying wishful thinking of traditional monotheism).

Although many people still cling to comforting traditional theologies, Watson suggests that the therapeutic core of religion has been extracted from traditional metaphysics and repackaged. Instead of priests we have counselors to handle our emotional crises, and instead of geocentric security we have the strange inspirations of evolutionary deep time and the staggering multiverse.

The common ingredient that Watson affirms in these secular paradigms of meaning involves an appreciation of *local* fulfillment and happiness, rooted in nature rather than the supernatural. After the totalizing trajectories of religious fundamentalism and imperialism, the *size* of life, Watson points out, was scaled back in the twentieth century, away from cosmic consciousness to almost bonsai scope. Watson affirms, "the age of overbearing ideas is over." He would probably approve of Candide cultivating his garden at the end of Voltaire's novel, or maybe Bill Murray at the end of *Groundhog Day* enjoying the simple pleasures of small-town life. I tend to agree with the humble importance of the local.

There is nothing like the *cosmic*, however, to get the blood flowing. I want to argue here that the religious believer has an entirely different kind of joy available to her, and it is not easily fungible with secular substitutes. Religious joy is a special case, a sui generis.

Perhaps the best way to approach the topic of cosmic joy is from its polar opposite, namely "cosmic fear." H. P. Lovecraft (1890–1937) is a name synonymous with horror, and many connoisseurs of the genre consider him the rightful heir to Edgar Allan Poe's distinguished mantle. His stories, such as the "The Call of Cthulhu," were sometimes published in the pulp magazine *Weird Tales* during his lifetime, but his influence has been acknowledged by many, including Jorge Luis Borges, Clive Barker, Stephen King, Neil Gaiman, and even a small army of heavy metal bands.

Lovecraft was a master at giving us blood-curdling monsters, but it is the emotion of eerie dread, which he excels in producing, that we need to consider. Lovecraft argues, in his 1927 *Supernatural Horror in Literature*, that good horror evokes a unique subjective emotion, which he refers to as "cosmic fear."[37] There is something in the horror experience, Lovecraft claims, that resonates a deep instinctual awe of the unknown. "The one test," Lovecraft explains, "of the really weird is simply this—whether or not there be excited in the reader a profound sense of dread, and of contact with unknown spheres and powers; a subtle attitude of awed listening, as if for the beating of black wings or the scratching of outside shapes on the known universe's utmost rim." Lovecraft suggests that all human beings have an instinctual awareness (some more refined than others) of the paltry state of human understanding—especially when compared with the almost limitless domain of the strange and unfamiliar. That lonely sense of fragility and vulnerability is a major aspect of the "cosmic fear" that horror triggers in us.

The same year that H. P. Lovecraft published his *Supernatural Horror in Literature*, German philosopher Martin Heidegger published his magnum opus, *Sein und Zeit, Being and Time*. From quite a different starting place, Heidegger, and other existential writers such as Jean Paul Sartre, argued that there is a radical kind of human experience, which is like fear but, in a way, deeper. Heidegger calls this radical dread "angst," a now famous German word for anxiety. Fear, he argued, is different from angst, because fear is a response to a definite, identifiable threat. One will have a fearful response to an assailant in a dark alley, an approaching aggressive animal, a felt earthquake or other natural disaster, and so on. But angst is an indefinite threat—the danger is nowhere in particular and yet everywhere. Like Lovecraft's "cosmic fear," Heidegger's angst is an ineffable mood of metaphysical proportion.[38]

It is interesting to find thinkers as diverse as Lovecraft, Poe, Heidegger, Schopenhauer, Freud, and so on, all trying to articulate a similar range of oblique irrational subjective experiences—dark, unsettling experiences that could not be discursively communicated (except in the poetic and visual expressions of the artists). When the horror genre pushes past the simple "fear-based" narrative of a monster chasing a victim, and instead, constructs an eerie world of foreboding, it crosses over into this more metaphysical pessimism of cosmic absurdity. Cosmic fear, or angst, or despair suggest, even if only temporarily, that the world *lacks* the secure structure and meaning that we ordinarily assume it to have. Both existentialism and horror, in their emphasis on human vulnerability, are critiques of rationalist enlightenment-based modernity, and traditional religious optimism.

We can think of existential dread as the angst of not existing, but cosmic fear goes further and ascribes nefariousness to reality itself. In the Book of Job, we find a powerful description of the unique nightmarish fear that lacks precise focus. "In thoughts from the visions of the night, when deep sleep falleth on men, fear came upon me, and trembling, which made all my bones to shake. Then a spirit passed before my face; the hair of my flesh stood up: It stood still, but I could not discern the form thereof" (Job 4:13).[39] Recent psychology and affective neuroscience give us a glimpse into the mental formation of this cosmic pessimism.

Neurologist Antonio Damasio and others suggest there are emotional settings or pathways, called "somatic markers," that help us make all kinds of decisions, especially automatic judgments.[40] The amygdala plays a major role in our emotions and the adjacent hippocampus handles memory, but these are in direct communication with the ventromedial prefrontal cortex—the new brain area of decision-making and executive control. Damasio suggests that somatic markers (created in the communication between the amygdala and the ventromedial prefrontal cortex) create weighted behavioral options for us. Should I run when I see the shadow approaching? Should I protect my friend? From the trivial to the sublime, fast decisions (including both survival and ethical decisions) are heavily biased by the emotional pathways that have been laid down by reward/punishment associations in our previous experiences. This differs from other forms of information learning. A computational view of the mind as data input, recall, and syntactical manipulation is not enough to account for the uniquely "instinctual" and imperative aspects of emotional judgments such as horror and fear.[41]

As we grow up, we meet our environment with associated physiological emotional states. These affective responses to stimuli become default emotional settings—for example, snakes give me the creeps. But on the positive side, family and friends give me feelings of love and affective bonds of loyalty (cemented by oxytocin and opioid production). These somatic markers are processed in the pathway between the ventromedial prefrontal cortex and the limbic brain. This means that our experience of the world is partly given by the outside world, and partly provided by our own emotional biases. We cannot, in the moment, dissect our experience into the objective and subjective ingredients. How we're feeling actually colors how the world is. Attraction (love) and repulsion (fear) color our world in an early encoded configuration, but these shift and modify according to later experiential patterns. Anyone who's ever been depressed knows exactly how dramatically our mood can color the whole world.

The point is that these emotional responses are not *instincts* in the sense of prewired or genetically engraved responses. The emotional systems of fear or joy are ancient in the sense that they have many similarities with nonhuman animals, but in our individual lives they are idiosyncratically assigned and have significant plasticity. Emotional tendencies and values can help us make fast appropriate responses to environmental challenges (which is why they evolved), but they can also be retrained or re-educated. The person gripped by cosmic fear has been retrained, or somehow acquired a set of somatic markers (in this case, fear), such that the whole world is colored sinisterly. Edgar Allan Poe was masterful at making the most mundane objects or events seem to throb with odious evil. Filmmakers like David Lynch are equally effective at giving the whole world an uncanny feeling.

Now, if there is cosmic fear, there is certainly cosmic joy. If the anxious or fearful person sees threat or instability everywhere, the joyful person sees security, justice, even love everywhere. For them God is everywhere in creation, so even when things look bad, they really aren't. For those of us on the pessimism continuum, this sanguine, cheerful mood is slightly irritating, but we cannot deny its sincerity. The great naturalist Stephen Jay Gould once contrasted these metaphysical outlooks as the "warm fuzzy" enthusiast versus the "cold bath" proponent.[42]

Gould and most everybody else characterized the difference between warm fuzzies and cold bathers as a cognitive difference. That is to say, each side has a different theory about how the world was made and whether it has purpose or not. No doubt this happens, and people's emotions sometimes follow their metaphysical theories. But I want to suggest that it is frequently the other way around. Even before the level of theoretical difference, the two groups have different emotional or affective readings of the world. I'm reversing the usual view—wherein one decides first whether God exists, and then feels positive emotions toward the world. Rather, very often the cosmic joy enthusiast already loves life and merely ascribes a Designer to justify the feeling. There is increasing evidence that emotional or affective personalities are stable, consistent platforms for lifelong behavioral and decision-making tendencies.[43] This may be because of the somatic marker pathways in the brain, or genetic makeup, or both. But warm fuzzies and cold bathers are not rigidly determined either, because we can sometimes move from one orientation to another.

Nonetheless, joyful people who *feel* that everything is ultimately okay, or the universe is intrinsically good, tend to be more resilient.[44] Some recent research reveals that spiritual and religious people are better at rebounding from trauma (e.g., see Dr. Harold G. Koenig's voluminous studies at Duke's Center for the Study of Religion/Spirituality and Health). The religious life usually contains the three key elements in responding positively to adversity; a strong social support group, a focus on empathy, and an ability to infer meaning—or as Dr. Donald Meichenbaum puts it, "an attempt to seek meaning, purpose and a direction of life in relation to a higher power, universal spirit or God."[45] The unique cosmic joy I've been sketching is part of this last key element.

Cosmic joy is a one-of-a-kind type of elation (sui generis) because it marks the entirety of reality and secondly it comes with concepts of purpose or meaning. That is to say, it is not just naked positive emotion (pleasure) associated with a specific experience. The advantage to cosmic religious forms of joy, compared with emotional management using music, for example, is that religious positive affect affirms cosmic meaning (e.g., the sense that all things are connected or that the Deity has a plan). For the believer, these additional cognitive elements (purpose and meaning) make the sweetness sweeter and the bitterness more endurable.

I need to underscore here that I'm not talking about the consolations of a naive theory or story, such as Creationism. I'm trying to get at the evanescent *feeling* that the cosmos is benign. If you don't have this feeling, then you have to believe that other people are sincerely having an experience that is unavailable to you; or, alternatively, they are not, but they're faking it or merely projecting wishful thinking.

Contrary to the critics of religion, I don't think the warm fuzzies are faking anything or projecting wishful thinking and mistaking it for reality. I do, however, think that they are feeling the world through a matrix of positive affective markers, and this permeates their perception and interpretation of the world. Perception itself is *feeling-laden* and cannot be easily or entirely decoupled. And even our awareness of existence itself—Why is there something rather than nothing?—can have an emotional tone.

In the early twentieth century, German theologian Rudolph Otto argued, in *The Idea of the Holy* (1917), that an experience of awe defines our notion of the holy or sacred—there is a sense of encountering something overwhelming. This mysterious feeling of wonder is both fascinating and terrifying at the same time. It may be the very core experience for all subsequent theology.

Intoxicants have a long history with artistic and mystical religious traditions, in part because they help engender this odd feeling of wonder. As the soma drinking Vedic authors of the Hindu pantheon understood, removing our executive cognitive functions with intoxicants not only frees the mind to form fantastical associations and simulations but also removes the little ego itself—making way for transcendent experiences of divine union (what Freud called "Oceanic experiences"). My suspicion is that the oceanic aspect of this experience comes not from a real metaphysical immersion with God, but from a phenomenological change—a psychological movement from centered egoistic consciousness to decentered states. The religious mystic and the artist have always shared a longing for the open water of consciousness.

These mystical aspects of religion do not attempt to track nature for accurate predictions, nor do they obviously improve the thriving of the person. Shamans, presumably, were not better at the hunt because they had seen the unity of all things. Rather, some mystical forms of religion endeavor to acknowledge the unique field-consciousness that seems to be a background for particular contents of consciousness.

Robert Bellah argues, following Jerome Bruner's work in developmental psychology, that humans can engage in various modes of representational thought.[46] In religious thinking, we employ these same modes of *enactive* thinking, *symbolic* thinking, and *conceptual* thinking. As young children, we develop enactive representations that pertain to our bodily actions. And in rituals, we act out religious meaning with our bodies; we bow, we supplicate, kneel, dance, and so on. Then we learn to think symbolically using iconography and story, to represent virtue, vice, heaven, hell, spirits, and so on. And finally, we think conceptually. In the religious domain, conceptual thinking drives theology and makes possible a more systematic representation of universals.

Before these modes of representation, however, lies what psychologists Piaget and Inhelder called the "adualism" of the child, the state of consciousness before an integrated self.[47] The distinction or boundary between self and world is not an early datum for the infant, because it emerges slowly through experience. Bellah calls this the "unitive" experience, and he suggests that it precedes the more content-rich representational modes, serving as a crucial touchstone for later religious thought. "The unitive event, then, is a kind of ground zero with respect to religious representations. It transcends them yet it requires them if it is to be communicable at all. Christian negative theology and the Buddhist teaching of emptiness (*sunyata*) attempt to express this paradoxically by speaking of nothingness, the void, silence, or emptiness. Yet the very negative terms themselves are symbolic forms, are representations, and therefore introduce an element of dualism into the unitive event even when they are trying to overcome the dualism of representation" (Bellah, 2011, p. 12).

It's safe to say that mysticism, supernaturalism, and religion generally have had a great interest in celebrating this presymbolic, unmediated experience. Whether it is the *sensus divinitatis*, the oceanic experience, or the Atman/Brahman consummation, religion and art affirm the transcendental experience. Such an experience need not have a true referent in order for it to be transformative. But it must have some emotional content, if only in the re-entry phase of consciousness. William James suggests four characteristics of mystical experiences.[48] Such experiences are ineffable and cannot be named. They have noetic content—that is to say, the person learns something. The mystic is passive—the event happens to the person. And the experience is transient, passing quickly.

We need to add a criterion to James's list, namely, mystical experience is emotional as well as intellectual. The unitive experience is potentially terrifying, but it's usually described by contemplatives as joyful, or blissful.

No doubt cosmic joy has several ingredients internal to it, like the psychological feeling of security, or safety, or refuge. As Psalms 4: 6–8 says, "Many, Lord, are asking, 'Who will bring us prosperity?' Let the light of your face shine on us. Fill my heart with joy when their grain and new wine abound. In peace I will lie down and sleep, for you alone, Lord, make me dwell in safety." Such feelings of security must accompany the cosmic experience, in order to render it empowering rather than debilitating.

Another important ingredient in cosmic joy may be what psychologist Jonathan Haidt calls "elevation."[49] Elevation is a feeling of inspiration and expansion, which comes from awe-inspiring experiences with nature, art, or moral beauty. "Elevation appears to be caused by seeing manifestations of humanity's higher or better nature; it triggers a distinctive feeling in the chest of warmth and expansion; it causes a desire to become a better person oneself; and it seems to open one's heart . . . to other people" (p. 864).

There is empirical evidence that people who experience elevation are more likely to help others and give more to charity (Haidt et al., 2003). This evidence dovetails with some striking data from the independent public policy group Philanthropy Roundtable.[50] According to their 2014 statistics, religious faith plays a central influence on giving. Religious people are more likely than the nonreligious to donate to charitable causes (including secular causes), and they give significantly more. People who attend religious services twice a month or more give over four times as much as people who never attend services. Moreover, religious people are more likely to volunteer. Among Americans who volunteered during 2014, three-quarters belonged to a religious organization, while one-quarter did not.

Finally, it is important to note that feelings of cosmic joy do not require a traditional "creator monotheism" to flourish. Rather, such feelings equally attend polytheism, deism, animism, and pantheism. As we pointed out earlier, Spinoza had fairly heretical views on religion and yet recognized that healthy religion was not brooding on misery and suffering, but enacting joy as much as possible. "No deity," he says, "takes pleasure in my infirmity and discomfort," nor does the deity think tears and fears flow from virtue. Rather, joy is virtuous and gives vitality. "The greater the pleasure wherewith we are affected, the greater the perfection whereto we pass; in other words, the more must we necessarily partake of the divine nature. Therefore, to make use of what comes in our way, and to enjoy it as much as possible (not to the point of satiety, for that would not be enjoyment) is the part of a wise man" (*Ethics,* Prop. XLV).

It is common for the critics of religion to grudgingly acknowledge religion's occasional social benefits, but it is invariably decried as an authoritarian fear-based coercion. Threaten and intimidate people, and they will get in line and behave. But I have been arguing that the positive emotions are equally, if not more, motivating for empathy, generosity, and cooperation. Anthropologist Richard Sosis did a comparative study of utopian communities and discovered that religious communities were more likely to survive than secular communities.[51] One way to interpret this finding is that fear of God's punishment structures better cooperative ethical behavior. But cosmic joy is an equally powerful resource for individuals and communities, and we must factor in its adaptive value.

In short, religion is particularly good at fostering and focusing a set of adaptive feelings and actions that can improve the vitality of the individual as well as the cooperation of larger groups. American pragmatist William James believed that "*feeling* is the deeper source of religion, and that philosophic and theological formulas are secondary products, like translations of a text into another tongue" (Varieties of Relig. Lecture XVIII). Going slightly further, I'd say that feeling is the deeper source of all metaphysics—from warm fuzzy to cold bath. Any number of nature/nurture developmental pathways generate the joyful personality, but once you've got it, you've got a highly resilient foundation for weathering the storms of life.

CHAPTER 6
Fear and Rage

When Moses approached the camp and saw the calf and the dancing, his anger burned and he threw the tablets out of his hands, breaking them to pieces at the foot of the mountain.

—Exodus 32:19

And He made a scourge of cords, and drove them all out of the temple, with the sheep and the oxen; and He poured out the coins of the money changers and overturned their tables; and to those who were selling the doves He said, "Take these things away; stop making My Father's house a place of business."

—John 2:15

A man said to the Prophet, "Give me advice." The Prophet, peace be upon him, said, "Do not get angry." The man asked repeatedly and the Prophet answered each time, "Do not get angry."

—Al-Bukhari, *Hadith* 16

Bertrand Russell says of religion that "fear is the basis of the whole thing—fear of the mysterious, fear of defeat, fear of death." More disturbing, Russell adds, "fear is the parent of cruelty."[1] In this view, Russell is echoing David Hume's character Philo, who says, "terror is the primary principle of religion, it is the passion, which always predominates in it, and admits but of short intervals of pleasure" (*Dialogues,* XII). And Russell's claim augurs the more recent criticisms by Christopher Hitchens, Sam Harris, and Richard Dawkins that religion is intrinsically terrorizing and prone to violence.

I concede that religion regularly produces fear and rage in its adherents, but I will argue in this chapter that it often attempts and succeeds in managing and minimizing fear and rage. Still, the goal of this analysis is not to get religion to play nice and only reinforce liberal values. Sometimes religion increases fear and anger and points them at enemies for the sake of defensive and offensive struggle. This may disturb our tolerant value system, but a tolerant value system will serve you poorly if real enemies are at your throat. Religion can help mobilize the adaptive uses of violence, which any anthropologist must admit is still a viable path to group success.

Critics of religion will often cherry-pick the most bizarre and violent religious events, and then damn the whole enterprise as poison from a prescientific era. I will argue instead that fringe forms of religion do not represent the mainstream, and more typical forms of religiosity are usually pacific and healthy. But I am not naive. Sometimes mainstream religion is also belligerent, and we will examine the occasional need for such belligerence. After discussing the ways in which religion manages fear and rage, I will examine ways to humanize religion further and avoid the dehumanizing elements.

WHAT IS FEAR?

Darwin, in *The Expression of Emotions*, points out that fear begins as a highly animating experience—a powerful stimulant. "A man or animal driven through terror to desperation, is endowed with wonderful strength, and is notoriously dangerous in the highest degree." But fear very quickly alters its victim and shuts down the human and animal, giving them an almost catatonic condition. "Fear," Darwin says, "is the most depressing of all the emotions; and it soon induces utter, helpless prostration."[2] The exception to this devitalization is when fear can be transformed into directed anger, which we'll discuss later in this chapter.

All mammals are equipped with adaptive instincts like fight or flight, but these are housed primarily in the brain stem. Built on top of these midbrain systems are the limbic emotional circuits. As we've already seen, emotional neuroscience has located seven major affective systems that mammals share: fear, care, lust, rage, panic, seeking, and play.[3] Each of these circuits has unique pathways through the brain, enlists specific neurotransmitters and hormones, and results in specific mammal behaviors. Fear, for example, has a neurocircuitry that passes from the amygdala through the hypothalamus to the periaqueductal gray (PAG), down to the brain stem, and out through the spinal cord. Natural selection built this operating system in most vertebrates. It helped them survive in a hostile world.

Human and other mammal fear is regulated largely in the amygdala, and neuroscientist Joseph E. LeDoux has mapped the pathway by which fear and memory (in the hippocampus) work in tandem to create conditioned learning.[4] When a person associates dogs with aggression (and biting), for example, and then crosses the street when dogs approach, her brain is cycling through a similar circuit that governs rodent lab learning (foot shocks and associated images/smells). Fear is homologous across the mammal clade—that is to say, it's the same basic ingredient across many species.

Like any other biological trait, fear is subject to evolution. We have evidence that mammals have heritable dispositional levels of fear or timidity. Levels of shyness, for example, can be artificially selected by breeders, resulting in more fearful populations. Rats, for example, have been analyzed in new threatening environments, and those animals that displayed fearful behaviors (e.g., immediate defecation and reluctance to explore) were bred together. In only ten generations of breeding, scientists were able to measure ten times more fear in the population, and thirty generations produced thirty times more fear.

In the last few years, biologists have discovered that fear (and probably other emotions) can be acquired in a rat's lifetime and be passed down to subsequent generations via epigenetics. "Epigenetic" formerly meant embryological development from simple to complex structure (as opposed to preformation), but the term has a new meaning these days. "Epigenetic" has been resurrected by biologists recently to refer to the newly discovered layer of molecular triggers and switches that ride on top of our genetic code. It sounds almost Lamarckian, but data suggests that expression tags can be triggered in an animal—say, a mouse's fear response to foot shocks during exposure to a specific odor. And the expression tag of conditioned fear during the odor can replicate in the next generation, such that the offspring is also afraid of the same otherwise neutral odor.[5] This is not a hereditary change in the genes per se, but a retained change in the expression switches that ride on top of the genome. Two generations of mice show increased fear of the scent of oranges, because their grandparent mouse ancestor was shocked during exposure to orange scent.[6]

Thinking about fear from an evolutionary perspective is revealing. Darwin himself repeatedly brought snakes (real and fake) down to the London Zoo primate house. He discovered that chimps had an extreme fear of snakes, and he concluded that some rudimentary taxonomic recognition-system seemed hard-wired into the animals—some classification system (probably morphological or shape-based) carried emotional responses with it, and helped give the chimps a useful instinctual dread of threatening species.

What would it be like to live without fear? Presumably, it would be great . . . while it lasted. Chances are, it would be a very short life. A woman, referred to as SM in neuroscience literature, suffers from focal bilateral amygdala lesions.[7] Her compromised amygdala means that she lacks the usual fear emotion that normal mammals experience. She is fearless. And researchers have studied her while they exposed her to fear-inducing experiences (e.g., real snakes and tarantulas, haunted houses, and horror films).

Experiments repeatedly showed that "frightening" stimuli elicited high degrees of attention arousal in SM, but no fear per se. She would approach many of the threats with great curiosity and cognitive excitement, but she did not have normal physiological or psychological fear responses. At a haunted house visit, "The hidden monsters attempted to scare SM numerous times, but to no avail," researchers reported. "She reacted to the monsters by smiling, laughing, or trying to talk to them. In contrast, their scare tactics typically elicited loud screams of fright from the other members of the group. More than showing a lack of fear, SM exhibited an unusual inclination to approach and touch the monsters" (Feinstein et al. 2011, p. 36). In some cases, she had to be prevented by the researchers from putting herself in actual danger because she seemed to lack the instinctual wherewithal.

Cultural theorist Mathias Clasen takes the SM case as evidence that "Horror monsters are not only terrifying; they are captivating."[8] He recognizes, in the pathology case of SM, a failure or breakdown of a universal affective system that explains some of the cross-cultural features of horror. "Why," he asks, "do horror stories generally travel well across cultural borders, if all they do is encode salient culturally contingent anxieties?" Cases like that of SM suggest that horror has a finite set of triggers/responses that were built during our hominid past. And we can glimpse how it works when the system goes wrong, as it did with SM.

One way to interpret the fearless woman is to see her as experiencing cognitive category jamming, in the sense, say, of categories such as "living man" and "headless," but then failing to experience the affective feelings (e.g., avoidance, retreat, dread) that usually spark the appropriate adaptive response. The default cognitive categories, laid down in SM's early childhood presumably, are violated by horror images—producing arousal—but the affective system of fear (based in the lateral amygdala) is never appropriately triggered.

It's possible that the cognitive category mismatch produces a fear response in most people, but alternatively, it is also possible that fear precedes all this cognitive machinery and triggers more directly from perceptual data. Fear, from this perspective, is not a result of cognitive confusion, but runs on a different physiological pathway altogether. Placing fear before cognition (rather than as a consequence) is more consistent with our understanding of evolution. Mammalian emotional adaptations (e.g., fear) were under construction for hundreds of millions of years before symbolic cognition arose in *Homo*.

As we already noticed, the emotion/cognition complex in fear is a Janus-faced experience, partly *imperative* (e.g., I should run away) and partly *indicative* (e.g., that creature is part-man and part-snake, or more likely, that man is a mugger). This Janus-faced representation is strongly coupled together in lower animals—mice, for example, simultaneously recognize cats as a kind of thing (in a category) *and* as dangerous (fear affect). Humans, on the other hand, can decouple these two pathways (indicative and imperative) and fear can be reattached to alternative kinds of creatures/perceptions. As we'll see shortly, this decoupling proves very helpful in some cases, and disturbingly maladaptive in others.

Not only the Darwinians recognize the adaptive uses of fear. Aristotle, in his *Rhetoric*, recognized that fear is helpful because it focuses one's mind and behavior on a threatening event or person. Fear brings intense salience to some person or thing in our perception and paves the way for rapid response. The furious face of some miscreant bearing down on me, or the slithering shape at my foot, or the ritualistic beheading of some innocent person—all produce intense fear and prepare the body and mind for fighting or fleeing. Our old-brain animal fear is immediate and fast, but we also have more protracted fear that can go on, via the ruminations of the neocortex, for weeks and years. Aristotle says, "fear is caused by whatever we feel has great power of destroying or of harming us in ways that tend to cause us great pain. Hence the very indications of such things are terrible, making us feel that the terrible thing itself is close at hand; the approach of what is terrible is just what we mean by 'danger'" (Bk. II, Ch. V). In cases of genuine danger and risk, fear is extremely helpful. As Aristotle says, "fear sets us thinking what can be done" (Rhet. Bk. II, Ch. V).

RELIGIOUS MANAGEMENT OF FEAR

I want to discuss several ways in which religion reduces fear, but then turn to ways in which it amplifies fear and employs it for adaptive goals. The most obvious area where religion traditionally offers a unique therapeutic balm is fear of death. No one wants to die, and religion says you don't have to. Veracity and credibility aside, that is a powerful analgesic.

Philosophy and psychology long have recognized that beneath many of our human projects lies deep existential fear. Terror management theory claims that the main explanation for most human behavior and achievement are our motivated fear and avoidance of death.[9] We realize that we're going to die, and that realization forces us to seek immortality—in reality (through religion and utopian medicine, etc.) or symbolically (through children, or creative work, etc.). We are terrified by the prospect of not existing.

Cultural beliefs, such as religious belief in an afterlife, relieve terror and promise literal immortality. But social and cultural institutions (such as tribes, schools, nation states, and even ideological world views) offer symbolic immortality, in the sense that they are bigger than my individual contribution, and they go on or persist after I am gone. Even the most scientific mind, according to terror management theory, is subconsciously seeking immortality. It's unclear if we are to read the religious person as just a more crude seeker (i.e., in pursuit of literal rather than figurative escape from death), or a more honest seeker. Or should we merely interpret them as more fearful? The theory is unclear.

It is difficult to study this theory experimentally. Generating the fear of death via threats is more ethically problematic for empirical research, but reminding people of death can be done via the Mortality Salience Induction Procedure. This procedure guides subjects to reflect upon their own death, and write about their feelings.[10] Subsequent tests are performed to determine whether such morbid priming influences deeper beliefs and attitudes.

Using terror management theory (TMT), psychologist Jonathan Jong explores the question of whether religious people are more or less afraid of death. It is not entirely clear what TMT predicts here. Are people who are more afraid of death more inclined to seek out religion, producing a strong correlation between religiosity and death concern? Terror management theory could mean that someone who is highly concerned with death is more likely to be an active religious devotee, because the promise of immortality motivates dramatically. Or is it the case that religious people are getting strong doses of fear reduction (via the promise of immortality) and, therefore, they will have measurably less concern about death than the nonreligious subject? In the first case, researchers might expect a positive correlation between fear and religious devotion, but in the second case researchers might expect a negative correlation. Some of this confusion about correlation can be clarified by assessing the base starting points, or belief contents, of the subjects. They're still working out the empirical research program, but it looks like significant correlations exist between fear of death and the perceived value of religion.

A comparative study of people from Turkey, Malaysia, and the United States confirmed a positive correlation between fear of death and religiosity.[11] That same study revealed that Muslims expressed considerably more fear than members of other religions, and females were more fearful of death and more religious than men.

Are there atheists in foxholes? The old saw suggests that even cool-headed, rational atheists will lose their cool when bullets are flying around them and their death seems imminent. In those dramatic situations, do we instinctively reach out to supernatural forces, or do we spontaneously pray? Some psychologists finally tested this old adage.[12]

Terror management theory predicts that when an atheist is presented with a mundane choice between religious belief and her secular world view, she privileges her world view over religion. In large part, this is because her world view is itself a form of symbolic immortality or terror management, and it consoles better than an incredulous literal immortality option (i.e., heaven). Subjects who are exposed to morbid priming and then asked directly to give a self-report, will usually stick firm and even double-down on their secular preferences. However, more indirect methods that measure reaction time and implicit association testing, reveal subconscious attitudes (implicit beliefs). And the old saw seems confirmed because those tests reveal that even atheists adopt more credulous and positive attitudes toward religion after morbid priming.[13] If you remind people of their death, they warm up to the gods.

An important study of terminally ill patients revealed the complexity of religion as terror management.[14] If patients have a religious orientation that provides order, existential meaning, and recognition of one's self worth or self-esteem in the broader cosmic context, then those patients attain "religious comfort" amidst physical suffering (end-stage congenital heart failure). They are also less likely to succumb to depression at the end of life. But if a patient's religious orientation creates a threat to self-esteem, uncertainty, and a sense of abandonment or punishment by God, the patient attains a state of "religious struggle" and succumbs easily to depression at the end of life. So, the *kind* of religion or one's place in the cosmic plan is highly relevant to the success or failure of this terror management. If you see God as a vengeful punisher and have doubts about your own piety, then religion can actually amplify your terror. Whereas a welcoming merciful God reduces depression and helps patients meet physical suffering with greater resilience.

Although it is common for believers and skeptics to assume that the comfort of religion consists primarily in its promise of literal immortality, psychologists have noticed that "self-esteem" is the more important aspect of religious comfort.[15] If subjects feel that they are relevant agents, albeit small, in the cosmic meaning of life, they are buffered from anxiety, even if they do not believe in their own literal immortality. Varieties of this view can be seen in people who feel they will personally disperse after death, but their energy will transform into other biological formats, and they will play a part in the ecological circle of life. However, nothing beats old-time religion when it comes to fostering a stable sense of purpose and meaning. Some studies find that people are much more likely to feel a sense of purpose (and reduced anxiety) when they have a sure conviction that a traditional monotheistic God exists as part of a unified metaphysical framework.[16] Well-structured religious ideologies (such as those in Christianity or Islam, etc.) give people a firmer sense of purpose than more flexible, ambiguous alternatives (such as New Age movements or interfaith pluralism).

Perhaps the crucial ingredient for stable terror management via religion is the idea of a cosmic author, who serves as a ground or foundation for the material world. My own view is that meaning and purpose are more ready-to-hand in our *local* relations of family, friends, and proximate politics. But all those dependencies can disappoint or fail, and my resilience may not be as robust as a traditional religious person who has an unbreakable, unfailing, and inexhaustible reservoir of purpose.

If dying is the deepest anxiety of life, it is by no means the only. Another area where religion appears to reduce fear is in our encounter with the unknown generally. Philosophers and anthropologists long have recognized that religion explains the unexplainable. Prescientific and folk cultures generally need to make sense of the changing environment (e.g., floods, droughts, earthquakes, volcanoes), as well as social changes (e.g., war, shifts in political power) and personal mysteries (e.g., disappearance or loss of a loved one, failed marriage, sudden good fortune).

Religious thinking about mysterious events often is dismissed by critics as juvenile magical thinking, because naturalistic explanations would better suffice. Two responses seem relevant however. First, on many pressing questions (e.g., the origins of the universe, or the loss of a child to cancer) there are no naturalistic explanations that satisfy—either because the mechanical explanation is still just a promissory note, or because the "how" answer fails to address the "why" question. Secondly, the supposed magical thinking is not quite as magical as first appears. When the believer traces the origin of some observed event into the unobserved spiritual domain, she invariably tethers the cause to a *mind* of some sort. The cause of this or that mundane mystery is another mind, albeit divine or otherwise invisible. It is a feature of the human mind to search for and even project intentions, motives, and desires into the world. This ability (i.e., the theory of mind mechanism) is part of our cognitive architecture, because it helps us read other human and animal agents. The religious believer may be over-projecting mind into nature—reading false positives—but the tendency is neither irrational nor juvenile. If the skeptic protests that the believer is projecting an unseen force (mental intention) behind some observable action or event, the same can be said of every other "theory of mind" attribution, because I don't see my mother's or brother's intentions either and only infer them from their observable behaviors.

The believer can be rightly accused of being overly anthropomorphic perhaps, but not obscurely magical. Many secular humanists are profoundly anthropomorphic about their pets, for example, and this is because tracing events (including behaviors) to mental intentions is irresistibly helpful. Will such attributions sometimes trace back, under the microscope of indicative science, to nonmental and nonintentional causes (physical causation)? Yes, of course, and frequently. But the imperative practical domain of the average layperson has no such analytical luxury, and he needs to press on with the business of surviving. In the same way that metaphysical naturalism becomes the skeptic's promissory note for her many uninvestigated phenomena, the divine mind becomes the believer's promissory note.

It is common for many contemporary critics to dismiss the age-old "design argument" (or teleological argument) as a species of creationism and to give it no further hearing. But this confuses the sad political battle with the philosophical debate. Yes, fundamentalist Christian school board members try to reintroduce creationism through the back door of "intelligent design" theory, but the latter is nowhere near as silly as the former. Creationism is disproven by every science, from geology, to cosmology, to evolution, and so on. The design argument, however, hangs on as a more respectable if somewhat embarrassing option. "Look round the world," Cleanthes says, in Hume's *Dialogues*, "contemplate the whole and every part of it: You will find it to be nothing but one great machine, subdivided into an infinite number of lesser machines, which again admit of subdivisions to a degree beyond what human senses and faculties can trace and explain. All these various machines, and even their most minute parts, are adjusted to each other with an accuracy which ravishes into admiration all men who have ever contemplated them. The curious adapting of means to ends, throughout all nature, resembles exactly, though it much exceeds, the productions of human contrivance; of human designs, thought, wisdom, and intelligence" (Part II).

Given that we don't see complex adapted machinery, such as solar systems, human eyes, and DNA, come about by chance, proponents can infer that such elegant machines are the product of mind. Some deity brought the ingredients together, decreed the natural laws by which they move, and composed the system of nature as an ongoing clock or watch.[17] As Cleanthes puts it, "the Author of Nature is somewhat similar to the mind of man, though possessed of much larger faculties, proportioned to the grandeur of the work which he has executed. By this argument a posteriori, and by this argument alone, do we prove at once the existence of a Deity, and his similarity to human mind and intelligence."

Of course, after Darwin, we can see that the "watchmaker" is "blind"—that is to say, natural selection is a purely mechanical process, without foresight, that adapts organisms to their environments. But while evolution explains the proximate creation of the elegant eye and the bird's wing, the believer can push the designer back to the more remote regions of ultimate causation. The design hypothesis is unnecessary and adds nothing to our understanding of biology, but it is not ruled out entirely either, given that it can take up residence further and further back in the shadows of deep history or in the "unseen intentions" guiding the surgeon's hand, or the mechanisms of DNA, or whatever. Design is a "blank cartridge," as William James pointed out (*Pragmatism*). But he should have noticed that a blank cartridge also makes a loud noise, and, in this case, it helps scare off the anxieties of many.

The design argument does not stand or fall with any specific religion, but rather operates behind many religions as a foundation. Critics are wrong, however, to think that "design" is a theory like other theories, and that it falls apart at the bar of empirical truth. For believers, the design hypothesis is not standing at the ready for predictions about future events. Believers rarely use the design hypothesis to forecast what will happen or what should happen. Rather, it is a cognitive closure that returns the affective or emotional systems to rest (or homeostasis). As such, it captures the past and present in a web of meaning, but its proponents have no interest in turning it into a research program.[18]

The idea that things happen for a reason provides a cognitive closure to stubborn mysteries. If such closure becomes dogmatic and zealously defended, it can become a flashpoint for doctrinal aggression. But if this idea provisionally rests and relaxes a constantly searching mind, and satisfies a neurotic obsession such that prosocial life can resume, then its faults are unclear. As psychologist Rami Gabriel puts it, "Believing that there is an answer might be, at least emotionally, more important. . . . It is no surprise that, in Abraham Maslow's hierarchy of needs, the need for safety and security (in this case, the belief that there is an answer) is prior to the need for self-actualization."[19]

As we've already seen, with Buddha's "avyakata" or unanswerable questions, some people can leave big metaphysical mysteries unsolved and get back to daily life. But others need to get off the fence and commit to a designer in order to get on with things. The therapeutic aspect of the design argument is even more obvious when we see that people cling to it, even when the "problem of evil" threatens to derail it. Some people, for example, would rather deny that the death and suffering of innocents is really a case of "innocent" suffering, believing instead that God only metes out justice. Or consider how polytheism nicely accommodates the problem of evil, because competing finite gods effectively explain the existence of holocausts, famines, and disasters. In all such cases, however, there is still an assumption of intelligent intentions at work behind the scenes. Most mainstream religious people accommodate suffering and "evil" with the expectation that it will one day be made clear.[20] Living in the imperative rather than indicative mode makes such pragmatism reasonable. The takeaway, here, is that metaphysics (in this case religion) is part of the emotional management cultural system.

Religious mystics may object that the design argument is too anthropomorphic, and we cannot assume that God's mind is anything like ours, nor can we assume that we can properly recognize or assess His handiwork in nature. God, for such mystics, is a giant question mark, looming in the great beyond, and our senses and minds are too puny to access Him. For mainstream religious believers, however, this vague God leaves them cold. How can one relate to a vague cosmic principle that has no human-like qualities? For the mainstream devotee, the radical mystic looks no different than the atheist, because both parties cannot relate to a divine power and pragmatically operate through life as if there were none.

Another area where religion impacts fear is its ability to boost confidence. Aristotle points out that the opposite of fear is confidence, "and what causes it is the opposite of what causes fear; . . . the nearness of what keeps us safe and the absence or remoteness of what is terrible: it may be due either to the near presence of what inspires confidence or to the absence of what causes alarm." Dissecting confidence further, Aristotle says there are two reasons why people face danger calmly. They may have no experience with the dangerous thing, or "they may have the means to deal with it" (Rhet. Bk. II, Ch. V).

Taking a boat out in a terrible storm, for example, might not cause you fear, because you've never been out in a boat before, and you have no clue that the storm can kill you. This is the confidence of naivete. On the other hand, you may feel calm because you've successfully piloted your way through many terrible storms and have the requisite skills to deal with it.

For the believer, God provides the "means to deal with" almost anything. It is hard for the skeptic to appreciate this point, but the believer feels a level of confidence that rises well above both the pessimist and the realist. The skeptic will object that it is nothing but the confidence of naivete, premised on ignorance of real conditions. But the religious person is more like the other case. She feels that fearful situations are real and challenging, but a powerful deity "has her back." The believer feels that no matter how bad it gets in the short term, the long term will be just, and good, and she will prevail. Believing that God or gods are helping you is like going into a knife fight with a gun in your possession. You're going to be all right.

No doubt this kind of confidence gets many people killed or harmed. When I lived in Cambodia, I met a former Khmer soldier who assured me that his special Buddha amulet—still worn around his neck—allowed him to survive many battles with Vietnamese enemies. The amulet, he said, prevented bullets from piercing his body. I find this literally dubious, and, of course, those amulet-wearing soldiers who didn't survive the battles are not here to damn the jewelry's supposed powers. But I've no doubt that his religious confidence helped him somewhat. Running at an enemy that is trying to kill you is a necessary part of war, and how you feel about it shapes how well you do it.

Like an athlete who needs to do an elaborate superstitious pregame ritual in order to feel calm or pumped-up or whatever, so, too, the confidence-building of religious ritual or belief is powerful when facing fearful events. The belief or ritual doesn't make it true (e.g., amulets stopping bullets), but it may make you better or more effective in the crisis. And if an individual fails or puts himself at greater risk because of a religious belief, he may still (as in the case of war) provide enough good for the group to survive, so religiously motivated sacrifice (martyrdom) has evolutionary benefits for the population.[21]

Fear management does not result primarily from religious beliefs, but from religious behaviors. Religion often is taken to be a set of ideas in the head, but is more frequently a set of obsessive-compulsive behaviors. The body of the believer is frequently engaged in repetitive perseverations that reflect the kind of embodied or hot cognition system we've already discussed. Consider how similar bodily supplication gestures look across cultures. Acts of supplication recreate or simulate the bodily submissions that entreat some favor from a dominant force. And when the repetitive behaviors are not successful manipulations of the external world, then they often continue as forms of adjunctive consolation for the devotee.

Animistic beliefs dominate the everyday lives of Southeast Asians. There are local spirits, called *neak ta*, in Cambodia, inhabiting almost every farm, home, river, road, and large tree. The Thais usually refer to these local spirits as *phii*, and the Burmese refer to them as *nats*. Even the shortest visit to this part of the world will make one familiar with the ever-present "spirit houses" that serve these tutelary spirits. When people build a home or open a business, for example, they must make offerings to the local spirits, otherwise these beings may cause misfortunes for the humans.

Everywhere in Cambodia, Laos, and Thailand, you'll find these miniature wooden houses with offerings dutifully placed inside them. The spirit houses are usually colored according to which day the owner was born, and they often contain miniature carved people who will act as servants to the spirits who take up residence there. The offerings can be incense or flowers, or fruit, or anything valuable and precious, but the spirits are particularly pleased by shot glasses of whiskey or other liquors. Quality alcohol is an expensive sacrifice and demonstrates the seriousness of the devotee.

The offerings are designed to please *neak ta* and *phii*, but also to distract and pull mischievous spirits into these mini-homes, thereby sparing the real homes from malady and misfortune. Most businesses and homes in Cambodia and Thailand, for example, have these shrines. The mix with Buddhism is so complete that monks frequently make offerings to these spirits, and the Buddhist pagodas have little spirit shrines built into one corner of the temple. The more recent Buddhist religion is built on top of this much older animistic system—animism was never supplanted by modern beliefs.[22]

The belief that nature is loaded with invisible spirits that live in local flora, fauna, and environmental landmarks is generally characterized by Westerners as "primitive" and highly irrational. And even religious devotees of monotheism in the developed West look down their noses at animism. The developed world usually tells a familiar Comtean narrative; early religion was animistic and polytheistic, but then we progressed to monotheism as we became better educated and advanced, while the less developed pagans kept on with their anachronistic animism. In this progress myth, animism is way down on the ladder, but a more nuanced appreciation of religion around the globe reveals both the ubiquity and the intelligence of animism.

Most of the world is made of animists. In actual numbers and geographic spread, belief in nature spirits outweighs the familiar Western Axial Age contenders. Almost all of Africa, Southeast Asia, rural China,

Tibet, Japan, rural South and Central America, as well as the indigenous populations of the Pacific Islands—that is, pretty much everywhere except Western Europe, the Middle East, and North America—are all dominated by animistic beliefs. Even places where later religions such as Buddhism and Catholicism enjoy *formal* recognition as national faiths, much older forms of animism constitute the daily concerns and rituals of the people.

The well-traveled Darwin himself noted the universality of animism when he said, in the *Descent of Man*, "I am aware that the assumed instinctive belief in God has been used by many persons as an argument for His existence. But this is a rash argument, as we should thus be compelled to believe in the existence of many cruel and malignant spirits, only a little more powerful than man; for the belief in them is far more general than belief in a beneficent Deity."[23]

Many Western theists assume that animists are highly uneducated and unscientific, and eventually they will "evolve" into a more scientific view of God—a rational God of natural laws (who is also omniscient, omnibenevolent, and omnipotent). For their part, many secularists contend that all theists will eventually join the evolution beyond even monotheism. We all previously believed that storms, floods, bad crops, and diseases were caused by irritated local spirits (invisible persons who were angry with us for one reason or another), but now we know that weather and microbes behave according to predictable laws, and there are no "intentions" behind them. This view of nature as "lawful" and "predictable" and "value neutral" has given those of us in the developed world power, freedom, choice, and self-determination. This power is real, and we can be sincerely thankful to benefit from dentistry, and cell-theory, antibiotics, birth control, and anesthesia.

But two things are worth noting. Contrary to its own self-image, monotheism has not really been "rational" since the brief reign of Deism during the Enlightenment; in fact, actual monotheism of the last few hundred years has been staunchly fideist, or faith-based. Martin Luther's suggestion, that a good Christian should "tear the eyes out of his reason," is still a default position for many believers. And the second point worth making here is that animistic explanations of one's daily experiences may be every bit as *empirical* and *rational* as Western science, *if* we take a closer look at life in the developing world.

I am not making the usual relativist argument that indigenous people have an equally good epistemology and logic—though entirely different from our own.[24] On the contrary, I want to suggest that a universally recognizable rationality (in animists) can be read as an understandable (albeit unfamiliar) response to radically different data (i.e., daily experience with a capricious Nature). Living in a hostile world produces the unique affective and cognitive responses of animism.

Consider animism in context. Animism can be defined as the belief that there are many kinds of persons in this world, only some of whom are human. One's task, as an animist, is to placate and honor these other spirit-persons.

It is important to remember, however, that the daily lives of people in the developing world (or even the world before the Industrial Revolution and urbanization a couple hundred years ago) are not filled with the kinds of independence, predictability, and freedom that we in the developed world enjoy. Frequently, one does not choose one's spouse, one's work, one's number of children—in fact, one does not choose much of anything when one is very poor and tied to the survival of one's family. In *that* world, where life is truly capricious and out of one's control, animism seems quite reasonable.

It makes more sense to say that a spiteful spirit is temporarily bringing one misery, or a benevolent ghost is granting favor, than to say that seamless neutral and predictable laws of nature are unfolding according to some invisible logic. Unless one could demonstrate the real advantages of an impersonal lawful view of nature (e.g., by having a long-term, well-funded medical facility in the village), the requisite experiential data to overcome the animistic view will never manifest. Our First-World model about neutral predictable laws will be an inferior causal theory for explaining the chaos of everyday Third-World life. In the developing world, animism literally makes more sense.

I've been arguing that religion provides some order, coherence, respite, peace, traction against the fates, and perhaps most importantly, it quells the emotional distress of human *vulnerability*. Many ritualistic practices (like those in animism) provide some genuine relief for anxiety and agony, by furnishing small behavioral gratifications. Religion's main function—especially animism—is not as a path to morality; nor can it substitute for a scientific understanding of nature. Its chief virtue is emotional management. Powerless people turn to religion and find a sense of relief there, and this helps them psychologically to stay afloat. Those who target religion and wish to abolish it—such as the Marxists and the New Atheists—seek to pull away the life preserver, mistakenly blaming the floatation device for the drowning.

Consolation has a significant physiological aspect and should not be overintellectualized. Yes, contemplative reflection on death and immortality is a uniquely human activity, and religion alleviates such existential anxiety via philosophical ideations. But most daily religious activity calms and/or distracts the devotee through *adjunctive behaviors*, which act as positive self-stimulation, or stimming. All humans engage in stimming behaviors (e.g., nail biting, hair twirling, constantly checking our smartphones), but more intense forms can be seen in those on the autism spectrum. Temple Grandin (2011) points out, "When I did stims such as dribbling sand through my fingers, it calmed me down. When I stimmed, sounds that hurt my ears stopped. Most kids with autism do these repetitive behaviors because it feels good in some way. It may counteract an overwhelming sensory environment, or alleviate the high levels of internal anxiety these kids typically feel every day. Individuals with autism exhibit a variety of stims; they may rock, flap, spin themselves or items such as coins, pace, hit themselves, or repeat words over and over (verbal stims)."[25]

Calming or distracting forms of self-stimulation are part of the larger phenomenon, described in animal ethology as adjunctive behavior.[26] During natural and artificial conditioning, animals key in to behaviors that are regularly paired with rewards, but which have no necessary connection or causal role in delivering the reward. Lab pigeons, for example, will peck a small light that turns on just before a food pellet is released. Eventually this irrelevant light-pecking behavior becomes a time-consuming intensive behavior in between feeding events.[27]

The Pavlovian adjunctive behavior takes on a life of its own, and persists even after experimenters omit the food reward whenever light-pecking occurs (i.e., punishing the behavior). Similarly, rodents, cows, and other animals will engage in adjunctive water consumption when hungry. Ordinarily water consumption is naturally paired with eating, but when experimenters reduce food or extend the temporal intervals between food rewards, animals will drink double and triple the amounts that thirst would dictate. Adjunctive drinking is a kind of stimming behavior that may reduce stress and regulate dopamine while the animal is in a frustrated SEEKING phase of anticipation. The stimming behavior is palliative when more productive or inducing behaviors do not work or cannot be executed.

Religion is filled with ritualized behaviors, including ceremonial body movements, routinized manipulations of prayer beads, talismans, and totems, candle lighting, supplications and prostrations, prayer recitations, collective singing, holy water rites, pilgrimages, sacrifices, and so on. When our SEEKING systems are aroused (e.g., the promise of food), but there is no way to satisfy it, we engage in adjunctive behaviors.[28] But this is also true of long-range human seeking or the teleological projects that we might generally call "hope." Our prayers are hopes for family benefit and other successes, both mundane and spiritual. For most mainstream religious believers, this long-range seeking or hope is not the juvenile desire to live forever, but more impressive and familiar. All parents, for example, want to protect their children from harm, but very quickly we encounter the impossibility of perfect protection. However, the painful ache and urge to protect does not diminish accordingly. It burns quietly at all times, even while our realism acknowledges its inevitable frustration. Religious stimming is a partial psychological rescue.

Adjunctive repetitive behaviors may be byproducts of adaptive behaviors, because certain kinds of repetitive actions ordinarily produce helpful results—as when repeated pecking on shiny trash releases food crumbs for city pigeons. Adjunctive light-pecking behavior in laboratory pigeons may be a byproduct of otherwise adaptive routines. For humans, prayer can be seen as an adjunctive version of the otherwise helpful habit of asking other people for help.[29]

Prayer and other rituals such as rain dances are forms of adjunctive behavior that make people feel better in situations where they have no better action possibilities. These behaviors make us feel better because our affective system (SEEKING or RAGE, etc.) has been ramped up to accomplish something, but there is nothing we can do in this circumstance—the pigeon cannot make the food come faster, the farmer cannot make the rain come, the mother cannot bring her baby back to life. "Could praying be an adjunctive behavior," Panksepp asks, "that gives human beings the illusion that they are somehow able to magically change their fates?" (2012, p. 116). These are the neural roots of religious beliefs that need further study.

I am suggesting that religious rituals are partly adjunctive behaviors (culturally sanctioned and transmitted) that help devotees to manage their emotional lives (e.g., hopes and vulnerabilities), and this makes sense out of many of the seemingly paradoxical behaviors of religion when considered from the inadequate rational agent model. Among other things, religion is a culturally structured set of psychobehavioral perseverations, often providing some return to equilibrium when other resources and consumption activities cannot do the work. When a loved one dies, we feel an overwhelming need to "do something." But, really, there is nothing to be done. Religion is helpful in those moments, not because it solves problems, or enlightens, or anesthetizes, but because it gives us something—usually very precise and elaborate—to do. It is not the beliefs that console, but the ritualized activities.

Oftentimes, the explicitly noetic aspects of religion reinforce and further articulate the physiological forms of anxiety reduction. The grooming touch of a warm hand on the grieving or anxious person is recreated in linguistic format to bring relief to the troubled heart. Even a cursory survey of gospel lyrics will make the case obvious. The consoling balm of a friend's or parent's care is transferred to God and made totalizing and absolute in the cultural poetry of religious song: "The Lord's our Rock, in Him we hide. A Shelter in the time of storm. Secure whatever ill betide. A Shelter in the time of storm."

FROM FEARING TO FIGHTING

It is common for defenders of religion to argue that it makes men more tolerant, more loving, and more generous. In short, defenders of religion often endeavor to show that it produces the goals of *liberalism*. In fact, my own project—an agnostic recommending the good qualities of religion—might appear to be just such a liberal defense of religion's social psychology. That interpretation, however, would be a misinterpretation of my project.

My goal has been to show that religion is a cultural mechanism of emotional management, and emotional management is adaptive—leading to the survival of human individuals and groups. But emotional management should not be confused with emotional taming or subjugation. Cooperation is good for human beings, but sometimes conflict works even better.

Sometimes it is necessary for illiberal emotions—ones that promote belligerence—to rise to the defense of a population. The adaptive value of anatomical traits is clearly relative to the animal's environment—cuddly fur, for example, is helpful in mammal bonding, but sharp teeth or dangerous antlers are helpful in mating competition and defense. Emotions are similarly relevant to specific life demands, and cultural mechanisms that elicit helpful emotions during appropriate environmental challenges constitute an important means of survival. Religious management of emotion acts like an external, cultural exoskeleton for Homo sapiens.

Religion not only defuses or reduces emotions, it sometimes transforms emotions for other goals. For example, blind fear or anxiety can be transformed through religious scripture, image, and sermon into a form of productive reverence. Admiration, respect, veneration, and reverence are crucial emotions for religious life, and they emerge as mixtures of ingredients including fear, adulation, and purity (the hygienic opposite of disgust).

Americans, priding themselves on unfettered individualism, forget or discount the importance of reverence and respect for authority. Earlier Western cultures (e.g., monotheistic theocracies), and Eastern cultures (e.g., Confucian influences in the Far East and caste-system Hinduism in South Asia) structured society on, among other things, emotions of reverence. Consider reverence in the context of human social evolution. The organization of human groups should be understood in relation to environmental resources.

The *Family-level group* refers to a foraging society of up to 35 people that re-forms each season. In this hamlet community, leadership is not permanent, but specific to the task at hand, whether that be hunting or making weapons. The *Local-level group* is five to ten times the size of the Family-level group and, being less nomadic, includes organization for food storage and common defense. The shift from hunter–gatherer band to agrarian state in the Holocene influenced a "release from proximity"—that is, a loss of immediate reciprocal dependence.[30] To facilitate better cooperation, religion helped humans develop fictive kin bonds (making "family" from non-blood related comrades). Homo sapiens expanded their care circle of empathy to nonrelatives, but also transformed fear to emotions of awe and reverence—because these contributed to chief or "big man" loyalty.[31]

The *Big-man group* is a type of local-level band consisting of 350 to 800 people featuring a leader who decides for the group how to manage risk in collective projects. In trade relations with other tribes, for example, the Big Man is the go-between, or, in arbitrating internal disputes, the Big Man decides who is right, who is wrong, and what is to be done. Additionally, the Big Man also serves as a master of ceremonies in ritual activities. The length and extent of any Big Man's rule depends upon the group's reverential loyalty, usually garnered via the Big Man's personal charisma. Subsequent levels of social organization emerge later, such as the *Regional polity,* with over 1,000 people, and eventually the *State* with its millions, but for our purposes we can stop here. Simply notice that reverence for authority is an ancient form of social cohesion, which assists in an adaptive, decision-making division of power. Reverence for God, for your leader, for your parents, and other authority figures, was a beneficial mood, provided those authorities were benign. Reverence flowed up, and benefits flowed down.

However, the case of emotional transformation I want to explore here is the transformation from fear to rage. There is a smooth transition from fear to anger, because fear forces us to focus our attention on potential dangers. Fear tends to produce tunnel vision, locked on the menace, and this is helpful if a real threat is imminent.[32] Fear stops you from pursuing your own pleasures and goals, and prioritizes safety over everything else. Fear is extremely helpful in a hostile environment, because it motivates defensive action.

"Fear," religion scholar Robert Fuller explains, "not only mobilizes us to defend physical territory but also mobilizes us to defend our cultural territory. Such defense invariably requires heightened loyalty and conformity on the part of the threatened group" (p. 33). Fuller has noticed that dramatic scriptural stories, such as the apocalyptic *Book of Revelation* in the Bible, are very effective in transforming fear into fear-induced anger.[33]

The *Book of Revelation*, or the *Apocalypse of John*, was written in the early nineties of the Common Era (during the reign of Emperor Domitian). It is a beautiful, frightening, jumble of end-time forecast, conspiracy history, and veiled sociopolitical manifesto. The description of monsters involves, among other things, a giant red dragon (12:3), a hybrid leopard-bear-lion beast (13:2), and a two-horned beast that emerges from underground (13:11). There are also many plagues and pestilential trials in the story, including human-headed locusts, and Jesus crushing impious people in a giant winepress—making a river of blood.[34]

Originally, these terrifying stories would have been read aloud to a public audience. With repetition and drama, these narratives would have created an intense fear and dread in the listeners. Even in today's secular age, ghost and monster stories are highly effective in activating our old-brain emotional systems, so imagine how powerful they are in a literal paradigm in which the end of the world is imminent.

The goal of religious terror is not to whip up fear and leave it at that. Rather, religious emotional management uses fear for two main purposes, both of which employ fear-driven anger. First, fear of hell, or being smashed in a human winepress, or any number of Hieronymus Bosch scenarios, serves as the great motivation for increasing anger at oneself. One does not generally improve one's moral habits until after one has become angry enough at one's own behaviors. And this is because guilt and repentance are acts of aggression against one's own hedonistic tendencies. Impulse control is generally good for social animals like us, and most impulse control is a kind of aggression toward the self. It is adaptive aggression because it constitutes self-discipline, but it is an emotional transformation from fear to anger.

Too much anger at the self, however, creates a masochistic person and culture—focused on guilt, shame, and the ascetic denial of all pleasure and happiness. This tendency ebbs and flows in religion, and we see it in the overboard self-loathing of some Hindu mendicants, Catholic priests, fundamentalist Islamists, starving Buddhist monks, and so on. Mainstream religion tends to bring just enough self-loathing to the devotee to improve his virtue, but not enough to grind down his self-esteem.

Subsequently, religion is very effective in getting the fear-driven anger directed outward, toward threatening enemies. According to psychologist Robert Plutchik, anger "blunts feelings of personal insecurity and prevents feelings of helplessness from reaching levels of conscious awareness."[35] If directed at a perceived enemy, fear-driven anger unifies a group into greater loyalty and cooperation against this common enemy.

The stories, imagery, and rituals of religion have long managed these emotional ingredients into adaptive strategies. "Apocalyptic literature linked experiences of fear, anger and resentment with culturally elaborated eschatological hopes, and thereby forged lasting communal and theological bonds among early Christians" (Fuller 2007, p. 35). Other religions, too—particularly more fundamentalist strains—are fond of apocalyptic stories and imagery, because these tend to furnish convenient cosmic enemies and an urgent need for purity and allegiance among the devout.[36]

It is here that the critic of religion often will lose all patience and denounce the whole enterprise as an outmoded tribal source of violence against outsiders. Hasn't religion drummed up hostility against innocent out-groups and pursued their destruction (e.g., Catholics vs. Protestants during the Thirty Years' War, the Crusades, the Second Sudanese Civil War, etc.)? Sadly, yes, this is true. Many contemporary liberal intellectuals, however, have not had the requisite experience to realize that some of your perceived enemies are indeed your real enemies.

People who dismiss religious-fueled rage as intrinsically evil or primitive, have usually never faced real enemies. In prosperous Western liberal democracies, it is easy to think of one's enemy as a misunderstood force, whom one can eventually negotiate with and come to some détente. In such genteel circumstances, religious rage is indeed too much. Would that such circumstances were long-lived and ubiquitous. But they are neither.

We might cherry-pick cases of melodrama, and dismiss pugilistic cultures who saw "foreign hordes at the gate," or some such paranoia. But it is easy to forget that sometimes there really are foreign hordes at the gate. Sometimes real enemies want your destruction and want what you have. The no-borders assumptions of the Left are only noble and righteous if (1) the émigrés share liberal values, and (2) the ecological and economic resources are plentiful enough that no one will have any competition for survival. Because there has never been such a benevolent ecology, for anything longer than an historical blink of an eye, it seems unlikely that all parties will tolerantly endure their own miserable decline. American tolerance has been premised on the expanding wealth of frontier and empire, but reduce that expansion, or reverse it, and see the return of adaptive tribalism.

Sometimes enemies must be fought and stopped, and religion has played a role in mobilizing loose collaborators into a unified defense front. The open-hearted humanitarian person wonders: How bad can the threats be? Do we really need the melodramatic narratives of religion to help us fight our battles? Well, consider some notorious invaders. Millions of people died during the Mongol invasions of Eastern Europe in the thirteenth and fourteenth centuries. Timur's bloodthirsty campaign to establish a Muslim caliphate killed an estimated 15 million, during the fourteenth century. Or consider more recent conflicts, such as the Rape of Nanking, the Nazis, the Lebanese Civil War, the Hutu and Tutsi conflict in Rwanda, the Khmer Rouge Killing Fields, and the Syrian conflict. Confronting organized enemies who want your demise and your resources sometimes requires culturally structured counterviolence. Religion sometimes comes to the rescue, by forging a force of resistance, and, to put it embarrassingly and honestly, a force for plundering, too. This is not in keeping with our contemporary liberal views of religion, but such liberal views are not in keeping with the history or anthropology of religion.

Art, like religion and political rhetoric, can cultivate moral sentiments and inspire moral action. As "affect management," culture has the potential to paint the Other as horrifying (e.g., Islamophobia, homophobia, anti-Semitism) or to paint the Other as brethren. Reconfiguring antisocial somatic markers created by religious demonization is fundamentally a cultural therapy project, too. Religion often demonizes the Other (stirring fear and anger), but then when threats subside, religion heals and unifies (fostering prosocial care emotions across boundaries).[37]

Recent social psychology suggests that human tribalism (underwritten by amygdala-based fears about out-groups) might be inevitable, but also highly susceptible to revision. So flexible and promiscuous is in-group favoritism that it can be weaned off the usual nefarious criteria of blood ties, race, sex, and class, to be reassigned to more benign affiliations. Psychological experiments reveal a whole range of criteria for in-group bias.[38] For example, test subjects have been shown to award higher payoffs to arbitrary in-groups, such as people who just happen to share the same birthday as the test subject. And in-group bias can be demonstrably strong when subjects share allegiance to the same sports teams, and so on.

A fickleness of tribalism is potentially good news for re-educating bigots, giving new hope to liberalism generally. But, of course, such promiscuity or flexibility of affective bonds also reduces positive solidarity mechanisms, including loyalty.[39] Liberalism often forgets that strong tribal forms of socioeconomic organization—families, for example—still do most of the day-to-day living, dying, cooperating, and conflicting well below the radar (and the ideals) of abstract state-level egalitarianism. Many small subsistence groups, such as families, tribes, and chiefdoms, continue to struggle for resources inside the larger political frameworks of nation-states, and this means that the psychology of vulnerability is a daily experience. These smaller us–them dynamics continue to draw on the ancient dialectic between xenophobia and xenophilia. Therefore, fear-induced anger, like other emotions, may continue to have adaptive utility in our contemporary biological and social environments. But positive virtues, too, like loyalty, are strong in these smaller subsistence groups, and their ethical orientation can hardly qualify as utilitarian.

At the more personal level, consider this transformation from fear to anger. Earlier in this chapter, we quoted Darwin's claim about fear. Recall his observation that "Fear is the most depressing of all the emotions; and it soon induces utter, helpless prostration."[40] One way we've seen this helplessness overcome is the movement to outwardly directed anger. Nothing rousts a person from depressed, fear-based torpor like a fit of rage. Anger never fails to put a spring in your step. It may horrify us to acknowledge such an ignoble root of the purpose-driven life, but my defense of religion cannot be a whitewash. More horrible still, for some readers, might be the fact that I'm also praising even these illiberal aspects of religion. But these, too, are part of religion's adaptive success, and nobody said the survival of our species would be pretty.

WHAT IS RAGE?

In a sinister but playful mood, Freud quotes the Romantic poet Heinrich Heine's description of the good life: "Mine is a most peaceable disposition. My wishes are: a humble cottage with a thatched roof . . . and a few fine trees before my door; and if God wants to make my happiness complete, he will grant me the joy of seeing some six or seven of my enemies hanging from those trees. Before their death I shall, moved in my heart, forgive them all the wrong they did me in their lifetime. One must, it is true, forgive one's enemies—but not before they have been hanged."[41]

This bit of gallows humor helps us, Freud thinks, to recognize a true aspect of ourselves—an aspect that usually lies submerged under the surface of the sunnier socialized image of ourselves. He argues that "men are not gentle creatures who want to be loved, and who can at the most defend themselves if they are attacked; they are, on the contrary, creatures among whose instinctual endowments is to be reckoned a powerful share of aggressiveness." My neighbor, Freud says, is not just a potential helper or sexual object, but also a prospective target for me to vent my aggression. I am tempted to "exploit his capacity for work without compensation, to use him sexually without his consent, to seize his possessions, to humiliate him, to cause him pain, to torture and to kill him. *Homo homini lupus* (man is a wolf to man)."

Freud derived his pessimism from *experience* (via the headlines of any newspaper, plus his own personal familiarity with anti-Semitism), as well as from a Darwinian view of the human animal. We must have a fair share of aggression in our "instinctual endowments," else we would never survive the severe challenges of living to adulthood (e.g., avoiding predators, outstripping competitors, fighting enemies). In his structural model of the psyche, Freud calls this selfish, instinctual, amoral aspect of the self, the "it"—the Id.

Rage is a powerful force that, along with other socially deleterious impulses, lives like a frustrated virus in the dark cellars of the Id. The Ego (the "I") emerges slowly in the post-uterine life of the baby and forms a node of conscious awareness—a locus of self-identity. Later, in toddler life, the child internalizes the values and mores of the external society (the nuclear family), regulating its own behavior by internal conscience rather than parental punishments. But, unfortunately, sometimes it all goes wrong. When conditions are right, the viral rage escapes the usual superego subjugation and vents its terrible energy on hapless victims.

Developmental psychology suggests that we all get a "policeman" in our own heads if parents do a decent job of raising us. A child's basic mix of love and fear toward her parent is utilized in the earliest forms of discipline. If the parent scolds the child after some infraction, the child will feel the direct fear of the parent but also the fear of the loss of parental love. These two fears combine to form a powerful motive to accommodate the wishes of the parent. The move from external control (parent) to internal (conscience) happens when a more mature child encounters reasonably consistent and just punishments from the parent. The natural aggression that a child points outward toward its external punisher, can turn back upon the self when the parent remains a lovable (nonabusive) and consistent force in the child's life.

When the child's aggression turns upon its own behavior and desires, it provides the repressive force requisite for self-mastery and the formation of conscience. If a child is brought up by an unloving and overly strict parent, then the child's own aggression stays trained outward (on its abuser and subsequent surrogates), failing to turn inward. But if the parent is overindulgent and too lenient, then the child's aggression has nowhere to go but inward—causing an overly severe superego. Thus, abusive parents create outwardly rageful offspring, and indulgent parents create inwardly rageful (self-punishing) offspring.

In reality, of course, human character formation is much more complicated than this, but Freud's explanation continues to be highly influential in our understanding of aggression. As we mentioned earlier, religion helps this process of managing or directing anger. Turned in on the self, anger facilitates the repression that is necessary for us to live in a large collective of competing desires and interests. Religion teaches us to "turn the other cheek," and "do unto others," and so on. But then, when the collective is under threat, religion redirects our anger away from the self and the in-group, and outward to the "infidels," or "pagans," or "heathen," or "idolaters."

Rituals such as the New Zealand *haka*—practiced by Maori people, and now by many non-Maori "Kiwis," reveal how group behaviors can amplify rage for potential battle. Engaging in the body gestures (e.g., chest thumping, foot stomping, tongue protruding grimaces) in a collective group is an overwhelming experience. These activities really create a level of intensity inside the actor that is alarming and exhilarating. Even performing the *haka* at a trivial sporting event can make you feel like you're able to do superhuman violence and irresponsible acts of altruism and vengeance. Imagine how similar forms of embodied cognition can motivate a group of religious warriors.

Is rage always an impulsive expression, without calculation, planning, or forethought? Is it explosive, like a mysterious animal that bursts out of a human being? Or is it merely the last culminating violent gesture in a long series of mental meditations on one's own wounded pride? Is ego-consciousness quietly fomenting rage for long stretches before rage finally sheds its cognitive tutor and makes its own terrible way?

According to the affective neuroscience view we've adopted through out most of this book, anger is like the other basic emotions in the sense that it originates in the old brain (brain stem and limbic system), but it wends its way elaborately through the neocortex and, in particular, the frontal lobes. Unlike nonhuman animal rage, human anger cycles through a feedback loop of cognitive calculations and affective feelings. Our frontal lobes help us to expand anger into our future planning, and to retrieve historical injuries from memory, weaving together a narrative of mistreatment and threat by enemies and righteous revenge. Religion helps us sustain this long-range anger, focusing it and nurturing it into a tool of ruthless competition.

Rage is intimately connected with indignation, which is closely linked to subjective notions of justice. The emotional shades into the intellectual and vice versa. One of the common aspects of narcissistic monsters is the inability or unwillingness to confront existence and accept it on its own terms. Healthy socialized human beings learn to live with and even accept some degree of anxiety, frustration, hostility, and aggression in their lives (in their romantic lives, their role as parents, children, siblings, schoolmates, office colleagues, etc.). Of course, even for a healthy person, there's a limit to the amount of frustration one can and should bear, but the poorly socialized person finds that limit very nearby.

Sociologist Jack Katz, who masterfully analyzes the criminal mind in *Seductions of Crime*, points out that many murderers see themselves, at least at the moment of slaughter, as righteous avengers.[42] "What is the logic of rage," Katz asks, "such that it can grow so smoothly and quickly from humiliation and lead to righteous slaughter as its perfectly sensible (if only momentarily convincing) end?" In both cases, when a subject feels humiliation or rage, he has a feeling of impotence or powerlessness—something or someone has forced or compelled the subject. The person feels victimized by forces outside himself, in the case of humiliation, and by forces inside himself in the case of rage. Spouses who feels repeatedly humiliated by their partners, may feel, according to Katz, like their very *identity* is being broken and degraded by the other person. Rage promises to retake the situation.

Humiliation "lowers" one. It makes one feel small. Humiliation reduces, diminishes, lessens, shrinks, dispirits, depresses, casts down, and so on. Rage reverses this downward trajectory. Rage "rises up," "blows up." "It may start in the pit of the stomach," Katz explains, "and soon threaten to burst out of the top of your head." The rageful are cautioned to keep their lids on and not to blow their tops. In response to humiliation, rage might be said to be a psychological ascent (with terrible consequences).

Religion can quell this exploding *elan vital* of rage, or it can stimulate or direct it. But what is "it"? What is the frighteningly powerful energy that we call rage? We share this terrible energy with many other mammals, but ours is uniquely flexible and capable of cultural (religious) sculpting.

Most of us think that an animal behaves in *response* to lots of environmental information, and that's partially true. A male lion or gorilla gets stimulated into procreative behavior by a thousand environmental perceptions—he responds to specific stimuli, such as the smell of the female, the sense that his belly is full, the fact that it's raining, and so on. But as we've seen, affective neuroscience has discovered a finite set of emotional systems (e.g., lust, play, seeking, rage) and these, in turn, operate complex sequences of behaviors once they get triggered. Using electrical stimulation on different parts of the brain (ESB), Jaak Panksepp could trigger lab animals to engage in attack behavior, aggressive behavior, fearful behavior, and even playful behavior—all without the presence of environmental stimuli. In other words, we mammals have "responses" that can be turned on even when they are not *responding* to anything.

When Panksepp first attempted his ESB technique on a cat (whose medial hypothalamus had been surgically implanted with an electrode), the cat was perfectly peaceful. When he administered an electrical stimulation, the cat leaped viciously at his head, a hissing spitting tangle of fangs and claws. As soon as he turned off the ESB, the cat relaxed into a peaceful state and could be petted with no sign of danger. Behaviorists, who resisted the idea of animal emotions, wanted to describe this stuff as "sham rage," but Panksepp called it what it looked like—rage. The fact that humans have had ESB in these precise brain locations and reported intense rage lends credence to the idea that we share a palette of instinctual emotions.

The key brain areas that activate during rage episodes are the medial amygdala to the bed nucleus of the stria terminalis (BNST), as well as the medial and perifornical hypothalamic to the periaqueductal gray (PAG). Affective neuroscience also has identified the main neurotransmitters in rage episodes: substance P, acetylcholine, and glutamate.

The evolutionary functions of rage in mammals can be broken into three main categories: predatory behavior, response to restraint or threat, and in-group competition. Killing another animal obviously has survival advantages for predators, and it looks like the aggression system is mobilized to help aid in executing that difficult act. Additionally, a slightly different form of panic rage emerges when an animal is cornered or restrained. And finally, a slightly different form is elicited when males fight each other for access to females. These are not diverse responses stemming from the same brain activity. Each form of rage behavior is stimulated by a slightly different area of the brain (in ESB experiments), and this suggests that they are natural kinds or discrete emotional-behavioral circuits. It would be interesting to study the brain activity of angry religious zealots (in fMRI studies) to see what circuitry is activated in their hostility phase. Interestingly, increases in the neurotransmitter serotonin reduce all these forms of aggression.

Adaptive anger did not need to wait until Darwinian theory to receive its due. Aristotle also praised the usefulness of anger in certain situations. Contrary to purely pacifist approaches, Aristotle argued that anger was a useful part of the virtuous life—provided one was angry at the right person, about the right thing, for the right amount of time, in the right measure, and for the right purpose. Those important considerations reveal the general complexities of affective management and the specific intricacies of anger management.

Religion has an important role to play here, too. Modern liberal religious traditions—tolerant and egalitarian—have shunned anger as intrinsically destructive, but, of course, the God of the Pentateuch is notoriously and unapologetically angry. Recent sectarian violence in the Islamic world, as well as interfaith clashes (e.g., Buddhists and Muslims in Sri Lanka and Burma) raise afresh the question of religion and rage. But even social justice movements, such as engaged Buddhism and Christian civil rights movements, employ righteous anger to positive ends. The reason, according to Aristotle, why anger is so helpful in moral struggles, is that we are made confident by the sense that we are the wronged, not the wrongers.

Rage can rescue the depressed, and motivate the righteous to fight for justice, but it also can get tangled up in related antisocial emotions like resentment. Resentment is the hunger for revenge, fed by the feeling of powerlessness. According to Nietzsche, Christianity and its moral vision is born out of this specific feeling. Nietzsche and other philosophers use the French word *ressentiment* to emphasize that it is more than a psychological feeling. Ressentiment is also a value system and a moral appraisal of others' actions. According to Nietzsche, when the powerless Jewish minority inside the Roman Empire could not attain status, they slowly reversed the Roman value system—making suffering into a virtue and weakness into "the good." The meek will inherit the kingdom of God.

Freud expanded Nietzsche's genealogical approach toward resentment to a more wide-ranging psychodynamic phenomenon—one that occurs in all of us, yet still fuels social values and norms. Our obsession with fairness, for example, emerges out of our childhood resentment that others have more, e.g., more things, more status, more favor (Panksepp 2012).[43] "If one cannot be the favorite oneself, at all events nobody else shall be the favorite."[44]

Religion can take private resentments and contextualize them in a larger cosmic struggle. The young man feels miserable because he can't get satisfaction in his romantic life? It must be the infidels. The laborer can't get work? It must be the immigrant heathen. This may be unhelpful for the individual devotee, who now has a confused causal picture of his grievance to add to his resentment troubles. But it may be therapeutic in another sense, because it gives target to diffuse animus and promises mechanisms of redress and restoration. The means and the goals of the purpose-driven life do not need to be benevolent. They only need to be dramatic, and exhilarating. Moreover, religious management of anger (or any emotion) did not come about for the sake of individual happiness. If the group is served by religious rage, then the individual's plight becomes secondary.

Rage and fear are basic ingredients in monotheisms, according to Freud because God is simply an abstract version of your parent (usually your father). "Thou shalt not commit adultery," is a well-known edict from the Pentateuch's Ten Commandments (Exodus 20:14). Along with many of the other commandments, it strictly manages social behavior and can be seen as yet another form of cultural domestication. Divine commandments from a transcendent realm help humans dial down intragroup aggression, or RAGE. Violent competition for mates becomes culturally managed by religious rules, because bonds are strenuously protected from interlopers. This, together with elaborate creeds of purity, chastity, asceticism, and guilt, stabilizes the group significantly. But this regulation of LUST and RAGE is often only possible with the counterbalancing weight of religious FEAR.

Religion, particularly monotheism, up-regulates fear in adaptive ways. Freud (1927) recognized the strict *surrogate father* in monotheism, and we now consider it almost obvious that belief in a strict patriarchal God restrains human violence and fosters civilization. Religion helps dial fear up to paranoid levels, because the tribe comes to believe that an invisible all-seeing God is watching our every move (as a toddler perceives his all-seeing parent). In small hunter–gatherer tribes there is great difficulty in violating your neighbors, because everyone lives in the "glass-house" context of small-band moral reputation. As societies get more complex and anonymous, monotheism creates the ultimate glass-house of supernatural omniscience.

God is so much more powerful than any earthly chief or strong man, that He acts as a constant check on power. Before modern law, God was the ultimate insurance against the unchecked tyrant—and the Chinese notion of the Mandate of Heaven (*tiānmìng*) did the same normative work in the Warring States period.

Specific virtues of humility rather than pride and hubris are consistent and inevitable, when even the biggest Big-Man realizes that he is not an alpha after all, but a mere beta.

The ultimate antibullying mechanism is to have an invisible giant bully in a more dominant position than the local alphas. God is that giant, and fearful awe is his emotional signal.

As Paul Seabright points out, even in hunter–gatherer contexts we have "coalitions of losers" who check the power of aggrandizers.[45] Countervailing power is the way that many fragile cooperatives are sustained. Power unseats entrenched power. In small-bands, coalitions of losers can keep aggrandizers from ruining the collective, but much bigger societies, like ours, can benefit from an invisible and totalizing "police" apparatus.

DEVELOPING "EON PERSPECTIVE"

As we saw earlier, religion often reduces anger and other emotions by methods both bodily (e.g., prayer and meditation) and cognitive (reframing negative thoughts in positive frames). Sometimes religion manages anger by "cooling off" the devotee. According to an Abu Dawud Hadith, Muhammad suggested, "If one of you is angry when he is standing, let him sit down so that the anger will leave him, otherwise let him lie down."

The adaptive peace of mind, and the psychological freedom that comes from Buddhist meditation, originate from the ability to contemplate the ephemerality of reality—including the temporariness of my pain and pleasure. Liberation from suffering and anger follows upon the realization that "this too shall pass."[46] Anger and addiction are reduced when we cease to cling to things and experiences. Religion can amplify resentment, or it can decrease it.

Most anger is caused by one or more of these experiences: you feel hurt (you've been rejected somehow), your sense of justice is violated (your sense of right and wrong is disrupted), you are afraid (your or your loved ones' future is threatened).

When I became a parent, I felt—as most other parents feel—like I was growing some totally new *emotions* inside my psyche. Like a new limb emerging on your body, complex emotions—previously unfelt—start to twist their way into your mood lexicon. When I reached my thirties, I imagined that I had experienced the full range of human emotions. I had not lived a sheltered life and I had, by then, felt many very strong emotions. But nothing prepares one for the unprecedented emotions of parenthood. Of course, there are the obvious changes (i.e., you can't believe how much you love this little person). But other darker emotional material emerges as well. For one thing, the guardian feelings of protection and defense became heightened to the stratosphere. I almost drove us off the road once, while trying to keep a mosquito from landing on my baby. This and other ridiculous warrior emotions come flooding in. In China, a car came vaguely close to my son's stroller, and I stepped into the street and punched the side mirror clean off the car. The same "near miss" happened a month later in China (it happened a lot, given the overcrowding), and I almost went to jail. These levels of aggression were quite unknown to me before my son was born. The angry dad is a common literary and Hollywood trope, but the origins of this chronic anger often stem from the frustrated desire to protect loved ones.

Guardian aggressions often stem from a sense of terrible *vulnerability.* Of course, everyone feels vulnerable now and then. But standing with your sick child in an emergency room, while he screams in pain, is an emotion that a nonparent cannot understand. That feeling of vulnerability comes in a magnitude that truly dwarfs everything else. Watching your child suffer, and being unable to fix it, is one of the worst feelings that humans can experience. And the anger that it spawns is truly frightening. My point here is that becoming a parent not only brings new responsibilities (that's obvious to anybody), it also brings totally new "ingredients" into your inner life. It creates new and difficult emotional organs.

Religions seek to reduce some of this suffering. One tactic that we've already seen in Buddhism, Hinduism, Christianity, and Judaism is the adoption of the long-range perspective. I'll refer to this as *eon perspective*. When we are feeling overwhelmed by anger, or despair, or fear, the Buddha asks us to think about the impermanence of our problems and ourselves. Similarly, Stoic philosopher Marcus Aurelius asks us to contemplate the human drama of families, cities, and even nations that lived hundreds of years ago. They all did just as we do. They married, worked jobs, had children, loved and lost, felt great joys, killed each other, and engaged in every other emotional human endeavor. But, Aurelius reminds us, "of all that life, not a trace survives today." It will be no different with the dramas of our own generation.

Of course, eon perspective won't cure every kind of worry and anger regarding family; it will do little, for example, to assuage the anxieties of the emergency room visit. But it might help parents when they're stressing out about the thousand daily anxieties and outrages that accompany domestic life.

When people asked the Buddha why his followers were so joyful and healthy when they lived so simply, he replied: "They do not repent the past, nor do they brood over the future. They live in the present. Therefore they are radiant. By brooding over the future and repenting the past, fools dry up like green reeds cut down in the sun." Most of us, of course, are "green reeds cut down in the sun," but we're all searching for a little more of that "radiance."

THE UPSIDE OF DEMONIZATION

On November 13, 2015, Paris was attacked by a coordinated onslaught of mass shootings and a suicide bombing. One hundred and thirty-five people were killed and over three hundred and fifty were injured. The Islamic State of Iraq and the Levant (ISIL or ISIS) claimed responsibility.

ISIS released an online statement, reveling in the bloodbath and promising more to come. The chilling rhetoric is worth consideration.

> In a blessed battle whose causes of success were enabled by Allah, a group of believers from the soldiers of the Caliphate (may Allah strengthen and support it) set out targeting the capital of prostitution and vice, the lead carrier of the

cross in Europe—Paris. This group of believers were youth who divorced the worldly life and advanced towards their enemy hoping to be killed for Allah's sake, doing so in support of His religion, His Prophet (blessing and peace be upon him), and His allies. . . .

And so eight brothers equipped with explosive belts and assault rifles attacked precisely chosen targets in the center of the capital of France. . . . The result of the attacks was the deaths of no less than two hundred crusaders and the wounding of even more. All praise, grace, and favor belong to Allah. Allah blessed our brothers and granted them what they desired. They detonated their explosive belts in the masses of the disbelievers after finishing all their ammunition. We ask Allah to accept them amongst the martyrs and to allow us to follow them.

Let France and all nations following its path know that they will continue to be at the top of the target list for the Islamic State and that the scent of death will not leave their nostrils as long as they partake in the crusader campaign, as long as they dare to curse our Prophet (blessings and peace be upon him), and as long as they boast about their war against Islam in France and their strikes against Muslims in the lands of the Caliphate with their jets, which were of no avail to them in the filthy streets and alleys of Paris. Indeed, this is just the beginning. It is also a warning for any who wish to take heed.

Allah is the greatest.[47]

Most of the Americans I know have grown up in a relatively safe and prosperous environment—created largely by the postwar boom and the golden age of capitalism (c. 1945–1970s). An economic tide kept ebbing and flowing through the 1990s and the start of the new millennium, when a series of bubbles burst, leaving us with a struggling middle class and an obnoxious wealth concentration in the top 1 percent. But through all of this, we have not faced many enemies on our own shores, nor have we felt the same universal conviction and dread that the Greatest Generation felt toward the Nazis. My point is that life may be getting economically harder in recent times for the middle class, but with rare exceptions people have not been trying to kill us in our own streets.

Most of the people reading this have never had a true *enemy*—someone who wants to kill you. For those lucky people, even the idea of "real enemies" seems melodramatic and paranoid. Surely, they think, we can negotiate our disagreements and celebrate our common humanity. But if you have survived an attack on yourself or your family, you have very different views on strangers, on security, and on universal love.

Even the Catholic activist Dorothy Day, wondered if too much mercy and "cheek turning" transforms us into human doormats. "This turning the other cheek, this inviting someone else to be a potential thief or murderer, in order that we may grow in grace—how obnoxious. In that case, I believe I'd rather be the striker than the meek one struck".[48] Even the saints can't help but feel the tug of war between our sense of mercy and our sense of justice. If a group's religion is all mercy and has no grit or fight for justice, then the group and its religion will go extinct in the competition with even vaguely aggressive neighbors. That would be a case of maladaptive or deleterious religion. Such cases can be found in history (e.g., Mahavira in Jainism, or Albigensians), but they do not survive long.

When I was living in Cambodia, I had the good fortune to meet the very powerful Cambodian monk Maha Ghosananda. He demonstrated the strength of Buddhism by defying the anti-Buddhist Khmer Rouge in the 1970s and by leading many peace marches in the face of terrible threats and even attacks. He tells a story about the need to balance compassion with strength. One must strive for tolerance, openness, and compassionate acceptance, but one shouldn't be naive about it.

Maha Ghosananda's parable tells of a violent dragon who met a bodhisattva on the road one day. The bodhisattva told the dragon that he should not kill anymore and should instead adopt the Buddhist precepts and care for all life. The bodhisattva inspired the dragon, and afterward the dragon became completely nonviolent. But now the children who tended to the animal flocks nearby, seeing that the dragon had become gentle, lost all fear of him. And they began to torment him, stuffing stones and dirt into his mouth, pulling on his tail, and jumping on his head. Soon the dragon stopped eating and became very sick. When the dragon encountered the bodhisattva again, he complained, "You told me that if I kept the precepts and was compassionate, I would be happy. But now I suffer, and I am not happy at all." To this the bodhisattva replied, "My son, if you have compassion, morality and virtue, you must also have wisdom and intelligence. This is the way to protect yourself. The next time the children make you suffer, show them your fire. After that, they will trouble you no more."[49]

Most contemporary religious believers and apologists, East and West, tend to emphasize religion's merciful traditions and liberal, pacifistic messages. But the historian of religion sees this correctly as a pendulum swing and not an expression of essential properties. In increasingly pluralistic countries, with diverse populations, fundamentalist religion (with its clear sense of us and them) is not an adaptive version of religion. But in a hostile environment, in which outside enemies are actively seeking one's destruction, fundamentalist passion, simplicity, and conviction prove beneficial for survival. Religion is good at adjusting its message to meet the changing situation—in part because scriptures are vague enough and diverse enough to mine for both pacifism and belligerence, and all points in between. The messy ambiguity of scripture is a favorite punching bag for critics of religion—whose *indicative* modality requires more coherence for truth evaluation. But scriptural inconsistency can be considered a virtue in a cultural system that needs to draw upon different messages as environmental conditions change.

There have been horrible cases of demonizing and dehumanizing the Other throughout all of history. I wrote an entire book, called *On Monsters* (Oxford, 2009), about the many ways that we culturally typecast and categorize strangers as monstrously threatening—thereby justifying our forms of subsequent aggression. But we must also face the embarrassing and impolite fact that demonizing and dehumanizing your enemy helps you fight him better. It is an adaptive strategy. And then there's the even more impolite fact that occasionally your enemy really is a monster—really is a nonnegotiable malignant force that seeks to destroy your loved ones. Of course, this monster is a product of nature, nurture, and experience generally (not supernatural), but that mundane origin story doesn't make him less terrible. One can tell a nuanced and humanizing story of how a particular ISIS fighter, say Jihadi John (Mohammed Emwazi), developed from a normal teenage boy, but he's still cutting an innocent man's head off.

Fear amplifies the size and strength of a perceived potential threat. If you are afraid of spiders, you see them as much bigger than actual size.[50] And many people who've been assaulted or had a home invasion report the size of the culprit as much larger than his actual size. The fact that fear is easily extrapolated and amplified stands at the very foundation of terrorist logic. The terrorist strikes a few victims directly, but a whole population indirectly.

Demonizing one's enemy is a significant ingredient of the transformation from fear to anger and then retaliatory action. If your enemy is bearing down on you, or your competitors are overcoming you, then you may have to fight them. Demonizing them helps prepare you for what you may need to do. By way of analogy, consider the way a field surgeon objectifies the person she is operating on. She must focus on issues beyond the immediate cutting and pain of the patient—and this may require a slight dehumanizing of the patient. Arguably, this is one of the reasons why medical training still requires cadaver anatomy, when three-dimensional computer modeling is so available. A kind of controlled "brutalization" may be the crucial feature of the traditional anatomy lesson. For example, if you're in dire need of a serious surgical procedure, you'd rather not have a squeamish surgeon who is too sensitive for the nasty trench work. William Hunter, the eighteenth-century British anatomist, pointed out that "Anatomy is the basis of surgery, it informs the head, guides the hand, and familiarizes the heart to a kind of necessary inhumanity." Or perhaps a better analogy is the way that divorcing couples frequently demonize each other during the process, realizing only later that the characterization was more caricature than reality. Such distortions are unfortunate but also efficient in cutting deep connections and speeding painful extrication.

My point is not to give some moral defense of demonization, but to explain it in the context of social conflict. Once demonization starts, of course, it is hard to get back in the box and eventually needs careful defusing. We ignore the adaptive success of such strategies because our moral sensibilities are affronted, but then we won't understand the psychodynamics of angry religious sects, either here or abroad.

Long before our rational higher cognition turns our emotions into principled ethics, it is the work of simpler social and cultural institutions, such as religion, to shape and sculpt our feelings into adaptive resources. Anthropologist Polly Wiessner (2014) studies how informal institutions, such as religion, rituals, and even songs, shape emotion and cognition.[51] Songs, especially in a religious context, are important mechanisms in cultivating and directing fear and anger.

The Enge peoples of New Guinea, for example, solve ecological and political challenges, in part, by musical group manipulation. When a group of friends splits into two hostile factions, as sometimes happens during competition for resources, the newly opposing groups will rile-up violence by singing songs that demonize their new enemies—songs that describe the opponent families as practicing incest, or describe the opponent women as having thorns in their vaginas, and other dehumanizing narratives. But after six months of warfare and several dead, the enemies grow weary and begin to sing peacemaking songs and songs of consolation. The new songs tone down the anger and shift the emotional state to one of reconciliation. This leads to expressions of care, and then meals are shared together between the groups. The songs and the meals pacify the rage and foster prosocial emotions and behaviors.[52]

These high-repetition informal institutions—rife in religious life—do most of the goading and prodding work that humans need in order to work together. Such interactive institutions bond the group, define the transgressions, enact the punishments, and clarify the important ecological demands (i.e., resource acquisition, predator protection) from the perceptual, cognitive, and emotional noise that is always present.

It's safe to say that mass media has almost entirely supplanted religion and other cultural mechanisms as the main engine of enemy demonization. It's unclear whether the intrinsically conflict-driven mass media can also generate the healing phase of reconciliation that is necessary after violent clashes. It would be interesting, for example, to do a comparative study of local religious versus mass media narratives about Japanese people after World War II, because that pendulum swung so successfully from hatred to approval in the decades after Hiroshima.

Ultimately, we need to remember that religion is not nearly as pacifist as currently portrayed. Although enemies of religion, like Richard Dawkins and Christopher Hitchens, have used that point against religion, I have argued that aggression is part of a larger adaptive strategy for group survival. Religion is a major player in the cultural packaging of foes and friends, but it does not seem, contrary to Bertrand Russell's pronouncement, to make humans more *cruel* than their ordinarily available instincts. Sometimes religion helps us to aid the stranger (e.g., the "good Samaritan" story), but sometimes it helps us meet a violent enemy with violence (e.g., the conquest of Canaan in the Old Testament and the Book of Revelation in the New Testament). There is no *absolutely* right thing to do, in the struggle for adaptation. Despite the pretenses of religion, which are absolutist in spirit, it succeeds by fine-tuning and changing its message to the immediate social and environmental pressures. Some of our early pre-Axial religions (e.g., Brahminism, Judaism) facilitated and celebrated xenophobia as an adaptive strategy, while some Axial Age movements (e.g., Buddhism in India, Mohism in China), and then Pauline Christianity, sought to reduce xenophobia.

Can we just love our enemies into submission? Can our own piety transform all our enemies into friends? Sometimes, that is a real option. ISIS magazine *Dabiq* makes it clear that sometimes that is not an option. "The fact is," ISIS warns us, "even if you were to stop bombing us, imprisoning us, torturing us, vilifying us, and usurping our lands, we would continue to hate you because our primary reason for hating you will not cease to exist until you embrace Islam. Even if you were to pay *jizyah* [tax for infidels] and live under the authority of Islam in humiliation, we would continue to hate you."

We might debate the *number* of people who hate you, but there's no debating that ISIS hates you. As I will point out in the next section, ISIS hostility should never be confused with Muslim attitudes generally. But ISIS is, of course, demonizing the West. From the perspective that some fights are justifiable and necessary, it may be strategic and beneficial for the Western soldiers fighting ISIS to return the insults.

THE CHALLENGE OF ISLAM

Throughout this book we've seen that religion is adaptable and adaptive. That is to say, any specific religion has enough scriptural and ritual flexibility to offer guidance on wide-ranging behaviors, and the immediate environmental challenges (e.g., poverty, wealth, war, unrest, peace, catastrophe) select for the most adaptive or fitting behaviors. Those behaviors are guided by emotions, which are managed by religion's imaginative cultural work (e.g., images, dramatic stories, rituals). And human agents have some conscious and intentional role to play in all this—it should not be seen as a purely mechanical play of genes and memes.

Islam is like every other religion in terms of its diverse and even contradictory messages. It should not be expected to be otherwise, because religious "internal contradiction" is a reflection of the fact that some life challenges elicit exactly opposite strategic responses. Sometimes, for example, you need to walk away from a bully, and sometimes you need to punch him in the face. The context usually decides the "contradiction."

Two quotes from the Qur'an reveal the issue clearly. The famous "sword verse" from *surah nine* "Repentance," suggests that Muslims should allow polytheist idolaters a time to convert to Islam and repent. But when the time for repentance has passed, then "wherever you encounter the idolaters, kill them, seize them, besiege them, wait for them at every lookout post; but if they repent, maintain the prayer, and pay the prescribed alms, let them go on their way, for God is most forgiving and merciful" (9:5).[53]

This violence-condoning passage has troubled Qur'an exegetes, but most scholars agree that the violence was a defensive strategy against oppressive polytheists who actively targeted early Muslims. Nonetheless, Muslim proponents of jihad, like Abdullah Azzam (who influenced Osama bin Laden) cited this Qur'an passage as a justification for war against the Western infidels. In fact, the Lebanese branch of al-Qaeda calls itself the Abdullah Azzam Brigades, demonstrating the intellectual debt to Azzam as a spearhead of "scripturally based" radical Islam.

Now contrast that pugilistic passage with the surprisingly tolerant sounding line, "There is no compulsion in religion: true guidance has become distinct from error, so whoever rejects false gods and believes in God has grasped the firmest hand-hold, one that will never break" (2:256). It's not exactly a version of the modern "to each his own," given that the passage later reminds us how the disbelievers "are the inhabitants of fire, and there they will remain." But the passage is for peaceful religious interaction and clearly relaxes any compulsion the zealot might feel to force Islam upon another person.

Those who argue that Islam is more dangerous than other religions because the Qur'an is more pugnacious have not read many religious scriptures generally. The Qur'an is very diverse in its emotional qualities and its behavioral norms. Moreover, the Pentateuch, the Vedas, Puranas, Hindu epics, and even cultural epics of Buddhism, such as *Xi You Ji* (Journey to the West), are filled with violence and righteous recommendations for violence.

We can certainly find oppressive policies—for nonbelievers and believers alike—in the subsequent cultural structures of sharia law, but these often have only the thinnest tether to the theology of Islam. Still religion *is* as religion *does*, and calls for reforming Islam are entirely reasonable if the costs of repressive tribalism have outweighed the benefits. The problem with contemporary Islam is that a small number of ferocious death cults have emerged (e.g., Boko Haram, ISIS, Al-Qaeda, and the Taliban), that do horrible things in the name of Allah. People argue whether these fringe groups are real Islam or not, but there is no "real Islam" or "real Christianity"—only the diverse "waterways" of mainstreams, rivers, and rivulets.

Although I think Islam needs reformation—particularly regarding apostasy, homosexuality, blasphemy, and women's rights—I want to argue that mainstream Islam is engaging in the same emotional management project as all other religions. In particular, mainstream Islam is providing therapeutic consolations, meaning frameworks, emotional domestication for family life, and occasional emotional agitation for defense and security.

Throughout this book, I have assumed a workable notion of "mainstream" religion without bothering much to define it. A few delineations now will be especially helpful in thinking about Islam (and other religions by extension). First, the mainstream religious community can be contrasted with clergy or clerical branches of the same religion. The goals of the lay Buddhist, or lay Christian, or lay Muslim are quite different from the monk, priest, or imam. Secondly, mainstream believers are more down-to-earth than the much smaller *mystic* branches of any given religion. The mainstream lay devotee does not usually have time, energy, or even interest in carefully plumbing the depths of consciousness for epiphanies and cosmic insights. Life in some form of religious isolation is not an option for the mainstreamer, who is strongly attached vertically (to parents, children, and even grandparents and grandchildren) and horizontally (to siblings, cousins, and friends). Additionally, the mainstream believer tends toward moderation in general, because work and family usually restrain extremist tendencies from taking deep root. Usually, for the mainstreamer, dogma and doctrine are secondary to social relations. The mainstream believer contrasts with the radical extremist, the fundamentalist, and the otherwise antinomian. The mainstream believer is a stakeholder in the family and property structures of the majority. This is not some consciously adopted conventionality, but the necessary outcome of being immersed in familial survival. Islamic scholar Maajid Nawaz sometimes calls these mainstream stakeholders "citizens who happen to be Muslims."[54]

It goes without saying that there are many more of these mainstreamers than fringe believers, but how many more? No one really knows. It is reasonable to calculate some approximate figures. If one parish priest, rabbi, or imam can serve approximately two hundred families, and we consider the average family at four persons, then we arrive at one cleric per eight hundred people. That is not an unreasonable ratio given that most religious people are interacting with their leader once a week or biweekly, and in collective activities. By that calculation, clergy make up one-eighth of 1 percent of the overall religious community. Even if we have eight clergy for these eight hundred believers, we only have 1 percent of the overall community. Similarly, we could subtract a 15 percent figure for mystical branches within a religion—which I suspect is extremely generous. Christian, Buddhist, or Jewish mystics tend to engage in idiosyncratic readings of scriptures (or alternate scriptures), and place more emphasis on inner psychological states (such as ecstasy), rather than on doctrines and orthodox teachings. The mystics often lack the strong vertical and horizontal familial and social ties I mentioned earlier.

Finally, we can consider the numbers of radicals or extremists in religion. It is difficult to establish such numbers, because terms like "extremist" are rarely adopted as a positive designation in polling data. More importantly, the meaning of "extremist" or "fundamentalist" is equivocal and more like a family resemblance of related convictions. Certain tendencies, however, are common. The extremist usually reads scripture as literally true, with minimal interpretation. Also, the extremist is zealous about beliefs and behaviors, advocating extreme actions. Purity and disgust loom large in the extremist's sensibilities. Rational debate and empirical evidence have little to no impact on the beliefs of the extremist. For the extremist, social life is secondary to the primacy of religion. And the "seen world" with its "superficial" markers of success, is less important than the transcendental realm.

Although it is hard to measure it accurately, extremism is rare. The reason why it is rare is simple but powerful. Life keeps getting in the way of extremism. It is a rare personality that can shut out the social world of family and friendship, and work, and aging, and sickness, and love. Indeed, the success of most extremist groups hinges on their ability to provide a strong social life (i.e., band of brothers), rather than on their religious devotion per se. The disaffected and the estranged gravitate toward extremism. But even if we generously grant another 15 percent to extremists—again, very generous in my estimate—we still arrive at approximately 69 percent of religious people as moderate mainstreamers. We'll see next that the estimate of extremist Muslims may only be near 3 percent, which strengthens my argument further.

Without this all-important distinction—between mainstream and peripheral religiosity—it is too easy for critics of religion to pick the weirdest antisocial parts of religion to lambaste the whole enterprise. Moreover, it is not arbitrary but essential to my argument to focus on the majority or mainstream, because such gigantic cultural systems as Judaism, Christianity, Islam, and so on, could never persist in idiosyncratic forms that violate survival imperatives. Looking at mainstream religion is tantamount to looking at religion's most adaptive ingredients for survival, given the broad similarities in the evolutionary landscape of Homo sapiens.

Altogether, there are over 1.7 billion Muslims worldwide. How many of those are moderate mainstreamers, who are working through the common trials and tribulations of family, work, education, death, and so on, and how many are extremists? Approximately 85 percent of Muslims are Sunnis (a denomination designated by the belief that Abu Bakr was Muhammad's rightful heir and caliph). The smaller group of Shia (who claim Ali ibn Abi Talib as Muhammad's heir) are divided primarily among Iran, Iraq, and Lebanon, with Alawites in Syria. The explicitly extremist group Taliban (in Afghanistan) are Sunni and are estimated at around 60,000 members. Al Qaeda are also Sunni (spread through the Middle East and Africa) and are estimated between 20,000 and 30,000 members. ISIS or ISIL are Sunni and are estimated at 20,000–30,000 inside Iraq and Syria, with another 30,000–60,000 spread outside Syria and Iraq. Total estimate of ISIS is between 60,000 and 250,000.

So far, these numbers are very small in comparison with the big picture of 1.7 billion Muslims. Still, a handful of lunatics with the right weapons can wreak total devastation, so one cannot be complacent. The anxiety-producing data, however, is the very large number of Sunni Wahabi Muslims from Saudi Arabia and beyond. Wahabism is an extreme interpretation of Islam that takes an ultraconservative view on social issues and scriptural literalism. A Freedom House 2006 study of Wahabi educational literature, available in Saudi Arabia and even at mosques in the United States, revealed frightening levels of anti-Semitism and explicit hatred of non-Muslim Americans—including suggestions that it is a religious duty to hate Christians.[55] The report suggested that this kind of hatred was mainstream in Saudi Arabian Wahabism—a group estimated to be around 5 million in the Persian Gulf region. That is disturbing data, because when we add up these hateful groups we arrive at roughly 5.5 million people who hate non-Muslims, with, of course, a much smaller subset taking up explicit violence.

There is also some disturbing data (from a 2013 Pew Research Study) revealing that very high percentages of all Muslims believe sharia law is divine (a revelation from God) and should be the official law of the land in their country.[56] Essentially, a majority of Muslims worldwide favor theocracy. The same report reveals extremely high support throughout the Muslim world for brutal punishments for law breakers, including cutting off hands for theft, stoning for adultery, and even death for those who try to leave the faith (apostates).

Now these are disturbing data, but the question is whether these larger populations are "radical" in the same sense as the extremists (that is to say, potentially violent), or whether they are just expressing intensely conservative social values (without malignant intent). No one really knows for sure.

American critics of Islam, such as *Act! For America*'s founder Brigitte Gabriel, argued at a 2014 Heritage Foundation forum that 15 to 25 percent of Muslims were radical extremists, and that percentage translated (according to Gabriel) as 180 to 300 million Muslims "dedicated to the destruction of Western civilization."[57] If she is correct, that is a frightening number of hostile Muslims, but it is very unclear how she arrived at her numbers.

Former Muslim Ayaan Hirsi Ali, who has been an active critic of Islam for years, puts the figure of extremism much lower, at around 3 percent.[58] Ali has every motive to inflate the numbers, given that she has received death threats and her own friend Theo van Gogh was stabbed to death by a Muslim extremist in the Netherlands (2004), but she puts the figure at a mere 3 percent. That is still a big number, when you remember the total. It could mean that around 50 million Muslims are extremely hostile to non-Muslims. Importantly, the extremist is just as hostile toward mainstream Muslims, and it is these moderate Muslims who suffer the full brunt of extremist orthodoxy. This point deserves to be underscored, because we tend to see Islamic extremism as directed at the West, but it is equally motivated to purge moderate Muslims and the mainstream "citizens who happen to be Muslim."

The good news, however, is that approximately 1 billion, 650 million Muslims are mainstreamers and do not have a belligerent orientation. Ayaan Hirsi Ali is still worried. "It simply will not do," she writes, "for Muslims to claim that their religion has been 'hijacked' by extremists. The killers of Islamic State and Nigeria's Boko Haram cite the same religious texts that every other Muslim in the world considers sacrosanct."(Ali 2016)

This is not a particularly persuasive argument to fear Islam in general. For one thing, as I've repeatedly argued, every possible adaptive emotional strategy can be found in every major religious scripture. Violence is condoned in every religious scripture because violence has always been adaptive under certain conditions. The same is true of the peaceful passages that instill emotions of care, compassion, and love. Secondly, most Muslim extremists do not appear to be very interested in or even clear about the basic teachings of Islam.

Maajid Nawaz and his group *Quilliam* are working to reform Islam from the inside out, and he is hopeful. But he points out that even though jihadism (seeking sharia via violence) is tiny, and Islamism (seeking sharia via political roads) is around 15 percent, huge segments of mainstream Islam nonetheless are still very illiberal—anathema to the values of human rights (e.g., gay rights, freedom of religion, gender equality, humane punishment).

The impatient skeptic of religion thinks the solution to all this is simply increased secularism. But Nawaz points out that secularism was already introduced to the Muslim world as a correlate to the modernization of the Imperialist and even Ba'athist movements.[59] The failures of such secularism—corrupt puppet governments—have left a pronounced stigma on the secular approach generally. Making Islam more liberal, according to Nawaz, must come from within the Islamic tradition itself. And there are ample resources within Islam for such reformation, but so far little political will to drive it.

Ultimately, resentment, not religion, is the engine of extremism. Religion only masks a deeper dynamic of social grievance, and especially, warped and frustrated masculinity. It is no accident that most extremists are disaffected young men. Yes, there are political and economic grievances among jihad proponents, but there are libidinal forces at work, too. Young men, without positive cultural guidance, can acquire distorted masculinity—such that aggression fails to serve and protect, and instead spills out into antisocial pathways.

The jihadi loser emerges from great frustration: As he develops through puberty, he acquires some of the most intense emotional drives of the human operating system—in particular, lust—but his culture informs him that his own desire, his own body, and the bodies of women, are impure and require repudiation. That interminable frustration can be channeled into a zealous mission to purify everything in the acid of Islamism. Male power is thought to be diminished—a kind of purity defilement—from uncontrolled women (the alluring single woman or the infidel), but when a woman is in some "appropriate" state of affiliation (the obedient wife), there is no pollution and the male's power is increased by his domination of her.

This is not essentially different from the sanctioned sexuality one finds in other Axial Age religions, East and West. Indeed, Islam is historically far less concerned with sexual asceticism than Christianity, as the role model of the many-times-married Muhammad demonstrates in contrast to that of Jesus. Yet the fear and loathing of emancipated female sexuality is a palpable drive within contemporary radical Islam. And the rape cultures of Boko Haram and ISIS represent a further devolution of the "controlled female" fantasy, with rape and slavery sanctified as an act of worship.

There's little to no theological underpinning for this stuff, but there is an irresistibly tempting psychodynamic for frustrated young men who are easily drafted into a pathological band of brothers. For the terminally frustrated male, the promise of women slaves is an enticing, albeit horrifying, recruitment tool.

The pre-modern West also demonized desire. But in the contemporary West, natural sexual frustration is intensified by a culture that throws sex in your face at every turn, reminding you that you're not getting any. These are existential issues because they resonate—rightly or wrongly—at the core of how men see themselves. The problem is that many of our social norms and cultural narratives increase rather than defuse resentment. And resentment is the psychological fuel that gets the fire of violence going, whatever the ideological justification.

Resentment is the hunger for revenge, fed by the feeling of powerlessness. Recall that it was Friedrich Nietzsche who built upon Søren Kierkegaard's use of the French word *ressentiment* to emphasize that this is far more than a subjective feeling. *Ressentiment* is also a value system and a moral appraisal of others' actions. The individual who feels oppressed and excluded is feeling envy and insecurity, but he tells himself that he is, in fact, the morally superior being. Nietzsche argued that the whole of Christianity was born out of *ressentiment*: When the powerless Jewish minority inside the Roman Empire could not attain status in the oligarchic structures and the martial virtue system, they slowly reversed the Roman value system—making suffering into a virtue and weakness into "the good." The arrogant Romans might run the empire, but the meek would inherit the kingdom of God. Sigmund Freud expanded Nietzsche's genealogical analysis of resentment into a more wide-ranging psychodynamic phenomenon—one that occurs in all of us, and still fuels social values and norms.

These insights are important because it is not enough to simply label lone-wolf shooters and ISIS fighters as "mentally ill." Toxic maleness and the specific hydraulics of hate are grounded in originally adaptive biological structures, which need cultural management to find healthy expression. As the neuroscientist Joe Herbert pointed out, young men are coiled tight by testosterone, which drives risk-taking behavior in the service of competition for females (the ancient adaptive imperative). Tilt the balance of young intermale aggression just slightly, and you get the fanatic mindset that we see in jihadist movements and U.S. antifederalist extremism alike.[60]

My suspicion is that the lone-wolf and the jihadi fighter don't have a theory as much as a feeling. These feelings of resentment are a combination of thwarted affective drives (limbic system) plus cognitions about culpability (neocortex). The weaponized loser tries to make sense of his emotions by supplying causal stories and moral judgments about *why* he doesn't have the sexual satisfactions, wealth, or status that he expects. The people he thinks *do* have those satisfactions and freedoms must be brought low or punished, and the unattainable women who withhold their pleasures must be humiliated and destroyed. This is how boys with no specific grasp on Islam can find a convenient "religious" backdrop for their revenge fantasies.

The discrepancy between what the angry man wants and what he gets is eventually theorized, but in a lazy way—he adopts the ISIS ideology, or a Westboro Baptist Church-style Christianity, or homophobia, or antifederalist patriotism, or whatever is ready to hand. The frustrated male casts about for a "cause" of his misery, and mistakes the increasing power of newly emancipated communities for his depletion. Whether it is the son of Muslim migrants who turns his rage on the LGBT community, or the hater of Muslim migrants who turns his rage upon the political champion of migration, the same hydraulic of hatred is at work.

The lone-wolf mass shooter and the jihadi fighter are not as far apart as one might think. The fanatical ideology of ISIS or Boko Haram is just the last ingredient added to a bubbling cauldron of male frustration, rage, and resentment. Anthropologist Scott Atran confirms that most jihadists don't know much about Islam. A few well-chosen pugilistic Quran quotes and homophobic or misogynistic slogans can rileup a resentful male to all kinds of evil. The wellspring of this evil is not in the religion, nor even the economic conditions, or the socially constructed patriarchy, but in profound, implacable resentment. Other factors converge, as Atran notes, to help sculpt resentment into warfare, including the "band of brothers" promise of jihad—which answers to deep-seated social yearnings in isolated and alienated young men.[61]

In short, Islam is like every other long-lasting religion. It has cultural resources within it that can up-regulate or down-regulate specific emotions. If 3 percent of the worldwide Muslim population is using Islam to justify hatred and violence, 97 percent are using it for prosocial and positive ends. If the critic of religion optimistically imagines that a secular cleansing would wipe out even this tiny 3 percent of belligerence, then I simply redirect his gaze to the wake of carnage provided by twentieth century secular revolutions.

Epilogue

Religion is Promethean. Like fire, it is capable of great good and also destruction. At this moment in history, its destructive power may seem dominant—flashing out like bright yellow flames. But I've been showing the value of religion—burning blue flame at the core of the fire.

As we've seen repeatedly in this book, the duality of religious convictions and cultures—at one time, egalitarian and peaceful, at another time tribal and belligerent—flows from the fact that two hearts beat within our breasts. We are that duality. But this is not the juvenile duality of the devil on one shoulder and the angel on the other. Rather, we are each endowed with a handful of adaptive emotional systems (e.g., anger, fear, play/joy, lust), and these are neither good nor bad, but helpful as the specific conditions require. We have anywhere from four to seven "hearts" beating within our breasts. Religion, I've shown, is one of the main coordinators of all that passion.

Religion modulates many of our emotions and behaviors, but who or what will modulate religion when it gets stuck? Sometimes a religion gets caught in a sclerotic mode, unable to adapt to an environmental or social change. Sometimes a religious community becomes terminally aggressive or ascetic, or fearful. In these cases, religions reform or go extinct.

Because I've been arguing that emotions are smarter than we thought, it might seem surprising for me to endorse *reason* as a good moderator of religious excesses. But evolution built a powerful neocortex, with impressive executive functions and impulse control. So, of course, cold cognition (from the frontal cortex) can help slow down the intensity and immediacy of hot cognition (from the limbic system). Unlike most other mammals that share our same affective systems, we can detach enough from our feelings to consider them.

However, I want to be very clear here. Unlike the contemporary rationalists, who see rationality as a cost-benefit calculator that churns out "effective altruism," I think ethical and religious improvement requires "practical reason." When philosophers try to make ethics into geometry or physics, they do so with the best intentions (i.e., objectivity, they assume, reduces squabbles). But they make a terrible error in thinking that mathematical or theoretical rationality is the only true reasonable approach to problems. Subjective experiences, biases, personal histories, emotions, and even friendship and kin-ties, are not compliant in a grid of universally binding rules. But my family, friends, and community members are not variables in a hedonic calculus or coordinates on a Cartesian lattice. Practical reason, originally formulated by Aristotle, is more capacious and capable of handling the realities of our local environment, our social hierarchies, and even our familial preferences.

Practical reason is the best way to analyze and reorient your religious community, because it does not pursue theoretical mathematical certainty, but probable, fallible, and context-dependent problem solving. Newtonian-inspired universalist rationality tries to make all people fungible, and quickly becomes incoherent when real-life values such as favoritism and love crash the grid. Kantians see all persons as idealized equals, guided by logical consistency. And the utilitarians see pleasure itself as an equal and transposable element or variable in the system. Aristotle, however, starts from *real life* and acknowledges that people are already in a value hierarchy—and the *good* comes in many qualitatively distinct forms.

Aristotle sees ethics as an inexact art, but that is a good perspective for regulating the complex cultural system of religion. For example, Aristotle recognizes that family and friendships are not utilitarian cost-benefit relations. There are some important inequalities.[1] Parents, he explains, are responsible for their children—responsible for their existence, their nurture, and their upbringing. He considers this to be a case of positive unequal friendship, and thinks there are many forms of friendship (e.g., teachers and students) that imply the "superiority of one party over the other." Now, this talk of superiority rings strange to our egalitarian ear, but his general point is not very controversial. "The justice," he continues, "that exists between persons so related is not the same on both sides, but is in every case apportioned" to merit, to excellence, to usefulness, and to proximity (emotional and blood). Justice is not "the same on both sides"—it is not the commutative relation of secular egalitarianism. We ought, he says, to render *different* things to parents, brothers, comrades, and benefactors. Religious reformation requires this kind of situated reasoning.

Reforming religion, or moderating it, is not like geometry, but it *is* like medicine and other practical sciences (e.g., engineering). A good doctor does not diagnose simply by applying universal rules to particular cases, nor does she treat all bodies alike. Clinical knowledge is acquired by taking a case history. Philosopher Stephen Toulmin characterizes some typical questions in a patient's case history: "To what extent is a patient's condition a result of earlier diseases, accidents, or other misadventures? To what extent must we explain it, rather, by the patient's family background, upbringing, and experience in life? And what pointers do we need to attend to, if we are to see just what the patient's problem is, and how it can best be remedied?"[2]

These techniques are concerned with the particulars of the patient. Health, like *the good*, is not an abstraction that exists independently of patients or people—the actual contingent history of the person will explain the condition, and perhaps even suggest the medical way forward. An applied science like medicine is a good analogy with *reasonable religion*, because the more particular detail we get—or the more concrete complexity—the more likely we are to resolve decisions wisely. As Toulmin puts it, "Set against any fully described problem, abstract principles do not measure up."[3] Rationality is not a policeman for religion. And Aristotle reminds us that "we must not expect more precision than the subject matter admits."

Although reason can help to catch and redirect wayward religious cultures, it is ultimately a weak and unreliable solution. The answer is not more book learning and science, but better childhoods—in the sense of emotional maturity. Children who don't learn to manage their emotions (via parental discipline and cultural conditioning) are not going to be emotionally mature as adults. No increase in secularism or science literacy will turn emotional extremists into emotional moderates. The best way to reduce religious extremism is to provide children with more stable, nurturing, social environments. They will be less prone to cruelty later in life, and religion will speak to their higher natures.

Some critics of religion have suggested that scientific literacy will prevent the dark machinations of the passions, while others have suggested that we need an alternative adventure narrative—dedicated to heroic liberalism—to capture the teetering hearts of disgruntled teens. This latter option has the advantage of engaging the emotional systems through imagination—something ISIS is good at, for example—but I doubt whether anything generates emotional maturity as well as a childhood of secure attachment with caregivers. There's no panacea, but being loved comes close.

Religion, even the wacky, superstitious stuff, is an analgesic survival mechanism and sanctuary in the developing world and wherever people are suffering. I'm an agnostic and a citizen of a wealthy nation, but when my own son was in the emergency room with an illness, I prayed spontaneously. I'm not naive—I don't think it did a damn thing to heal him. But when people have their backs against the wall, when they are truly helpless and hopeless, then groveling and negotiating with anything more powerful than themselves is a very human response. It is a response that will not go away, and that should not go away if it provides genuine relief for anxiety and anguish.

We might be inclined to remove the supernatural magic of religion and arrive at an enlightened Deism, on the grounds that it is more reasonable and consistent with science. If you can attain this level of wisdom, then no one will be happier than I, but do not mistake it for religious progress. Many of the consoling and therapeutic aspects of religion that I've been praising in this book flow from the magical stuff—God hears my prayers, for example, or the spirits intervene. In mainstream religion, God helps me *in real time*, not as an indirect Deist lawmaker. We cannot get rid of magical thinking, and in most cases don't want to.

In 2017, I spent some time in the Kingdom of Bhutan, studying the unique Vajrayana Buddhism of the region. My guide, Namgay, who is a very devout Buddhist, often cited the maxim, "If you cannot help, then at least do no harm." This idea, "do no harm" (Sanskrit, *ahimsa*) is an important feature of Indian religion generally, and it persists in the far-flung regions, like Bhutan, where Buddhism eventually landed. Principles such as "do no harm" and "increase compassion" (*karuna*) form an ethical umbrella over all manner of metaphysical and supernatural beliefs—forming a protective layer of humanism around some otherwise magical thinking.

Culture doesn't get much more magical than Vajrayana Buddhism, practiced in Tibet, Bhutan, and the Himalayan regions of India: Carved phalluses spout holy water; dreams contain real visitations of the dead; mermaids live at the bottom of some lakes; Buddha statues speak; deities and special monks fly; and astrologers are consulted on most major life events. In fact, Bhutanese people believe that the founder of Bhutanese Buddhism, Guru Rimpoche (8th century CE), is a second Buddha, who brought a more magical tradition because his predecessor's rationalist approach was not effective on the stupid human race. His predecessor, Gautama Siddhartha or Shakyamuni (563–483 BCE), taught a naturalistic psychological dharma of mental training, but the second Buddha brings mystery, magic, and authority. The Vajrayana practitioner is untroubled by the shift to magic, because the best "medicine" for increasing compassion and enlightenment is simply the one that works. Like a bell on a giant mountainside prayer-wheel that dings every revolution in order to bring your meditating mind back to the present, so, too, the magical stories and practices indirectly return the mind to the cosmic project of increasing liberation for all sentient beings.

How does it do this? A simple example might suffice to reveal the chain. And it can easily extrapolate to most other religions. My friend in Bhutan told me that his mother-in-law needed an operation to remove a tumor. She consulted with the local Buddhist astrologer who told her that the best way to build up good karma for the impending surgery was to practice more compassion for sentient beings. She was instructed to decrease the suffering of those less fortunate than she. She donated money to help poor children acquire craftsman skills, and she released some captive fish and birds into the wild. By these merit-making techniques she supposedly improved her chances for a successful surgery (which any skeptic can legitimately doubt), but it's also clear that she slightly diminished the suffering of other sentient beings (which even the skeptic cannot doubt).

My point in this discussion is to show that even the most supernatural religious beliefs can coexist with and even underscore the goals of tolerant humanism. Principles such as "do no harm" and "increase compassion" (karuna), form a kind of *virtue canopy* over all manner of metaphysical and supernatural beliefs. Christianity, Islam, Judaism, and other religions also have such a virtue canopy, but it usually only unfurls when cultural threats abate.

I have argued throughout this book that religion's primary function is not to provide a path to morality or to substitute for a scientific understanding of nature. Its chief virtues are as a "coping mechanism" for our troubles, and as social glue for our community. I am not simply rehearsing the adage "reason for the few, magic for the many." Instead, the slogan should be revised to the less catchy but more accurate, "Reason for the surmountable problems, and magic for the insurmountable."

Critic of religion Sam Harris, in his book *The Moral Landscape*, thinks he sees my argument coming. "Because there are no easy remedies for social inequality," he states, "many scientists and public intellectuals also believe that the great masses of humanity are best kept sedated by pious delusions. Many assert that, while they can get along just fine without an imaginary friend, most human beings will always need to believe in God."[4] He considers this position to be "condescending" and "pessimistic." But my argument—that religion soothes emotional vulnerability—can't be "condescending" if I'm also applying it to myself. I, too, get religious when I hit the insurmountable troubles. Besides, even if it *is* condescending—and I don't think it is—so what? Many true arguments have been condescending.

Like Sam Harris, I know a fair share of neuroscience, but that didn't alleviate my anguish and desperation in the emergency room with my son.

The old saw "there are no atheists in foxholes" obviously doesn't prove that there is a God. It just proves that highly emotional beings (i.e., humans) are also highly vulnerable beings. Our emotional limbic system seeks homeostasis—it tries to reset to calmer functional defaults when it's been riled up. There are aspects of religion, detailed throughout this book, that go straight into the limbic system and quell the adrenalin-based metabolic overdrive of stress.

How do we discriminate between dangerous and benign religions? That is a fruitful question, because it invites all world religions into the discussion. Both the developed and the developing worlds can profitably examine their unique belief systems in light of larger human values. We should employ a broad base of anthropological experience and a healthy dose of practical reason to make the necessary discriminations. Religious ideas that encourage dehumanization, violence, and factionalism should be reformed or diminished, while those that humanize, console, and inspire should be fostered. But as a historian of religion and an evolutionist, I have argued that some of the more quarrelsome emotions will inevitably remain in the adaptive reservoir. David Hume, trying to sift the good from the bad, said, "The proper office of religion is to regulate the hearts of men, humanize their conduct, infuse the spirit of temperance, order, and obedience" (*Dialogues*, p. 82). I have argued that this "proper office" is maintained not by top-down cultural policing, but by natural forces of familial affection, small group cooperation, and the demands of domestic life. These forces create the mainstream of religiosity.

In 2009, in Brazil, the archbishop excommunicated doctors for performing an abortion on a nine-year-old girl who had been repeatedly raped by her stepfather. The stepfather had impregnated her with twins. The girl's mother, too, was kicked out of the church, but the rapist was not. That is the kind of dehumanizing and dogmatic religion that should be reformed. Catholics deserve a better religion than that, and they seem to have gotten one with the election of Pope Francis in 2013. Pope Francis appears to be recalibrating Catholicism back toward its humanizing, consoling, and inspirational dimensions. In large part he does this by his own emotional example, not by didactic doctrine. Are there Catholic extremists? Of course there are. But the natural piety of the mainstream practitioner lives well below the corrupt levels of big church institutions, and below the arid inflexibility of theology. It has always been so, and always will be. Whether it is Catholicism, Protestantism, Islam, Buddhism, or animism, the adaptive virtues can be intensified while the maladaptive vices are reduced. In short, the reduction of human suffering should be the standard by which we measure every religion. Oftentimes, that is the same standard most religions adopt for themselves, but when occasionally it isn't, then we will need vigilance, and a mix of charity, skepticism, and possibly cultural intervention.

The phrase "cultural intervention" is fraught, but the future of interreligious interaction need not be like the past. Although there is still a great deal of religious illiteracy, most us know far more about one another's religions than generations past. How religion goes forward and how it embraces its "proper office" will depend a great deal on the development of globalization. Religious ideologies will certainly struggle with one another—as they always have. But if globalism could reveal the deeper shared project of diverse practitioners, then mainstream religious believers—householders and stakeholders in emotional communities—might find remarkable solidarity.

When I lived in Cambodia many Christian missionaries had recently come to the country to try to win it over for Christ. Cambodia, like other war-torn developing countries, had lost a generation to violence and with that human loss came a cultural loss. Buddhism was targeted as an "outmoded tradition" by the Khmer Rouge, and it was almost completely stamped out. This left a huge ideological hole in the Cambodian psyche. Aggressive Protestant Evangelicals, from the West, explicitly target such vulnerable communities and descend, as soon as it's safe, to convert the "heathen." In developing countries, they go to poor communities and offer the starving locals a bag of rice if they come to church and get baptized as Christians. These rice briberies are common in Southeast Asia, and demonstrate the state of religious "warfare" in a globalized world. Granted, this kind of "warfare" is much better than the old bloody versions, but it's still repugnant.

Evangelicals who want to supplant Buddha with Jesus are convinced that Buddhism is simply false, whereas Christianity is true. The Evangelical missionaries I met in Cambodia were confident that Jesus was God incarnate, whereas Buddha was a mere man—and why would anybody prefer a man to God himself?

A refreshing alternative to this myopic form of religious intervention can be seen in the Catholic missions, particularly the Jesuits in Southeast Asia. Unlike Evangelical missionaries who give food with the ulterior motive of winning conversions, the Catholics just give food because people are starving. There is no means/end negotiation, just charity.

French priest Francois Ponchaud has been a strong humanitarian force in Cambodia since the 1970s, and he opened Western eyes to the tragedies that were occurring under Pol Pot with his famous book, *Cambodge Anee Zero*.[5] Father Ponchaud and many Catholics worked tirelessly in the refugee camps during the 1980s, and today continue to bring relief and support to poor Khmer people. But their conversion policy is very clear, and very different from the rice Christian fundamentalists. The Catholics say that they only wish to "evangelize" through their humanitarian actions—not through preaching, or Bible thumping, or offering rice bribes.

The Catholics don't want to convert the Buddhists, they just want to help them with food, clean water, housing, education, and so forth. The Catholics have a great deal of respect for Buddhism, and they work *within* those ancient spiritual/social structures, not *against* them. In fact, some overly polite Cambodians, who are already familiar with rice Christian conversions, occasionally ask Father Ponchaud if they should convert to Catholicism—now that they are receiving Catholic charity. Ponchaud responds by asking them, "First, can you tell me what you know about Buddhism?" And if the Khmer do not know much, Ponchaud tells them to go learn more about Buddhism first. In fact, the Catholic Church makes the rare convert go through a rigorous three-year catechism before they will baptize them. Criticizing the rushed baptisms by the Mormon Elders, Ponchaud says, "They make pressure, pressure, pressure. Christ liberated us. [Mormon conversion] is not liberation; they make more slaves."[6]

It remains to be seen how these religious competitions will play out. Religions meet each other like tectonic plates. They can press against each other interminably, building up a mountain of strain—with neither side giving an inch; or, the meeting can become a subduction zone, where one tradition folds under the other and slowly melts away. This century promises to bring many such seismic shifts. At the core, however—even below the ideological plates—churns the white-hot emotional sources of all religion. Those volcanic forces will continue to sometimes rupture and explode in hot spots, but they will also build new formations.

NOTES

INTRODUCTION

1. Joanna Rothkopf, "E.O. Wilson: We Should 'Diminish, to the Point of Eliminating, Religious Faiths'," *Salon*, January 28, 2015, http://www.salon.com/2015/01/28/e_o_wilson_we_should_diminish_to_the_point_of_eliminating_religious_faiths/.
2. Ed Kiernan, Nancy Ing, David Wyllie, Robert Windrem, Jim Miklaszewski, and Jason Cumming, The Associated Press and Reuters contributed to this report, "Charlie Hebdo Shooting: 12 Killed at Muhammad Cartoons Magazine in Paris," NBC News, January 7, 2015, http://www.nbcnews.com/storyline/paris-magazine-attack/charlie-hebdo-shooting-12-killed-muhammad-cartoons-magazine-paris-n281266.
3. "IS Claims Paris Attacks, Warns Operation Is 'First of the Storm'," in SITE Intelligence Group Enterprise, November 14, 2015, http://ent.siteintelgroup.com/Statements/is-claims-paris-attacks-warns-operation-is-first-of-the-storm.html.
4. "Vatican Reveals How Many Priests Defrocked for Sex Abuse Since 2004," CBS News, May 7, 2014, http://www.cbsnews.com/news/vatican-reveals-how-many-priests-defrocked-for-sex-abuse-since-2004/.
5. Cary Funk and Lee Rainie, "Evolution and Perceptions of Scientific Consensus," Pew Research Center, July 1, 2015, http://www.pewinternet.org/2015/07/01/chapter-4-evolution-and-perceptions-of-scientific-consensus/.
6. See Chapter Two, "The Nature of Belief," in Sam Harris's *The End of Faith* (W. W. Norton, 2005). Also see Dawkins's Chapter Two, "The God Hypothesis," in *The God Delusion* (Mariner Books, reprint, 2008).
7. A. Damasio, *Descartes' Error: Emotion, Reason, and the Human Brain* (G. P. Putnam, 1994). Robin W. Simon and Leda E. Nath (2004) "Gender and Emotion in the United States: Do Men and Women Differ in Self Reports of Feelings and Expressive Behavior?" American Journal of Sociology, Vol. 109, No. 5. 1137–76. Thoits, Peggy (1989) "The Sociology of Emotions" Annual Review of Sociology 61: 837–57.
8. John Dewey, *A Common Faith* (Yale University Press, 1934), 27.
9. Unfortunately, Dewey's road has failed to accept the robust connection between denominational metaphysics and meaning, and more recent kindred spirits have agreed to celebrate merely aesthetic and ethical aspects of religion while denouncing the magic as reprehensible or primitive. These purely diplomatic maneuvers have been stopgap measures, and do not get to the heart of the tension.
10. Pascal Boyer, in his *Religion Explained* (Basic Books, 2001), uses the fact of religious terror as a counterargument to the "therapeutic argument" that religion survives because it soothes. In my view, he throws in the towel too early

on "religion as comfort," pursuing instead a more cognitive theory of shuffling mental categories/templates. Dialogues Add Hume Ref

11. Jonathan Edwards, *Sinners in the Hands of an Angry God* (1703–1758), Enfield, Connecticut, July 8, 1741.
12. Sarah F. Hoyt, "The Etymology of Religion," *Journal of the American Oriental Society*, 32, no. 2 (1912): 126–129.
13. Bernard Williams, *Moral Luck: Philosophical Papers 1973–1980* (Cambridge University Press, 1981).
14. See Charles Taylor's *A Secular Age* (Belknap Press, Harvard, 2007).
15. M. Twain, *Autobiography of Mark Twain,* Vol. 3 (University of Chicago Press, 2015), 3.
16. Jean Kazez discusses her religious fictionalism at her site: http://kazez.blogspot.com/2011/04/religious-fictionalism.html. But also see the provocative piece by William Irwin, "How to Live a Lie," in The Stone, *New York Times*, November 2, 2015, where I first learned of Kazez fictionalism.
17. W. Irwin, "How to Live a Lie," in The Stone, *New York Times*, November 2, 2015.
18. This famous quote is from the Introduction of Karl Marx's 1843 "A Contribution to the Critique of Hegel's Philosophy of Right." The full text is available online: https://www.marxists.org/archive/marx/works/1843/critique-hpr/intro.htm.
19. Some suggest that the nuclear family is the original human institution. I suspect, however, that it's not an institution at all, but a biological individual, distributed through space and time. See Stephen Asma, "You Are an Abstraction," at *3 Quarks Daily*, June 2013, http://www.3quarksdaily.com/3quarksdaily/2013/06/you-are-an-abstraction-mistakes-of-metaphysical-individualism.html.

CHAPTER 1

1. Is there room for this quirky creature, the Creation Museum, on today's ark of natural history museology? Scientific orthodoxy requires the evangelical museum to walk the plank so to speak, but historically speaking natural history museums have always been eccentric treasure chests of weirdness. Nature museums, with their displays of the exotic and the rare, have always existed at the frontier of credulity and wonder.

   Natural history museums began to emerge as public and professional institutions in the seventeenth century. Prior to that, collecting and displaying were active private fetishes for bourgeois Europeans. These *wunderkammer* or *kunstkammern* were jumbled, unsystematic cabinets that contained natural and artistic exotica. Whenever some overarching narrative of meaning was applied to the collections, it was invariably a celebration of the Creator's ingenuity and fecundity—as in the case of Konrad Gesner's explanation (*Historiae Animalium*) of his insect collection: "These little creatures so hateful to all men, are not yet to be despised, since they are created by Almighty God for diverse and sundry uses. First of all we are forewarned of the near approaches of foul weather and storms; secondly, they yield medicines for us when we are sick, and are food for diverse other creatures, as well as birds and fishes. They show and set forth the Omnipotency of God, and execute his justice."

   In many ways, Ham's new Creation Museum is more in keeping with this early museology. The purpose of investigating and displaying the Book of Nature is to further amplify the Holy Book. But as the budding sciences began to organize into disciplines and savant societies during the late seventeenth and early eighteenth centuries, private collections were bequeathed, purchased, and consolidated into real "Solomon's Houses" (an influential term invented by Francis Bacon to describe fictional wisdom warehouses of specimens). The professional science institutions (e.g., London's Royal Society, the American Philosophical Society, the Academie des Sciences) developed hand-in-hand with the growth of theoretical collecting (taxonomic, medical, and eventually evolutionary). By the time flagship American museums, such as Chicago's Field Museum, New York's American Museum of Natural History, and the National Museum of Natural History came to life in the nineteenth century, the theoretical map was squarely Darwinian. And the educational or rhetorical mission of the museum was to help average citizens to appreciate the general evolutionary history of the fossils, skeletons, and taxidermy on display.

In the 1940s and 1950s museum directors like Albert Eide Parr, at the American Museum of Natural History, began to redirect their giant institutional "arks" toward the new mission of ecology education and research. In 1943, for example, Parr begged an esteemed group of curators at the Field Museum to follow his lead and focus the new message on local ecology issues rather than exotic entertainment. And besides, he argued, the old mission of educating citizens about evolution had been successfully accomplished by now. That's right—curators in the 1950s believed that evolution theory was now firmly entrenched in the common-sense of mainstream America. The irony is delicious. Dim the lights, cue the diorama of Ham's evangelical anti-Darwin displays, and watch the rapid spinning of Dr. Albert Parr in his grave.

But while the respectable museums have standardized and harmonized their messages to accurately portray our state of scientific knowledge, the smaller-scale museums have always continued to percolate their mess of idiosyncratic specimens and ideologies. In the twentieth century, the difference between respectable and suspicious institutions is usually signaled by money. Oddball museums typically don't have much money, so the rhetoric or persuasiveness of their message is usually tarnished by the seedy patina of low-budget constraints. But the $30 million Creation Museum, which continues to pick up steam in big-budget patronage, is poised to bring new celebrity to unorthodox curating.

My reference to contemporary species numbers is taken from Jane Reece, et al (2012) *Campbell Biology* textbook (Pearson).

2. Aristotle distinguished science from other kinds of knowledge on the grounds that it gave a *causal* explanation for observable experience, and its claims were *systematic* (logically coherent). Science can't be just a bunch of associations, impressions, correlations, and anecdotes. It seems unlikely that anyone will find a real causal connection between star alignment and personality type. But by these Aristotelian criteria, things like Traditional Chinese Medicine look fairly scientific—the system of *qi* energy provides the *causal* foundation for specific associations within acupuncture healing, kung-fu skills, feng shui architecture, herbal remedies, and so on.

Starting in the seventeenth century, however, the definition of science changed. It wasn't enough to have a systematic causal story, because many competing stories could fit the same observable phenomenon. Retrograde planetary motion could be explained by Ptolemaic epicycle causation, for example, but that causal picture was eventually unseated by a shift to heliocentric astronomy. What's needed is the correct causal explanation, and the hypothetico-deductive model arose to put causal explanations through a gauntlet of empirical tests.

Can *qi* energy, creationism, and ghosts be scientifically corroborated in this more rigorous sense? Skepticism seems reasonable here because no one has seen *qi* directly, only indirectly. Even the meridians or channels of *qi* energy in the body remain undetectable to Western instruments, yet practitioners of Chinese Medicine spend years mastering the meridian anatomical charts. Are they chasing an illusion that takes authority from tradition alone, or are we still only at the commencement stage of discovery? *Qi* energy looks unfalsifiable, but maybe the promissory note will soon be paid. After all, scientists theorized, hypothesized, and assumed the reality of the gene (a unit of heredity) long before anyone actually observed one under a microscope. And the Higgs boson was posited in the 1960s, but only confirmed in 2012. Will *qi* energy be confirmed as the causal underpinning for the often-reported correspondence between acupuncture and healing?

In the nineteenth century, Darwin's scientific revolution didn't correspond to the experimental method of the falsifiability model. Galileo had been rolling balls down inclined planes and making direct observations to evaluate his gravitation theory, but Darwin's theory of natural selection was less observable. Instead, Darwin's natural selection attained increasing scientific acceptance because it explained so many diverse phenomena (e.g., the fossil record, adaptive structures, anatomical homologies). The paradigm of *qi* energy is as explanatorily resourceful and deeply rooted in China as Darwinism is in Western science. But there's a major difference, too, and it needs articulation. Darwinism only posits three major ingredients for evolution: offspring vary from their parents and siblings, offspring resemble their parents more than non-kin, and more offspring are born than can survive in their environment. Each of these facts is easily observable, and when you put them together you get adaptive evolution of populations. No additional metaphysical force, such as *qi*, is being posited.

It seems entirely reasonable to believe in Traditional Chinese Medicine and still have grave doubts about *qi* energy. In other words, it is possible for people to practice a kind of "accidental medicine"—in the sense that symptoms might be alleviated even when their causes are misdiagnosed (it happens all the time in Western medicine, too). Acupuncture and many similar therapies are not superstitious, but may be morsels of practical folk wisdom. The causal theory that's concocted to explain the practical successes of treatment is not terribly important or interesting to the poor schlub who's thrown out his back or taken ill. Ultimately, one can be skeptical of both *qi* forces and a sacrosanct scientific method, but still be a devotee of fallible pragmatic truth.

3. See Section VII of William James's "Will to Believe," in *Pragmatism and Other Writings* (Penguin, 2000).
4. R. G. Millikan, "On Reading Signs: Some Differences Between Us and the Others," in *Evolution of Communication Systems: A Comparative Approach*, edited by D. Kimbrough Oller and Ulrike Griebel (MIT Press, 2004), 15–30.
5. With some disinterested analysis we can distill the horror experience of predator fear, and other emotionally charged judgments, into a parallel process of affect and cognition, a process usually so interwoven that it appears as one unified experience (and in animals always remains so).
6. See Galileo's "Letter to the Grand Duchess Christina" (1615) in *The Essential Galileo* (Hackett Publishing, 2008).
7. W. James, "The Sentiment of Rationality," *Mind*, 4, no. 15 (1879): 317–346.
8. Where do these values come from, if not the indicative world? Many philosophers have suggested that values cannot emerge from the factual world, leaving them to take up a mystical view of transcendental truths or a mystical view of human reason (e.g., Kantian "pure" reason). I will argue throughout this book, however,

that they emerge as a species of what Aristotle called phronesis (practical wisdom). They come via hot cognition from the social animal world of mammal interaction. They are not propositional facts, nor are they mysterious intellectual intuitions, but they are empirical, and they are motivational. Their motivational or conative force comes from their affective or emotional weights, stabilized by habit.

9. Tanya Lurhmann, *When God Talks Back* (Vintage, 2012), 73.

CHAPTER 2

1. See Hitchens's *God Is Not Great* (Twelve Books, Hachette, 2007) and Harris's *The End of Faith: Religion, Terror, and the Future of Reason* (W. W. Norton, 2004).
2. See C. S. Lewis's *A Grief Observed* (Harper One, 2001), 3.
3. Charles Darwin's *The Expression of Emotions in Man and Animals* (Penguin Classics, 2009).
4. Deborah Hastings, "Baby Elephant in China Can't Stop Crying After Being Stomped by Mom," *New York Daily News*, September 23, 2013, http://www.nydailynews.com/news/world/baby-elephant-weeps-uncontrollably-mom-kill-article-1.1455224.
5. Marc Bekoff, "Do Elephants Weep as an Emotional Response?" *Psychology Today*, September 16, 2013, https://www.psychologytoday.com/blog/animal-emotions/201309/do-elephants-weep-emotional-response.
6. The same triggering of maternal behaviors in nonmother rats can be achieved by directly injecting oxytocin (OT) into their brains (OT can't cross the blood brain barrier). Studies like these have also established that OT is necessary for the onset of maternal behaviors, but not the maintenance of mothering activities. Once OT flips the switch, mothering care is sustained on its own momentum, so to speak. See Thomas R. Insel, "The Neurobiology of Affiliation: Implications for Autism," in *Handbook of Affective Sciences*, edited by Richard J. Davidson, Klaus R. Scherer, and H. Hill Goldsmith (Oxford University Press, 2002): 1010–1020.
7. See K. M. Kendrick, E. B. Keverne, and B. A. Baldwin, "Intracerebroventricular Oxytocin Stimulates Maternal Behaviour in the Sheep," *Neuroendocrinology*, 46 (1987): 56–61. Endocrinologists Kendrick and Keverne have published extensively on this area over the last two decades.
8. Among mammals, infanticide is a very common albeit horrifying mechanism by which males enter a new territory and take over. When a male, whether it's a rat or a lion, enters new territory, it usually kills the babies of the group. This activity stops breastfeeding, which stops lactation in the mothers, which then restarts ovulation. This brutal pattern creates the opportunity for the new male to mate with the females and create a new gene line. In rats, the postcoital oxytocin spike correlates exactly with the gestation period (three weeks) of its own offspring. In other words, after sex, males calm down long enough to bond with their own offspring (not kill them), and then they slowly resume normal levels of pup killing.
9. See Bowlby, *Attachment* (1969, Hogarth Press), and the second and third volumes, *Separation: Anxiety and Anger* (1972, Hogarth Press), and *Loss: Sadness and Depression* (1980, Hogarth Press).
10. See Alison B. Wismer Fries, T. E. Ziegler, J. R. Kurian, S. Jacoris, and S. Pollak, "Early Experience in Humans Is Associated with Changes in Neuropeptides Critical for Regulating Social Behavior," *Proceedings of the National Academy of Sciences*, 102, no. 47 (November 2005): 17237–17240.
11. See J. Panksepp, *Affective Neuroscience: The Foundations of Human and Animal Emotions* (New York: Oxford University Press, 1998), 263.

12. See Fabrizzio Benedetti's *Placebo Effects: Understanding the Mechanisms in Health and Disease* (Oxford University Press, 2008).
13. Alia Crum and Ellen J. Langer, "Mind-Set Matters: Exercise and the Placebo Effect," *Psychological Science*, 18, no. 2 (February 2007): 165–171.
14. C. Draganich and K. Erdal, "Placebo Sleep Affects Cognitive Functioning," *Journal of Experimental Psychology: Learning, Memory and Cognition*, 40 (2014): 857–864.
15. The quotes are from the Order of Christian Funerals, approved for use in the United States by the National Conference of Catholic Bishops and confirmed by the Apostolic See.
16. Sandra Blakeslee, "Placebos Prove So Powerful Even Experts Are Surprised" *New York Times, Science Times* (October 13, 1998), D1.
17. See, for example, Usha Lee McFarling, "Doctors, Studies Assert Faith's Healing Powers," *Knight Ridder Newspapers*, December 23, 1998; and Usha Lee McFarling, "The Power to Heal," *San Jose Mercury News*, January 23, 1999, 1E. Also see W. J. Strawbridge et al., "Frequent Attendance at Religious Services and Mortality Over 28 Years," *American Journal of Public Health*, 87, no. 6 (June 1997): 957–961. And more recently, H. S. L. Jim, J. Pustejovsky, C. L. Park, S. C. Danhauer, A. C. Sherman, G. Fitchett, and J. M. Salsman, "Religion, Spirituality, and Physical Health in Cancer Patients: A Meta-Analysis," *Cancer*, 121, no. 21 (2015): 3760–3768.
18. "Camp Erin: Where Children and Teens Learn to Grieve and Heal," The Moyer Foundation. Accessed July 23, 2017, https://www.moyerfoundation.org/programs/camperin_about.aspx.
19. Feminist philosophers, like Carol Gilligan (1982), noticed that the typical model of the Western ethical man was an utterly detached, impartial self. This autonomous self was supposed to have pulled himself out of the subjective quagmire of emotions and biased attachments in order to view the objective fair distribution of goods with a disinterested eye. Gilligan and other philosophers pointed out that this "autonomous self" was a total fiction (or perhaps a twisted pathology). Moreover, women pointed out that social knowledge itself must be particular, not universal; concrete, not abstract; and emotionally valenced, not just mathematical. Care is an alternative to principle-based ethics because it acknowledges the inextricable intimacies of human social life, and it places emotions at the root of those intimacies. But the intimacies of care also create special obligations and duties that constrain us, and act as quasilaws (more particular than universal, but still binding). Also see Rosemarie Tong's *Feminine and Feminist Ethics* (Wadsworth, 1993) for a good contrast of the autonomous man and communal woman paradigms of social and ethical knowledge.
20. E. Kubler-Ross and D. Kessler, *On Grief and Grieving* (Scribner, 2005), 230.
21. Philip K. Dick, *Flow My Tears, the Policeman Said* (Houghton Mifflin Harcourt, 2012), 121.
22. "Promissory Note" by Galway Kinnell, from *Strong Is Your Hold* (Houghton Mifflin, 2006).
23. "This American Life," radio broadcast, 2007. Accessed July 23, 2017, http://www.thisamericanlife.org/radio-archives/episode/324/my-brilliant-plan?act=2#play.
24. P. Ellsworth and K. Scherer, "Appraisal Processes in Emotion," in *Handbook of Affective Sciences*, edited by R. Davidson, K. Scherer, and H. Goldsmith (Oxford University Press, 2003), 572–595.
25. Kenneth I. Pargament, Harold G. Koenig, and Lisa M. Perez, "The Many Methods of Religious Coping: Development and Initial Validation of the RCOPE," *Journal of Clinical Psychology*, 56, no. 4 (2000): 519–543.

26. R. E. Phillips III, Q. K. Lynn, C. D. Crossley, and K. I. Pargament, "Self-Directing Religious Coping: A Deistic God, Abandoning God, or No God at All?" *Journal for the Scientific Study of Religion*, 43, no. 3 (2004): 409–418.
27. See Kenneth Pargament's *The Many Faces of Religion in Coping* (Guilford Press, 2001), 173.
28. The Pali word for impermanence is *anicca*, and it forms one of the central pillars of Buddhist philosophy. Pali, which was contemporaneous with Sanskrit, is the original Indian language of Buddhism. Many Buddhist terms and even scriptures have two versions, reflecting the different ancient languages. The better-known term *nirvana*, for example, is Sanskrit and its Pali version is *nibbana*. Likewise, the Sanskrit *dharma* is *dhamma* in Pali. This is worth noting because all of Southeast Asian Buddhism, Theravada, is based on the voluminous Pali scriptures, called the *Tipitika* (three baskets). The three baskets of Pali scriptures are the *Vinaya* (rules for monks), the *Suttas* (teachings for lay people), and the *Abhidhamma* (teachings for philosophers).
29. In the third century BCE the Indian emperor Ashoka converted to Buddhism and sent missionaries through contemporary Afghanistan and throughout the subcontinent and on to Sri Lanka. He began the highly successful dissemination of the dharma throughout all of Asia. And the dharma flowered into unique forms depending on the ingredients of the local "soil."
30. See Batchelor's *Confessions of a Buddhist Atheist* (Spiegel and Grau, 2011); Hagen's *Buddhism Plain and Simple* (Broadway Books, 1998); and Harris's *Waking Up: A Guide to Spirituality Without Religion* (Simon and Schuster, 2014).
31. Consider Dostoyevsky's famous *Grand Inquisitor* scenario (*Brothers Karamazov*), in which Christ comes back to the modern world and is arrested by the Church. Dostoyevsky, a devout Orthodox Christian, unfolds a story in which the Church captures Christ and the chief Inquisitor asks him to go away because the challenge of righteousness that He brings is way too difficult for weak human nature to accomplish. The Inquisitor explains to Christ that "The Church" is much better than Jesus at giving humans what they need: "miracle, mystery and authority." When the Inquisitor is finished with his rant, he really seems like a person who loves humanity more than Christ, because he (the Church) can give average people the comfort and ease that their daily suffering requires. The real teachings of Christianity, the Inquisitor argues, are just too difficult for such weak beings to live up to. *The Brothers Karamazov* (Farrar, Straus and Giroux; 12th ed., 2002).
32. See Orwell's "Reflections on Gandhi," in *All Art Is Propaganda: Critical Essays* (Houghton Mifflin Harcourt, 2009), 357.
33. R. J. Davidson and A. Lutz, "Buddha's Brain: Neuroplasticity and Meditation," *IEEE Signal Processing Magazine*, 25, no. 1 (2008): 176–174.
34. See Nina Strohminger, Jay Garfield, and Shaun Nichols's research, a summary of which is available here: "Is There Life After Death? Buddhism and the Loss of Self," *Slate*, June 2015, http://www.slate.com/bigideas/is-there-life-after-death/essays-and-opinions/buddhism-and-the-loss-of-self. "Buddhist monks and nuns—those who were steeped in these religion doctrines day in and day out—exhibited significantly more fear of self-annihilation than Americans or Indians. Buddhist laypeople, who were less versed in the details of the doctrine of selflessness, also exhibited less fear than the monastics. If we consider only the other possible reasons to fear death, such as fear of the unknown, Buddhists were no less fearful than anyone else. In short, the no-self doctrine, rather than equipping the Tibetan lamas with serenity regarding end of life, seems to provoke a deep-rooted anxiety of self-annihilation, and does nothing to reduce overall fear of death."

35. Theravada has a rather macabre emphasis on decaying flesh and bloated, bursting corpses. Search some reproductions of "dhamma paintings" from the mid-nineteenth century. The Chaiya manuscript, for example, is indicative. They depict, in detail, the "Ten Reflections on Foulness" (*asubha kammatthana*). The paintings illustrate the various uses of corpses as objects for contemplating impermanence. Following the great Theravadan philosopher Buddhaghosa's *Visuddhimagga* text ("Path of Purification"), the artist rendered decaying corpses in rather comprehensive stages of dismemberment and putrification. Staring at a bloated corpse will be particularly useful to me if I'm feeling overly attached and arrogant about the shape and morphology of my body, but if I'm feeling snobby or bigoted about my skin's color or complexion, then I should focus on the livid corpse that ranges from green to blue-black in color. If I mistakenly feel that my body is my own, I am to rectify this error by meditating on a worm-infested corpse (*puluvaka*), for as Buddhaghosa explains, "The body is shared by many and creatures live in dependence on (all parts and organs) and feed (on them). And there they are born, grow old, and die, evacuate and pass water; and the body is their maternity home, their hospital, their charnel ground, their privy and their urinal. . . ."
36. "Chinese Communist Party explains wedding and funeral rules," BBC News, February 19, 2016. Accessed July 17, 2017, http://www.bbc.com/news/world-asia-china-35610194.
37. See Terry Eagleton's *Culture and the Death of God* (Yale University Press, 2014), 188.
38. See Allen W. Johnson and Timothy Earle's *The Evolution of Human Societies* (Stanford University Press; 2nd ed., 2000), 250.
39. Sociologist Emile Durkheim inspired a century (and counting) of anthropology of religion—an approach that revealed the obvious social solidarity functions of religion. Using ceremonies and stories, religions manage our emotions and bond us into us–them groups. In a dubious dodge of this Durkheim tradition, Eagleton rejects the explanation of religion as social cement, by cherry-picking rebellious gospel passages. Almost desperate to say something controversial, Eagleton doesn't recognize that religion is primarily about *identity*. He emphasizes the Marxian view so strongly that he's forced to deny the anthropological view of religion as a positive, prosocial mechanism. Arguing instead that Christianity is "disruptive," Eagleton says that Jesus has come "to tear father away from son in the name of his mission." But that is willfully ignoring the obvious role that religion plays in forging stronger kin and even "fictive kin" groups. And, ironically, he undercuts his own argument here. He cannot claim that the essence of Jesus's message is disruption, if the lasting role of religion (according to his Marxian approach) is supposed to be human domestication. Which one is it, opium of the masses or spark of rebellion? The real answer is both, but Eagleton can't quite break out of his class-struggle paradigm.

CHAPTER 3

1. See Martha Nussbaum's *The Fragility of Goodness* (Cambridge University Press; 2nd ed., 2001).
2. *Forgiveness: A Sampling of Research Results* (American Psychological Association, 59th Annual DPI/NGO Conference, United Nations, 2006; 2008), 5.
3. See J. J. Gross, "The Emerging Field of Emotional Regulation: An Integrative Review," *Review of General Psychology*, 2, no. 3 (1988): 271–299.
4. As theorists Eva Jablonka, Ginsburg, and Dor (2012) suggest, language itself requires some emotional domestication because we need to calm down and inhibit our selfish and aggressive tendencies in order to engage in cooperative

communication. But language itself also helped *Homo sapiens* increase such emotional domestication because we could use arbitrary, agreed upon signals that do not have any inherent emotional push or pull. See "The Co-Evolution of Language and Emotions," *Philosophical Transactions of the Royal Society of London: Series B Biological Sciences* (August 5, 2012): 367.

5. J. Panksepp, *The Archaeology of Mind: Neuroevolutionary Origins of Human Emotions* (New York: W. W. Norton & Company, 2012).
6. Lucius Annaeus Seneca, "De Ira (On Anger)," in *Moral and Political Essays*, edited and translated by John M. Cooper and J. F. Procopé (Cambridge University Press, 1995), 1–116.
7. See Nussbaum's *Upheavals of Thought* (Cambridge University Press, 2001).
8. Panksepp (2011) describes (A) primary-process emotions as (i) sensory affects (sensorially triggered pleasurable–unpleasant feelings), (ii) homeostatic affects (hunger, thirst, etc. via brain-body interoceptors), and (iii) emotional affects (emotion action tendencies); (B) secondary-process emotions as (i) classical-conditioning, (ii) operant conditioning, (iii) emotional habits; (C) tertiary affects and neocortical awareness functions as (i) cognitive executive functions, (ii) emotional ruminations and regulations (medial frontal neocortex), (iii) free will, or intention to act (frontal cortical executive functions). See Panksepp's "Cross-Species Affective Neuroscience Decoding of the Primal Affective Experiences of Humans and Related Animals," *PLoS One*, 6, no. 8 (2011): e21236. Also see Izard et al. "Emotion Knowledge, Emotion Utilization, and Emotion Regulation" Emotion Review. Vol. 3. No. 1 (2011) pp. 44–52. Panksepp J. Affective neuroscience of the emotional BrainMind: evolutionary perspectives and implications for understanding depression. *Dialogues in Clinical Neuroscience*. 2010;12(4):533–545.
9. See Piotr Winkielman and Kent C. Berridge, "Unconscious Emotion," *Current Directions in Psychological Science*, 13, no. 3 (2004): 120–123.
10. L. Ostojić, M. Tkalčić, and N. S. Clayton, "Are Owners' Reports of Their Dogs' 'Guilty Look' Influenced by the Dogs' Action and Evidence of the Misdeed?" *Behavioural Processes*, 111 (2015): 97–100. Also see A. Horowitz, "Disambiguating the 'Guilty Look': Salient Prompts to a Familiar Dog Behaviour," *Behavioural Processes*, 81 (2009): 447–452.
11. William James famously reversed this sequence, suggesting that the behavior is first, and the emotion follows. See James's "What Is an Emotion?" in *The Heart of William James* (Harvard University Press; reprint ed., 2012).
12. See June Price Tangney and Ronda L. Dearing's *Shame and Guilt* (Guilford Press, 2002).
13. Environmentalism, as a substitute for religion, has come to the rescue. Nietzsche's argument about an ideal God and guilt can be replicated in a new form: We need a belief in a pristine environment because we need to be cruel to ourselves as inferior beings, and we need that because we have these aggressive instincts that cannot be let out. Instead of religious sins plaguing our conscience, we now have the transgressions of leaving the water running, leaving the lights on, failing to recycle, and using plastic grocery bags instead of paper. In addition, the righteous pleasures of being more orthodox than your neighbor (in this case being more "green") can still be had—the new heresies include failure to compost, or refusal to go organic.
14. See Pascal Boyer's *Religion Explained: The Evolutionary Origins of Religious Thought* (Basic Books, 2001), 187.
15. See Charles Griswold's excellent discussion of ancient and modern forgiveness in his *Forgiveness: A Philosophical Exploration* (Cambridge University Press, 2007).

16. Aristotle's view about the soul was more nuanced, and he admitted the possibility that external misfortunes could penetrate the eudaemonia of even the most righteous person. Stoics, however, pushed this notion of psychological immunity to extremes.
17. There is an interesting theological issue here, too. Notice that the Judeo-Christian God is interested enough in humans to offer or bestow forgiveness, when we ask for it. But the pagan God—both the Aristotelian and the Deist God of the Enlightenment—is too perfect to notice or care about our human peccadillos. God is too great to be injured by even your worst sins, and so He has no need to forgive you. Asking Him to forgive you is implying that you've hurt him or injured him, which is impossible for the philosopher's God, who is omniscient, omnipotent, and omnibenevolent.
18. See Solomon's *In Defense of Sentimentality* (Oxford University Press, 2004), 33.
19. See Joel Harrington's excellent biography of Schmidt, *The Faithful Executioner* (Farrar, Straus and Giroux, 2013).
20. See the Confucian *Analects*, Book 14, Chapter 34 for the clearest expression of this ethics. Translation Robert Eno (2013), online version available. Accessed on July 17, 2017, http://www.indiana.edu/~p374/Analects_of_Confucius_(Eno-2015).pdf.
21. Again see Martha Nussbaum's articulation of the judgmental structure of emotions in *Upheavals of Thought* (Cambridge University Press, 2001). But for a more extreme form of cognitive emotion, one that denies the animal instincts and places full emphasis on our conceptual construction of emotions, see Lisa Feldman Barrett's work, "Are Emotions Natural Kinds?" *Perspectives on Psychological Science*, 1, no. 1 (2006): 28–58. And see Feldman's more recent *How Emotions Are Made* (Houghton Mifflin Harcourt, 2017).
22. See *The Jatakas*, translated by Sara Janet Shaw (Penguin Classics, 2007).
23. See Stephen Asma's *The Evolution of Imagination* (University of Chicago, 2017).
24. Stoics used what might now be called "creative visualization" in order to imagine consoling narratives. Ironically, the consolation comes from imagining how much worse your situation could be, and then taking solace in the differential. The imagination plays an important role in recasting a troublesome event in a new context that defuses the negative emotions. When your enemy is screaming at you, the Stoics suggest that you reimagine them as a barking dog. Given that dog barking is not a personal insult or injury, just something dogs do, you cannot be offended when a dog barks at you. If you can imagine your enemy's abuse as merely the reflex of a poorly trained character, then you lose all feeling of injury.
25. G. K. D. Crozier, "Reconsidering Cultural Selection Theory," *British Journal for the Philosophy of Science*, 59, no. 3 (September 2008): 455–479.
26. Lucas Molleman et al., "Cultural Evolution of Cooperation: The Interplay Between Forms of Social Learning and Group Selection," *Evolution and Human Behavior*, 34 no. 5 (2013): 342–349.
27. This quote and the following from Sapolsky are drawn from an interview, "When Monkeys Make Up," from *In Character*, September 2008, http://incharacter.org/archives/forgiveness/when-monkeys-make-up-chimps-are-from-mars-bonobos-are-from-venus/.
28. F. Fincham, S. Beach, and J. Davila, "Forgiveness and Conflict Resolution in Marriage," *Journal of Family Psychology*, 18 (2004): 72–81.
29. F. M. Luskin, *Forgive for Good: A Proven Prescription for Health and Happiness* (Harper Collins, 2001).

30. N. A. Hawkins, D. N. McIntosh, R. C. Silver, and E. A. Holman, "Early Responses to School Violence: A Qualitative Analysis of Students' and Parents' Immediate Reactions to the Shootings at Columbine High School," *Journal of Emotional Abuse*, 4 (2004): 197–223.
31. See *Forgiveness: A Sampling of Research Results* (American Psychological Association, 59th Annual DPI/NGO Conference, United Nations, 2006; 2008), 17–19.
32. See E. Staub and L. A. Pearlman, "Advancing Healing and Reconciliation," in *Psychological Interventions in Times of Crisis*, edited by L. Barbanel and R. Sternberg (Springer-Verlag, 2006) pp. 213–243. Also, E. Staub, L. A. Pearlman, A. Gubin, and A. Hagengimana, "Healing, Forgiveness and Reconciliation in Rwanda: Intervention and Experimental Evaluation," *Journal of Social and Clinical Psychology*, 24, no. 3 (2005): 297–334. And E. Staub, "Reconciliation after Genocide, Mass Killing or Intractable Conflict: Understanding the Roots of Violence, Psychological Recovery and Steps Toward a General Theory," *Political Psychology*, December 2006.
33. See Jared Diamond's compelling analysis of the Rwandan genocide in Part Four of his book *Collapse: How Societies Choose to Fail or Succeed* (Penguin, 2005).
34. See *Forgiveness: A Sampling of Research Results* (American Psychological Association, 59th Annual DPI/NGO Conference, United Nations, 2006; 2008), 33.
35. There is a popular recent argument by rationalist optimists, like Stephen Pinker and Michael Shermer, that science and literacy (and democracy) have made the world a less violent place. I understand that the argument is usually based on statistical analysis of violent crime and war, but the statistical work is suspiciously massaged. This is not the place for a refutation of the statistical work (see John Gray's "Steven Pinker Is Wrong about Violence and War," *Guardian*, March 13, 2015, http://www.theguardian.com/books/2015/mar/13/john-gray-steven-pinker-wrong-violence-war-declining). But the twentieth century alone is the era of two World Wars, the Holocaust, the Killing Fields, the Russian Civil War, the Chinese Civil War, the Cultural Revolution, the French Indo-China War, the Vietnam War, the Persian Gulf War, the Rwandan Genocide, and much more. Frankly, it's hard to take the neo-Enlightenment optimists seriously. See Steven Pinker, *The Better Angels of Our Nature: Why Violence Has Declined* (Penguin, 2011) and Michael Shermer, *The Moral Arc: How Science and Reason Lead Humanity Toward Truth, Justice, and Freedom* (Macmillan, 2015).
36. M. J. A. Wohl and N. R. Branscombe, "Forgiveness and Collective Guilt Assignment to Historical Perpetrator Groups Depend on Level of Social Category Inclusiveness," *Journal of Personality and Social Psychology*, 88 (2005): 288–303.
37. D. McIntosh et al., "Forgiving the Perpetrators of the September 11th Attacks," in *Forgiveness: A Sampling of Research Results* (American Psychological Association, 59th Annual DPI/NGO Conference, United Nations, 2006; 2008), 18.

CHAPTER 4

1. Anthony's marvelous episodes have also fueled the pictorial tradition, from the medieval period to the present. Paintings by Hieronymus Bosch, Matthias Grunewald, and Salvador Dalí, for example, have helped to keep Anthony's tribulations in the popular imagination. Anthony's battle with monsters comes to us via his famous biographer Athanasius of Alexandria (c. 293–373). Athanasius chronicled Anthony's life in a work titled simply *Vita Antonii*, or *Life of Anthony*. The book was eventually translated into Latin and set the template for subsequent medieval monastic biographies. Athanasius is revered in all the major sects of Christianity as the first Church

Doctor. He served under Alexander of Alexandria, until succeeding him as Patriarch of Alexandria, and may have accompanied Alexander to the First Council of Nicaea in 325. Athanasius was adamant to stamp out the popular theory about Christ, called Arianism, named after another Alexandrian theologian named Arius (c. 250–336). Arians believed that God *created* Christ—Christ is not the same *substance* as God. This was anathematized by the Nicene Creed, which makes Christ, and the Holy Spirit, consubstantial with God the Father. Athanasius's position, that the holy trinity is the same being (*homoousia* in Greek, or *essentia* in Latin) and all are eternal, became the orthodox theology for Christianity. But this orthodoxy was not established until after a sustained attack on Arianism as heresy, some of which occupies the later sections of the *Life of Anthony*.

2. His faith revitalized him against his nightly attacks, and he rallied back. After throwing off the temptations of the flesh, Anthony was revisited by the devil many times—but the devil always shape-shifted to appear as some creature. "Changes of form for evil are easy for the devil," Anthony explained, "so in the night they make such a din that the whole of that place seemed to be shaken by an earthquake, and the demons as if breaking the four walls of the dwelling seemed to enter through them, coming in the likeness of beasts and creeping things" (*Life of Anthony*).
3. A. L. Bergman, M. S. Christopher, and S. Bowen, "Changes in Facets of Mindfulness Predict Stress and Anger Outcomes for Police Officers," *Mindfulness* 7 (2016): 851.
4. The form of Buddhism that entered America during the counterculture years was Zen. Zen, which I also love, is the hyper-puritan descendant of Buddhism—the neurotic cousin who's always disinfecting the furniture and showering off the impurities. It's so vigilant about eliminating dogma and anything outside of pristine meditation practice, that it no longer bears any resemblance to Buddhism (except its connection to the "mindfulness" discussion in the Buddha's *Mahasatipatthana sutta*). This is not really a criticism of Zen. But my humble observation is that American dharma has evolved into its rather narcissistic current form because Zen introduced Buddhism as a simple meditation practice and nothing more. Americans adopted the meditation idea but left behind the austere discipline of Zen and the cultural context. This neutered Zen Buddhism has no baggage whatsoever, so Americans felt that they could drape it over whatever beliefs they already enjoyed. That seems like a virtue at first ("Look, I'm a Christian *and* a Zen practitioner!"), but it lulled Americans into thinking that Buddhism was the Silly Putty of religions—infinitely malleable and conveniently fashionable. Buddhism becomes another accessory. Living in Southeast Asia or Japan, however, rids you of this confusion very quickly.
5. Artists have always been attracted to this aspect of Buddhism because, among other things, it provides a deeper impetus for creating poetry, music, painting, and so on. Our ordinary way of thinking and operating in the world assumes that our conscious minds reflect the real world—the mind discriminates differences because there are differences out there in nature. Buddhism rejects this ordinary thinking, suggesting that these discriminations are just illusions of the mind (fabrications) and do not reflect reality—which is "empty" (without inherent form). Consequently, according to these schools of Buddhism, literal language (like that practiced in everyday speech and science) cannot access reality. Art, however, can. The unexpected twist of the elegant haiku, for example, can suddenly reveal a nondiscursive truth that no literal language can represent.

6. Theravada legend holds that the Buddha transmitted the *Abhidhamma* teachings during his lifetime. The Pali Commentaries, written long after the Buddha's *parinibbana*, undoubtedly record the embellished oral traditions that slowly evolved in the popular imagination. According to the commentaries, the Buddha taught the entire *Abhidhamma* (seven books altogether, one of them alone is over 2,000 pages!) during a three-month rains retreat. (All monks are expected to take up a three-month residence, coinciding with monsoon season, from mid-July to mid-October, to study and meditate in retreat communities.) But he actually taught this full message to an assembly of gods (*devas*) in the Tavatinsa heaven, because mere humans are unable to sit still long enough in meditation to receive the deep, and apparently relentless, lessons. Legend has it that the Buddha would return to the human realm every day to go on alms-patrol, because he had to eat after all. During these nutritional-refueling stops, the Buddha summarized the heavenly lessons for his human pupil Sariputta. According to tradition, it was Sariputta who then wrote down the master's teachings and gave us the *Abhidhamma*. Scholars on the other hand, claim that the seven books of the *Abhidhamma* were slowly compiled during the three great Buddhist councils in India, reaching some final codification during the first century BCE.
7. See Emma Seppala's *The Happiness Track* (HarperOne, 2016).
8. The DMN was named as such in 2001. M. E. Raichle, A. M. MacLeod, A. Z. Snyder, W. J. Powers, D. A. Gusnard, and G. L. Shulman, "Inaugural Article: A Default Mode of the Brain Function," *Proceedings of the National Academy of Sciences*, 98, no. 2 (2001): 676–682.
9. "Heather Berlin on Genius and Creativity," *Big Think* website. Accessed June 7, 2016, http://bigthink.com/videos/heather-berlin-on-genius-and-creativity.
10. David Bashwiner et al., "Musical Creativity 'Revealed' in Brain Structure: Interplay Between Motor, Default Mode, and Limbic Networks," *Scientific Reports* 6 (2016).
11. The correlation of brain networks with meditation is very complex, in part, because there are different kinds of mediation, and indeed different conceptions of mindfulness inside the traditions of Buddhism. The early Pali sources suggest that it is the ability to keep something focused in mind, an attentional power. But later Buddhist developments (sometimes called nondualist Buddhism, e.g., Yogacara, Mahamudra) attempt to dissolve the subject/object barrier in reflection. These are different interpretations of mindfulness, and presumably correlate with different neural pathways. See John Dunne's "Toward an Understanding of Non-Dual Mindfulness," *Contemporary Buddhism*, 12, no. 1 (May 2011): 71–88.
12. Judson A. Brewer and Rex Jung et al., "Meditation Experience Is Associated with Differences in Default Mode Network Activity and Connectivity," *Proceedings of the National Academy of Sciences*, 108, no. 50 (2011): 20254–20259.
13. My thinking on this issue was influenced by several personal conversations with journalist Robert Wright, who is working on a book called *Why Buddhism Is True* (Simon and Schuster, 2017).
14. Elise Harris's " 'Contemplative Communities Are Not Immune': Pope Francis on Prayer," Catholic Online, July 24, 2016, http://www.catholic.org/news/hf/faith/story.php?id=70047.
15. Anthropologists Timothy Earl and Allen W. Johnson studied hundreds of human societies, in their *Evolution of Human Societies* (Stanford, 2000), and discovered that the nuclear family is the default form of human organization, because it allows for maximally flexible management of resources, limited demands on those resources, and trustworthy social ties.

16. Our early hominid ancestors (e.g., Australopithecus) probably had "fission-fusion" polygyny cultures, like contemporary chimpanzees. Their kin groups did not resemble our contemporary nuclear families. Mothers and infants had strongly bonded relationships, but adults drifted together into subgroups (for hunting or sex) and then separated again almost daily. The size of these groups (30–50 members) varied depending on the available resources (Dunbar, 2001). When unattached males entered a new group, or found a mother unprotected, they might kill the infant (as chimpanzees and other mammals often do). This terminates nursing, puts the mother back into estrus, and the interloper can then impregnate the female—hijacking the procreation system for his own gene line. Our hominid ancestors may have lived in just such a nasty and brutish world, but eventually males and females stumbled upon a new strategy of semistable partnerships. And this solved another important problem for pre-sapiens, namely paternity. It is much more likely that males will provision juveniles if their paternity is established. Female primates are promiscuous, and males ensure paternity by four possible methods: Alpha-male harems (e.g., gorillas), pair-bond mating (e.g., tamarins and humans), band-of-brothers kin groups (e.g., chimpanzees), and indiscriminate mating (e.g., bonobos). The evolution of the family probably played a significant role in creating the stable, secure environment for the amplification of social learning and information culture. Additionally, these longer, safer childhoods must have also contributed to the growth of inner-subjective headspace—no doubt leading to greater representational sophistication (and eventually language).
17. Buddhism, for example, recognizes that what we most want from life is happiness, so we set out to pursue it. This makes perfect sense, on the face of it. The problem is that happiness is universally confused with "pleasures" and then we're all off to chase gratifications. The basic assumption is that when we get that one last thing (the tank-sized SUV, the customized guitar, the trophy wife, the Gucci bag, etc.) or attain that one culminating gratification, we will finally be satisfied and fulfilled. We'll finally be who we wanted to be. But we are doomed, like a modern-day King Midas, to ruin every true happiness we have by touching it with our insatiable obsession. The life of hedonism cannot find its own termination—it's a fire burning inexorably across an infinite tinder field. Buddhism teaches us to see the beauty in this present moment or activity, rather than the pay-off pleasure that comes at the end of an activity. In this way, according to mindfulness traditions like Zen, you stop pursuing happiness, and actually become happy. What you should pursue, instead of gratifications, are activities that engage your creativity or your mental faculties or your physical powers. If you want to be happy, don't work on being happy—work on learning to play a musical instrument, study karate, take up small-engine repair, gardening, calligraphy, learn a language, paint a house, or try your hand at a soufflé. If you can keep your ego-consciousness from seeping in and turning these wonderful activities into manic fixations, then happiness (not always pleasure) will emerge out of the focused activity itself. A state of well-being and peacefulness comes forth as a byproduct of your mindful activity, because you have (perhaps only temporarily) dissolved the ego by distracting and luring it into a busy immersion with the minutiae of your chosen activity. This is the oblique pursuit of happiness.
18. Genesis 17:5: "No longer shall your name be called Abram, but your name shall be Abraham, for I have made you the father of a multitude of nations." Also,

"The angel of the Lord called to Abraham from heaven a second time and said, 'I swear by myself, declares the Lord, that because you have done this and have not withheld your son, your only son, I will surely bless you and make your descendants as numerous as the stars in the sky and as the sand on the seashore. Your descendants will take possession of the cities of their enemies, and through your offspring all nations on earth will be blessed, because you have obeyed me'" (Genesis 22:11–18). Or consider Ezekiel 47:22: "You shall allot it as an inheritance for yourselves and for the sojourners who reside among you and have had children among you. They shall be to you as native-born children of Israel. With you they shall be allotted an inheritance among the tribes of Israel."

19. Exodus 1:1–7: "These are the names of the sons of Israel who came to Egypt with Jacob, each with his household: Reuben, Simeon, Levi, and Judah, Issachar, Zebulun, and Benjamin, Dan and Naphtali, Gad and Asher. All the descendants of Jacob were seventy persons; Joseph was already in Egypt. Then Joseph died, and all his brothers and all that generation. But the people of Israel were fruitful and increased greatly; they multiplied and grew exceedingly strong, so that the land was filled with them."
20. Asian studies scholar Edward Slingerland offers a helpful discussion of these issues in Chapter Seven of his *Trying Not to Try* (Crown, 2014).
21. Deirdre McCloskey has developed a multivolume argument for how some of the more proximal virtues have scaled up in the modern period to inform and guide large-scale social institutions, particularly economic institutions. See *Bourgeois Virtues* (2006), *Bourgeois Dignity* (2010), and *Bourgeois Equality* (2016; all University of Chicago Press).
22. Robert A. Emmons and Patrick McNamara, "Sacred Emotions and Affective Neuroscience: Gratitude, Costly-Signaling, and the Brain," in *Where God and Man Meet: How the Brain and Evolutionary Sciences Are Revolutionizing Our Understanding of Religion and Spirituality*, edited by P. McNamara (Praeger, 2006), 11–30.
23. The Buddha often is interpreted as an "other-worldly" philosopher, but, in fact, he gave plenty of temporal advice for people who want to get along better with their spouse, their employer, their parents and children, their friends, and so on. His *Sigalovada Sutta*, or "Code of Lay Ethics" is widely known and followed throughout Theravada countries. It charts out the way husbands and wives should treat each other, as well as how children and parents, employers and workers, and teachers and students should. Buddha asks us to envision a social map with the four directional points of East, West, North, and South, along with a third-dimensional axis moving through the middle of the map. The Eastern point represents the relationship of parents and children, the Western point is the relationship between husbands and wives, the North represents friends, the South is teachers and students, the nadir of the central axis represents workers and employers, and the zenith symbolizes spiritual leaders. The Buddha gives five pieces of advice to each pair of relations. For example, parents should relate to their children by restraining them from doing evil, encouraging them to do good, training them for a profession, arranging a suitable marriage, and leaving them an inheritance. Whereas sons and daughters must relate to their parents by supporting them in old age, fulfilling their duties, keeping the family traditions, making oneself worthy of an inheritance, and honoring departed relatives. In the Western region of the social map, a husband should: respect his wife, be courteous toward her, be faithful to her, hand over domestic authority

to her, and provide her with adornment (jewelry, clothes, etc.). In response, a good wife is to: perform her duties well, be hospitable to relations, be faithful, protect her husband's earnings, be skillful and industrious.

24. See H. L. Mencken's *Minority Report* (Alfred Knopf, 1956), 3.
25. The great exception to this historical generalization is ancient China, and particularly the Confucian tradition. However, we cannot confuse the agnostic nature of Confucianism with modern secularism, given that Chinese Confucianism is heavily contoured by the metaphysics of *tian* (Heaven) and *de* (virtue). See Herbert Fingarette's classic *Confucius: The Secular as Sacred* (Waveland Press, 1998).
26. See Justin T. Mark, Brian B. Marion, and Donald D. Hoffman, "Natural Selection and Veridical Perceptions," *Journal of Theoretical Biology*, 266 (2010): 504–515. And see Amanda Gefter's article "The Case Against Reality," *Atlantic*, April 25, 2016. Hoffman's argument is not as new as some suggest. It updates the general fallibilism that one finds in American Pragmatism. The overarching theme of Dewey's philosophy, and William James before him, is that an *experimental* approach to life—one that tests ideas in the realm of action—should guide us in all domains, including religion, politics, ethics, art, and, of course, science. Dewey argued against sclerotic ideology, absolutism, and essentialism. Too many of us are overconfident about our opinions and tend to view them as gems of certainty, outshining those of other people, cultures, and eras. To all this confident certainty, Pragmatists pointed out that truth is fallible, and we can't be entirely sure when we've arrived at it. William James, in his *Will to Believe*, says, "the faith that truth exists, and that our minds can find it, may be held in two ways. The absolutists in this matter say that we not only can attain to knowing truth, but we can know when we have attained to knowing it; while the empiricists think that although we may attain it, we cannot infallibly know when. To know is one thing, and to know for certain that we know is another. One may hold to the first being possible without the second." Our ethical claims, like everything else, need to be treated as hypotheses that we test in the social realm. Morality does not fall from the sky as eternal truth. We try out notions of the good in the realm of social interaction, and we validate ones that work for us (e.g., sharing) and eliminate ones that don't (e.g., slavery). Dewey, in his essay "The Influence of Darwin on Philosophy," says ethics is not about utopian idealism, but about needful matters such as how to "improve our education, ameliorate our manners, advance our politics." Pragmatism, heavily influenced by Darwin, thinks that even ethics is an evolving adaptive response of Homo sapiens' social life.
27. Amanda Gefter's "The Evolutionary Argument Against Reality," *Quanta Magazine*, April 21, 2016, https://www.quantamagazine.org/20160421-the-evolutionary-argument-against-reality/.
28. In the 1990s Pope John Paul II announced that Darwinism was compatible with Catholicism. Shortly after the Pope's media blitz, the preeminent American Darwinist, Professor Stephen Jay Gould, wrote an influential article in *Natural History* magazine. Titled "Nonoverlapping Magisteria," the article was subtitled "Science and religion are not in conflict, for their teachings occupy distinctly different domains." In the piece, Gould mulls over the Pope's recent statements and uses them as a catalyst for a general theory about the relationship between science and religion. Using a Latin term that he adopts from Pope Pius's *Humani Generis*, Gould describes the different domains of science and religion as different "magisteria." A magisterium, which comes from the word for "teacher," is a domain of teaching authority. For example, one might argue,

given this concept, that the American separation of church and state is itself a division of magisteria. With this concept of magisteria, Gould explains that science and religion can never really come into conflict. The two groups can only be antagonistic toward each other if they have some common thing at stake; remove that common thing, and the clashes become ephemera. Gould supported the Pope's demarcation of two totally separate realms: evolution and religion. He explained: "No . . . conflict should exist because each subject has a legitimate magisterium, or domain of teaching authority—and these magisteria do not overlap (the principle that I would like to designate as NOMA, or 'nonoverlapping magisteria'). The net of science covers the empirical universe: what is it made of (fact) and why does it work this way (theory). The net of religion extends over questions of moral meaning and value."

29. Nowhere is the relationship between norms and adaptive impulse control more obvious than in the case of the Maasai peoples (North Kenya and Tanzania). In an age-old rite of passage, we find the interdependency of emotional control and economic/social future. *Emuratare* is the circumcision ritual performed on every boy sometime around the age of sixteen. An elaborate precircumcision ritual (*enkipaata*) leads up to the circumcision, including living apart from the village and engaging in endurance tests. The *emuratare* itself is considered the most important ritual for Maasai society, and it is how boys transition to men. All such coming of age rituals are complex stages in the emotional reconfiguration of boys to men, and girls to women. They are not just symbolic adjustments in how the tribe sees the individual, but actual transformations of the agent's emotional disposition (as well as cognitive self conception). Boys, for example, often recreate their emotional disposition from the highly expressive style of youth, to the Stoic style of householders and warriors. Their very survival in the group requires such emotional management. In the Maasai *emuratare*, the young man must endure the excruciating pain of having his foreskin removed without anesthetic or pain medicines. But more astonishing, he must do the ceremony before an audience of tribal villagers who watch his face carefully for any signs of flinching or grimace. If the boy winces and shows pain on his face during this procedure, he will fail his greatest test of manhood. There is no second chance. If the boy sustains a Stoic visage, then his father awards him with a goat or some other livestock. This is economically and socially crucial. The goat means that the young man now has wealth, and wealth means marriage, and membership in the community. If the boy flinches and fails this circumcision ritual, his father gives him nothing. Without the goat, he has no economic or social footing in the community, and he is ostracized and banished from the group. He must leave the protection and opportunity of the social group and live alone in the bush.
30. Marvin Harris, *Good to Eat* (Waveland Press, 1998), 77.
31. "Comic Jim Gaffigan on Stand-Up, Faith and Opening for the Pope," National Public Radio, *Fresh Air*, September 24, 2015, http://www.npr.org/2015/09/24/443070367/comic-jim-gaffigan-on-stand-up-faith-and-opening-for-the-pope.

CHAPTER 5

1. Simon Barnes's *How to Be Wild* (Short Books, 2008).
2. Ursula Goodenough's *The Sacred Depths of Nature* (Oxford University Press, 1998).
3. I first tried to articulate this notion of transcendental everydayness in my book *The Gods Drink Whiskey* (HarperOne, 2005). There the context was Southeast Asian

Buddhism, but I think it is a wider aspect of most religious thinking. And I want to connect it here, in this chapter, to recent moves in affective neuroscience.

4. See Alexander Roob's *Alchemy and Mysticism* (Taschen, 2014).
5. See Aldous Huxley's *Point Counterpoint* (Dalkey Archive Press, 1928; 1996), 247.
6. E. J. Dijksterhuis, *The Mechanization of the World Picture* (Clarendon Press, 1961).
7. Tomi Obaro's "Why Chance the Rapper's Black Christian Joy Matters," Buzzfeed News, May 19, 2016, https://www.buzzfeed.com/tomiobaro/why-chance-the-rappers-christian-joy-matters?utm_term=.ikV5EYPqM4#.srv4V8eXbQ.
8. See Paul Reps's 1957 collection of parables called *Zen Flesh, Zen Bones* (Anchor Books, Doubleday), 23.
9. See Chade-Meg Tan's *Joy on Demand* (HarperOne, 2016).
10. See B. L. Fredrickson, "The Role of Positive Emotions in Positive Psychology: The Broaden-and-Build Theory of Positive Emotions," *American Psychologist*, 56, no. 3 (2001): 218–226.
11. See J. Haidt, "The Moral Emotions," in *Handbook of Affective Sciences*, edited by R. Davidson, K. R. Scherer, and H. Hill Goldsmith (Oxford University Press, 2003), 862.
12. See Benedict De Spinoza's *Ethics, Demonstrated in Geometrical Order*, translated by R. H. M. Elwes (New York: Cosimo Classics, 2006).
13. See Jaak Panksepp and Jeff Burgdorf's "'Laughing' Rats and the Evolutionary Antecedents of Human Joy?" *Physiology and Behavior*, 79 (2003): 533–547.
14. See Sarah Blaffer Hrdy's *Mothers and Others* (Belknap Press, 2011).
15. See Kim Sterelny's *The Evolved Apprentice* (MIT Press, 2012).
16. See Simona Ginsburg and Eva Jablonka, "Memory, Imagination and the Evolution of Modern Language," in *Social Origins of Language* Eds. Daniel Dor, Chris Knight, and Jerome Lewis. (Oxford University Press, 2014) pp. 316–324.
17. Johan Huizinga, *Homo Ludends: A study of the Play-Element in Culture* (London: Routledge & Kegan Paul, 1949), 5.
18. Richard J. Davidson, "Toward a Biology of Positive Affect and Compassion," in *Visions of Compassion: Western Scientists and Tibetan Buddhists Examine Human Nature*, edited by R. Davidson and A. Harrington (Oxford University Press, 2001), 107–130.
19. Resilience is an affective style that can be measured by the rapidity of recovery time from adversity (Davidson and Begley, 2012). According to fMRI data, the resilient person shows a more rapid down-regulation of negative affect (observable in the interaction of the amygdala and ventromedial prefrontal cortex) after seeing painful images, whereas the nonresilient person has much slower restoration of positive affect (and cortisol homeostasis) after negative stimuli. See Davidson, R. J., & Begley, S. (2012). The emotional life of your brain: How its unique patterns affect the way you think, feel, and live—and how you can change them. New York: Hudson Street Press.
20. Stephen Michael Siviy and Jaak Panksepp, "Sensory Modulation of Juvenile Play in Rats," *Developmental Psychobiology* 20 (1987): 39–55.
21. See the excellent collection of essays in *Playful Religion: Challenges for the Study of Religion. Essays by André Droogers, Peter B. Clarke, Grace Davie, Sidney M. Greenfield and Peter Versteeg*, edited by Anton van Harskamp, Mirander Klaver, Johan Roeland, and Peter Versteeg (Eburon Delft, 2006).
22. See Scott Atran's *In Gods We Trust: The Evolutionary Landscape of Religion* (Evolution and Cognition) (Oxford University Press, 2002) and Pascal

Boyer's *Religion Explained: The Evolutionary Origins of Religious Thought* (Basic Books, 2001).

23. P. Boyer and C. Ramble, "Cognitive Templates for Religious Concepts: Cross-Cultural Evidence for Recall of Counter-Intuitive Representations," *Cognitive Science*, 25 (2001): 535–564.
24. W. James, "The Sentiment of Rationality," *Mind*, 4, no. 15 (1879): 317–346.
25. Becka A. Alper's "Millennials Are Less Religious Than Older Americans, but Just as Spiritual," Pew Research Center, November 23, 2015, http://www.pewresearch.org/fact-tank/2015/11/23/millennials-are-less-religious-than-older-americans-but-just-as-spiritual/.
26. The idea that love is a kind of madness is obvious to anyone who's ever been in love. In Plato's *Phaedrus*, he first denigrates love (eros) as a corrupting madness. The erotic drives, he suggests, are completely disruptive of the delicate psychological balance or harmony that makes up the "healthy" rational soul. Lovers are out of their minds. They are out of control—they are not themselves. After sketching the insanity of love and the slavery that flows from such self-alienation, Socrates radically shifts the discussion to praise love. The erotic drive gets reinterpreted as the "wings of desire" and these wings are how we humans rise above the mundane world to experience, if only briefly, the "higher realm." The process may be irrational and slightly out of control (like an unruly horse pulling your chariot)—but the intense energy of this drive is apparently necessary to lift us to such inaccessible heights. For Plato, love is a kind of insanity, but it is a form of ecstasy that reveals more truth to us than other forms of lunacy.
27. A. Pusey, "Of Genes and Apes," in *Tree of Origin*, edited by F. de Waal (Harvard University Press, 2001), 9–38.
28. A. Harcourt and K. Stewart, *Gorilla Society* (University Press of Chicago, 2007).
29. See Frans de Waal, *Our Inner Ape* (Riverhead Trade, 2006). It should be noted, however, that Gottfried Hohman's work with bonobos gives us a less sanguine picture, and reveals that aggression is still alive and well in the supposed hippies. See Hohmann, G., & Fruth, B. (2003). Intra- and inter-sexual aggression by bonobos in the context of mating. Behaviour, 140, 1389–1413.
30. J. Kingdon, *East African Mammals: An Atlas of Evolution in Africa,* Volume 3, Part 1 (University of Chicago Press, 1988).
31. I. Dupanloup, L. Pereira, G. Bertorelle, F. Calafell, M. J. Prata, A. Amorim, and G. Barbujani, "A Recent Shift from Polygyny to Monogamy in Humans Is Suggested by the Analysis of Worldwide Y-Chromosome Diversity," *Journal of Molecular Evolution*, 57, no. 1 (2003): 85–97.
32. Some paleoanthropologists (Reno et al., 2003) have suggested that pair bonding emerged as far back as 4 million years ago with the *Australophicines,* on the grounds that sexual dimorphism reduced significantly then (revealing cooperative rather than competitive body types). This argument seems undercut, however, by the fact that *Homo habilis* (2 million years ago) was highly dimorphic (although the theory might be sustained if we remember that bio-cultural patterns—like monogamy—need only endure in populations, rather than species, genera, or families). Pair bonding may have been like the fire-starting skill, in the sense that it came and went many times before it spread to more universal proportions. See Philip L. Reno, Richard S. Meindl, Melanie A. McCollum, and C. Owen Lovejoy Sexual dimorphism in *Australopithecus afarensis* was similar to that of modern humans PNAS 2003 100 (16) 9404–9409.

33. See S. Hrdy, *The Langurs of Abu: Female and Male Strategies of Reproduction* (Cambridge: Harvard University Press, 1977) and Mothers and Others: The Evolutionary Origins of Mutual Understanding (Cambridge: Harvard University Press, 2009).
34. The cultures of primate mating are complex, however, and one needs to be careful to avoid a simplistic cause-effect dynamic between resource availability and sexual politics. Yes, bonobo egalitarianism corresponds reasonably with easy food availability, but then again procreative fecundity also rises in most primates as food supplies increase. And the increased population density of males increases competition for female access in other primates. So, for example, in orangutans, sexual coercion has been observed to increase along with food availability (e.g., high fruit abundance) (Muller and Wrangham, 2009). Generally speaking, however, mating cultures vary according to ecological differences rather than differences in endogenous endocrinology and neurochemistry (i.e., the LUST system). See Muller, M. and Richard Wrangham *Sexual Coercion in Primates and Humans*. Harvard University Press, 2009.
35. E. R. Dodds, *The Greeks and the Irrational* (University of California Press, 1951).
36. S. Cacioppo, F. Bianchi-Demicheli, C. Frum, J. G. Pfaus, and J. W. Lewis, "The Common Neural Bases Between Sexual Desire and Love: A Multilevel Kernel Density fMRI Analysis," *Journal of Sexual Medicine*, 9, no. 4 (2012): 1048–1054.
37. See Lovecraft's *Supernatural Horror in Literature* (Dover Publications, 1973).
38. Angst doesn't make me aware of a particular threat, but instead draws me out of my ordinary utilitarian ways of operating in the day-to-day world and makes me aware of my existential quandary—who and what am I? "Being-anxious," Heidegger says, "discloses, primordially and directly, the world as world." And brings human beings into a face-to-face crisis with their own authentic potentiality. Angst is that unsettling philosophical sense that you, and every other thing in the world, is just "dust in the wind." But while this alienating mood can be debilitating, it is also, in the hands of the existentialists, the prime motivator for taking up a fresh authentic responsibility in the active composition of one's true self. The dark night of the soul eventually gives way to heroic existential strength, rather than nihilism. The contrast between fear and angst is articulated in Part I, Chapter 6 "Care as the Being of Dasein," in *Being and Time* (Blackwell, 1978).
39. See *The King James Bible*, Book of Job 4:13, available online. Accessed October 25, 2017, https://www.kingjamesbibleonline.org/Job-4-13/.
40. A. R. Damasio, D. Tranel, and H. C. Damasio, "Somatic Markers and the Guidance of Behavior: Theory and Preliminary Testing," in *Frontal Lobe Function and Dysfunction*, edited by H. S. Levitt, H. M. Eisenberg, and A. L. Benton (Oxford University Press, 1991), 217–229.
41. Neuroscience has begun to correct the computational model by showing how our rational, linguistic mind depends on the ancient limbic brain, where emotions hold sway and social skills dominate. In fact, the cognitive mind works only when emotions preferentially tilt our deliberations. Damasio (1991) worked with patients who had damage in the communication system between the cognitive and emotional brain. The subjects could compute all the informational aspects of a decision in detail, but they couldn't commit to anything. Without clear limbic values (that is, valenced feelings), Damasio's patients couldn't decide their own social calendars, prioritize jobs at work, or even make decisions in their own best interest. Our rational mind is embodied, and without this emotional embodiment we have no preferences. For our minds to go beyond syntax to

semantics, we need feelings. And our ancestral minds were rich in feelings before they were adept in computations.

42. See Stephen Jay Gould's *Rocks of Ages: Science and Religion in the Fullness of Life* (Ballantine Books, 1999).
43. J. Poncela-Casasnovas, M. Gutierrez-Roig, C. Gracia-Lazaro, J. Vicens, J. Gomez-Gardenes, J. Perello, Y. Moreno, J. Duch, and A. Sanchez, "Humans Display a Reduced Set of Consistent Behavioral Phenotypes in Dyadic Games," *Science Advances*, 2, no. 8 (2016): e1600451. doi: 10.1126/sciadv.1600451.
44. Resilience is an affective style that can be measured by the rapidity of recovery time from adversity (Davidson, 2012). According to fMRI data, the resilient person shows a more rapid down-regulation of negative affect (observable in the interaction of the amygdala and ventromedial prefrontal cortex) after seeing painful images, whereas the nonresilient person has much slower restoration of positive affect (and cortisol homeostasis) after negative stimuli. Different affective styles or emotional intelligence strategies may act as natural variations upon which natural selection can do its work. The clinical literature underscores a small normative palette of prosocial personalities on the one hand and many disorders on the other. But some temperaments (e.g., fixed insensitive strategy) may be better suited for some early rearing environments (e.g., nonsupportive, volatile households) (Allison Jessee et al. "Parents' Differential Susceptibility to the Effects of Marital Quality on Sensitivity Across the First Year." *Infant Behavior and Development* 33, no. 4 [2010]: 442–452.). Children with more sensitive or plastic developmental temperaments can benefit greatly from supportive caregiver environments, but they will also be more adversely affected by negative or abusive caregiver experiences. They are disproportionately advantaged because they can absorb high volumes of social information with high fidelity, compared with the less-penetrable style of the robust but fixed strategy. See Jessee, Allison et al. "Parents' differential susceptibility to the effects of marital quality on sensitivity across the first year." *Infant Behavior and Development* 33.4 (2010): 442–452.
45. See Olivia Goldhill's "Psychologists Have Found That a Spiritual Outlook Makes Humans More Resilient to Trauma," *Quartz*, January 2016, https://qz.com/606564/psychologists-have-found-that-a-spiritual-outlook-makes-humans-universally-more-resilient-to-trauma/.
46. Robert Bellah, *Religion in Human Evolution: From the Paleolithic to the Axial Age* (Harvard University Press, 2011).
47. See Jean Piaget and Barbel Inhelder, *The Psychology of the Child* (Basic Books, 1969). Original work published 1966.
48. William James, *The Varieties of Religious Experience* (Mentor Books, 1958).
49. See Jonathan Haidt's "The Moral Emotions," in *Handbook of Affective Sciences*, edited by R. Davidson, K. Scherer, and H. Goldsmith (Oxford University Press, 2003), 852–870.
50. See section "Statistics" on Philanthropy Roundtable website. Accessed July 22, 2017, http://www.philanthropyroundtable.org/almanac/statistics/.
51. Richard Sosis, "Religion and Intragroup Cooperation: Preliminary Results of a Comparative Analysis of Utopian Communities," *Cross-Cultural Research*, 34, no. 1 (February 2000): 70–87.

CHAPTER 6

1. Bertrand Russell's *Why I am Not a Christian* (Touchstone, 1927; 1967), 22.
2. See Darwin's *The Expression of Emotions in Man and Animals* (Penguin Classics, 1872; 2009), 82–83.

3. In addition to Jaak Panksepp, Paul Ekman and Richard J. Davidson are crucial researchers into the affective springs of human and animal emotions. And although they may quibble about Panksepp's master list of emotions, they all share an empirically grounded commitment to the importance of bio-social adaptive affect and expression . See J. Panksepp, *Affective Neuroscience: The Foundations of Human and Animal Emotions*. New York: Oxford University Press, 1998.
4. See Joseph LeDoux's "The Emotional Brain, Fear, and the Amygdala," *Cellular and Molecular Neurobiology*, 23, no. 4/5 (October 2003): 727–738.
5. Ewen Callaway's "Fearful Memories Haunt Mouse Descendants," *Nature*, December 1, 2013. Accessed July 23, 2017, http://www.nature.com/news/fearful-memories-haunt-mouse-descendants-1.14272.
6. The new epigenetics is rendering the old distinction between nature and nurture obsolete. It is also revealing how the mother's prenatal uterine environment can "communicate" features of the outside world to the baby's epigenome (switching system) and set new default traits that may last for multiple generations. For example, recent data from the "Dutch Hunger Winter" show an epigenetic switch for obesity. Nazis in 1944 Holland diverted food from the Netherlands to Germany. Longitudinal studies of the Dutch population have demonstrated that if a fetus was in its second or third trimester during this famine, the fetus "learned" that the environment was extremely poor in nutritional resources, so the brain/body adapted in utero by calibrating its physiology to aggressive conservation of incoming fat, sugar, and nutrition generally. The fetuses that were developing in this hostile uterine environment of the Dutch Winter, automatically reprogramed to store every bit of incoming calories. The result, many years later, was a high degree of obesity in the adults who were epigenetically changed during their fetal experiences. Lab testing on rodents has isolated the actual epigenetic switch for fat storage that can be turned on or off. See David Crews, "Epigenetics and Its Implications for Behavioral Neuroendocrinology," *Frontiers in Neuroendocrinology* 29 (2008): 344–357, and Nessa Carey's *The Epigenetics Revolution: How Modern Biology Is Rewriting Our Understanding of Genetics, Disease, and Inheritance* (Columbia University Press, 2012).
7. See J. Feinstein, R. Adolphs, A. Damasio, and D. Tranel's "The Human Amygdala and the Induction and Experience of Fear," *Current Biology*, 21, no. 1 (January 11, 2011): 34–38.
8. M. Clasen, "Monster Evolve: A Biocultural Approach to Horror Stories," *Review of General Psychology*, 16, no. 2 (2012): 222–229.
9. J. Greenberg, T. Pyszczynski, and S. Solomon, "The Causes and Consequences of a Need for Self-Esteem: A Terror Management Theory," in *Public Self and Private Self*, edited by R. F. Baumeister (Springer-Verlag), 189–212.
10. Objective measures have been devised to determine if the morbid priming is taking root in the test subjects. For example, subjects are given a partial word, and they are asked to complete the word, like "c-ff- -". The term "coffee" is more frequently completed by the control group of test subjects, while the word "coffin" is more common among the subjects who have meditated on their own death.
11. Lee Ellis, Eshah Wahab, and Malini Ratnasingan, "Religiosity and Fear of Death: A Three-Nation Comparison," *Mental Health Religion & Culture*, 16, no. 2 (February 2013): 179–199.

12. Nathan Heflick and J. Goldenberg, "No Atheists in Foxholes: Arguments for (But Not Against) Afterlives Buffer Mortality Salience Effects for Atheists," *British Journal of Social Psychology*, 51: 385–392.
13. Jonathan Jong, Jamin Halberstadt, and Matthias Bluemke, "Foxhole Atheism, Revisited: The Effects of Mortality Salience on Explicit and Implicit Religious Belief," *Journal of Experimental Social Psychology*, 48 (2012): 983–989. Also see Jonathan Jong and Jamin Halberstadt, *Death Anxiety and Religious Belief: An Existential Psychology of Religion* (Bloomsbury Academic, 2016).
14. D. Edmonson, Crystal L. Park, Stephenie R. Chaudoir, and Jennifer H. Wortmann, "Death without God: Religious Struggle, Death Concerns, and Depression in the Terminally Ill," *Psychological Science*, 19, no. 8 (August 2008): 754–758.
15. Mark Duchene et al., "Literal and Symbolic Immortality: The Effect of Evidence of Literal Immortality on Self-Esteem Striving in Response to Mortality Salience," *Journal of Personality and Social Psychology*, 84, no. 4 (May 2003): 722–737.
16. See Stephen Craney's "Do People Who Believe in God Report More Meaning in Their Lives? The Existential Effects of Belief," *Journal for the Scientific Study of Religion*, 52, no. 3 (September 1, 2013): 638–646. Also see Robert Emmons's "Striving for the Sacred: Personal Goals, Life Meaning and Religion," *Journal of Social Issues*, 61, no. 4 (2005): 731–745.
17. William Paley, *Natural Theology; Or, Evidences of the Existence and Attributes of the Deity* (Philadelphia: John Morgan, 1802).
18. A handful of intelligent design theorists are interested in turning design into a real research program (e.g., Michael Behe, William Dembski), but these approaches and goals are not representative of how mainstream religious people employ the design hypothesis. And, of course, the proponents of the research program have been rewarded with the appropriate measure of success, which is none.
19. See Rami Gabriel's "The Self Help Game," *Aeon*, February 6, 2017, https://aeon.co/essays/self-help-is-a-kind-of-magical-thinking-thats-why-it-works.
20. Perhaps the major point of contention between skeptics and believers is the problem of evil or suffering. C. S. Lewis famously saw suffering as a wake-up call. Pain and suffering, according to Lewis, are produced by Satan, but God uses that pain to produce good. Many believers are sympathetic to Lewis's attempted solution. By analogy, one critique retorts that we are asked to affirm a father's goodness after he has allowed an aggressor to torture one of his children so that the other children might learn a valuable lesson from it. Skeptics stand with Ivan Karamazov, in Dostoyevsky's *Brothers Karamazov*, who doesn't want to be there when, according to Christian doctrine, the lion will lie down with the lamb and the murder-victim will embrace the murderer.
21. A. Lieberoth, "The Evolution of Martyrdom? Considerations in the Study of Religious Self-Sacrifice," in *Human Characteristics: Evolutionary Perspectives on Human Mind and Kind*, edited by H. Høegh-Olesen, J. Tønnesvang, and P. Bertelsen (Cambridge Scholars Publishing, 2009), 274–295.
22. Stephen Asma's *The Gods Drink Whiskey: Stumbling Toward Enlightenment in the Land of the Tattered Buddha* (HarperOne, 2006).
23. Charles Darwin, *The Descent of Man* (Penguin Classics, 2004), 682.
24. Barry Barnes and David Bloor, "Relativism, Rationalism, and the Sociology of Knowledge," in *Rationality and Relativism*, edited by Martin Hollis and Steven

Lukes (Blackwell, 1982), 21–35. Also see Paul Feyerabend's *Against Method* (Verso; 4th ed., 1975; 2010).

25. Temple Grandin, "Why Do Kids with Autism Stim?" *Autism Asperger's Digest*, November/December 2011, http://autismdigest.com/why-do-kids-with-autism-stim/.
26. H. C. Fibiger and A. G. Phillips, "Reward, Motivation and Cognition: Psychobiology of Mesotelencephalic Dopamine Systems," in *Handbook of Physiology: The Nervous System*, edited by F. E. Bloom and S. R. Geiger (American Physiological Society), 647–675.
27. P. Brown and H. M. Jenkins, "Auto-shaping of the Pigeon's Key Peck," *Journal of the Experimental Analysis of Behavior*, 11 (1968): 1–8.
28. Jaak Panksepp and Lucy Biven, *The Archaeology of Mind: Neuroevolutionary Origins of Human Emotions* (Norton Series on Interpersonal Neurobiology). (New York: W. W. Norton & Company, 2012), 115.
29. In the case of humans, our limbic-based SEEKING system does not reflect on or think about experience, but our neocortex does, and tries to detect cause and effect patterns from all the possible correlating associations. See E. A. Phelps and M. S. Gazzaniga, "Hemispheric Differences in Mnemonic Processing: The Effects of Left Hemisphere Interpretation," *Neuropsychologia*, 30 (1992): 293–297.
30. Clive Gamble, "Palaeolithic Society and the Release from Proximity: A Network Approach to Intimate Relations," *Journal of World Archeology*, 29, no. 3 (1998): 426-449.
31. See Stephen Asma and Rami Gabriel, *The Emotional Mind: Affective Roots of Culture and Cognition* (forthcoming Harvard University Press, 2018).
32. Izard and Ackerman, "Motivational, Organizational, and Regulatory Functions of Discrete Emotions," *Handbook of Emotions* (2nd ed.), edited by Lewis and Haviland-Jones (Guilford Press, 2000), 253–264.
33. See R. C. Fuller, "Spirituality in the Flesh: The Role of Discrete Emotions in Religious Life," *Journal of the American Academy of Religion*, 75, no. 1 (2007): 25–51.
34. The author of *Revelation*, John of Patmos, spins an elaborate mystical vision of the end of the world and explicitly draws upon the earlier prophetic traditions to reinforce and validate the urgency of his call to repentance. His confusing visions entail a trinity of terror that focuses on the central demonic character of the giant seven-headed dragon (*draco*), "who is called the devil and Satan" (12:9). This satanic dragon first appears in a vision, alongside a woman who is about to give birth to a child (the messiah). The dragon menaces the woman, waiting to devour the child as it is born. But the creature's evil plan is thwarted because the son, once born to the woman, is immediately whisked up to God and his throne, and the woman escapes to the wilderness. A gigantic battle ensues in which the dragon and his minions fight unsuccessfully against Michael and his angels (who overcome the dragon by the blood of the lamb). The dragon and his army are hurled down from heaven and must continue their nefarious ways on the earth, where they persecute "the woman who brought forth the man-child" (*mulierem quae peperit masculum*).
35. Robert Plutchik, *Emotions and Life: Perspectives from Psychology, Biology, and Evolution* (APA Books, 2003), 329.

36. See R. Scott Appleby and Martin Marty, *Fundamentalisms Observed* (University of Chicago Press, 1991).
37. Some recent neuroscience pulls back the curtain on how such reconfiguring happens. Kateri McRea et al. (2008) conducted a series of fMRI studies on emotional regulation. The study measured brain activity first while male and female subjects were exposed to disturbing negatively valenced images, and then while the subjects engaged in calming methods (emotional regulation strategies). In addition to cognitive reappraisal strategies (for example, subjects reminding themselves that the horrible image is only a movie), many subjects—especially women—appeared to diminish negative feelings by enlisting positive feelings (for example, happy memories) to supersede the adverse emotions. In men, the amygdala down-regulates more rapidly upon cognitive reappraisal, but in women the amygdala stays more active and appears to be processing positive affect from the ventral striatum (a reward/pleasure processor). The gender issue aside for our purposes here, the interesting issue is that neuroscience reveals a brain system that helps us replace fear, horror, disgust, with positive affects. The brain has a therapeutic architecture. See McRae K, Gross JJ, Weber J, et al. The development of emotion regulation: an fMRI study of cognitive reappraisal in children, adolescents and young adults. *Social Cognitive and Affective Neuroscience*. 2012;7(1):11–22.
38. H. Tajfel, *Social Identity and Intergroup Relations* (Cambridge University Press, 2010).
39. Stephen Asma, *Against Fairness* (Chicago: University of Chicago Press, 2012).
40. See Darwin's *The Expression of Emotions in Man and Animals* (Penguin Classics, 1872; 2009), 82–83.
41. The Heine quote, and Freud's use of the adage *Homo homini lupus*, are taken from Chapter Five of *Civilization and Its Discontents* (W. W. Norton, 1989).
42. See Chapter One, "Righteous Slaughter," in Jack Katz's *Seductions of Crime* (Basic Books, 1988).
43. It's popular now to show the hilarious video of Frans de Waal's and Sarah Brosnan's famous experiment with capuchin monkeys, to "prove" the innate primate instinct of fairness. Two capuchins, in adjacent cages, were trained to take a token from a trainer and then trade the token back for a piece of food. Each monkey could easily witness the barter of the other. The food reward for this barter was usually a slice of cucumber, which capuchins like to eat. But grapes are loved by capuchins as a delicacy. If one monkey bartered her token and received only a cucumber slice, but then watched as the other monkey received a grape for the same kind of token, the first monkey would become incensed—refusing to play on, throwing cucumbers back at the experimenter, protesting, and even punishing the lucky grape recipient. (S. Brosnan and Frans de Waal, "Monkeys Reject Unequal Pay," *Nature*, 425 [2003]: 297–299.) This experiment has been widely overinterpreted by journalists to illustrate a fairness module in primates. Well-intentioned liberal academics also regularly intone the experiment as an ethical position that denounces unfairness from grape payment to Occupy Wall Street and beyond. But I submit that the experiment does not illustrate an ancestral fairness module or even a fairness instinct. The actions of the capuchin monkeys are more compatible with mammalian emotional systems, and do not appear to be moral (or normatively principled) at all. Envy and resentment are powerful in social animals, and although they may eventually scale up to social contracts, they are not moral

per se. Neuroscientists like Jaak Panksepp and Kent Berridge have shown that primates like us and other mammals have a very strong seeking or wanting system (driven by dopamine). Once this desire system is triggered, it ratchets up expectation—motivating the mammal in powerful ways (toward food, sex, etc.). (K. C. Berridge, "Pleasures of the Brain," *Brain and Cognition*, 52, no. 1 [June 2003]: 106–128.) The dopamine flood is at the high-water mark just before attaining the goal, not during the reward consummation. Now, thwarting or frustrating the culmination of that seeking drive immediately activates the RAGE system and results in behaviors as trivial as cucumber throwing tantrums or as profound as murder.

44. *Group Psychology and the Analysis of the Ego*, Part IX. 1921.
45. Paul Seabright, "The Birth of Hierarchy," in *Cooperation and Its Evolution*, edited by Brett Calcott, Ben Fraser, Richard Joyce, and Kim Sterelny (MIT Press, 2013), 109–116.
46. It is often assumed that the phrase "this too shall pass" appears in the Bible, but in fact it does not. It may have originated in Sufi poetry.
47. See Swarti Sharma's "Islamic State Claims Responsibility for Paris Attacks," *Washington Post*, November 14, 2015, https://www.washingtonpost.com/news/worldviews/wp/2015/11/14/islamic-state-claims-responsibility-for-paris-attacks/?utm_term=.05ce969c973a.
48. See Dorothy Day's memoir *Loaves and Fishes* (Harper & Row, 1963; reprint, Orbis Books, 1997), 61.
49. For a retelling of this story, see Maha Ghosananda's book, *Step by Step: Meditations on Wisdom and Compassion* (Parallax Press, 1991).
50. See Michael Vasey et al., "It Was as Big as My Head, I Swear!: Biased Spider Size Estimation in Spider Phobia," *Journal of Anxiety Disorders*, 26, no. 1 (2012): 20–24.
51. P. Wiessner, "The Embers of Society: Firelight Talk Among the Ju/'hoansi Bushmen," *Proceedings of the National Academy of Sciences*, 111, no. 39 (2014): 14013–14027.
52. See "CARTA: Violence in Human Evolution—Polly Wiessner: Violence: What's Culture Got to Do with It?" Youtube, published on July 31, 2014, https://www.youtube.com/watch?v=_ITnD8oz0sI.
53. The Arabic word *shirk* means to practice idolatry or polytheism. In the Qur'an it can refer to pre-Islamic polytheism, particularly the popular goddesses Al-lat, Al-Uzza, and Manat. But it can also be used more generically to denote non-Muslims, including Christian trinity worshippers, or even worshippers of money or intellect, rather than the righteous worshippers of Allah.
54. See Maajid Nawaz and Sam Harris's *Islam and the Future of Tolerance* (Harvard University Press, 2015), 31.
55. See "Saudi Arabia's Curriculum of Intolerance," published by the Center for Religious Freedom, 2006. Online version. Accessed July 23, 2017, https://freedomhouse.org/sites/default/files/CurriculumOfIntolerance.pdf.
56. See "Chapter 1: Beliefs About Sharia," in "The World's Muslims: Religion, Politics, and Society," Pew Research Center, April 30, 2013, http://www.pewforum.org/2013/04/30/the-worlds-muslims-religion-politics-society-beliefs-about-sharia/.
57. See "Brigitte Gabriel Gives Fantastic Answer to Muslim Woman Claiming All Muslims Are Portrayed Badly," Youtube, published on June 18, 2014, https://www.youtube.com/watch?v=Ry3NzkAOo3s.
58. See Ayaan Hirsi Ali, *Heretic: Why Islam Needs a Reformation Now* (Harper Paperbacks, reprint edition, 2016).

59. See Maajid Nawaz and Sam Harris's *Islam and the Future of Tolerance* (Harvard University Press, 2015), 123.
60. See Joe Herbert's piece, "What Every Dictator Knows: Young Men Are Natural Fanatics," *Aeon*, February 2016.
61. See Scott Atran's piece, "ISIS Is a Revolution," *Aeon*, December 2015.

EPILOGUE

1. This discussion is drawn from Books VIII and IX of Aristotle's *Nicomachean Ethics* (translated by W. D. Ross) in the *Basic Works of Aristotle*, edited by Richard McKeon (Random House, 1941).
2. I am very much indebted to Stephen Toulmin's career-long indictment that Modern philosophy abandoned practical reason, in favor of theoretical frames of meaning. And I agree with his call to reintroduce the contextual nature—historical, literary, and even emotional context—of knowledge and meaning. The quote is taken from Chapter Seven of Toulmin's *Return to Reason* (Harvard University Press, 2001).
3. See Chapter Eight of Toulmin's *Return to Reason* (Harvard University Press, 2001).
4. Sam Harris, *The Moral Landscape* (Simon and Schuster, 2011), 25.
5. Francois Ponchaud's *Cambodia: Year Zero* (Holt, Rinehart and Winston, 1978).
6. See "'When the Saints Go Marching In': Missionaries in Cambodia," by Liam Cochrane, *The Phnom Penh Post*, November 21, 2003.

INDEX